MW01610949

Walk in the Light Series

Appointed Times

An Examination of the
Scriptural Calendar
and the
Restoration of Creation

Todd D. Bennett

Shema Yisrael Publications

Appointed Times
An Examination of the Scriptural Calendar and the
Restoration of Creation

First printing 2012
Second Printing 2014

For information write:
Shema Yisrael Publications
123 Court Street
Herkimer, New York 13350.

ISBN: 0-9768659-9-8
Library of Congress Number: 2012900843

Printed in the United States of America.

Please visit our website for other titles:
www.shemayisrael.net

Appointed Times

An Examination of the
Scriptural Calendar
and the
Restoration of Creation

"Speak to the children of Yisrael, and say to them: 'The
Appointed Times of YHWH,
which you shall proclaim to be set apart gatherings,
these are My Appointed Times.'"
Leviticus (Vayiqra) 23:2

Acknowledgments

I must first and foremost acknowledge my Creator, Redeemer and Savior who opened my eyes and showed me the Light. He never gave up on me even when, at times, it seemed that I gave up on Him. He is ever patient and truly awesome. His blessings, mercies and love endure forever and my gratitude and thanksgiving cannot be fully expressed in words.

Were it not for the patience, prayers, love and support of my beautiful wife Janet, and my extraordinary children Morgan and Shemuel, I would never have been able to accomplish this work. They gave me the freedom to pursue the vision and dreams that my Heavenly Father placed within me, and for that I am so very grateful. I love them all more than they will ever know.

Loving thanks to my father for his faithfulness along with his helpful comments and editing. He tirelessly watched and held things together at the office while I was away traveling, researching, speaking and writing.

Special thanks to my friend and brother Eliyahu David ben Yissachar for all of his assistance relative to editing and, in particular, calendar and dating issues. Because of his efforts this work was made better, and most importantly, more accurate.

Introduction

This book is part of a larger body of educational work called the "Walk in the Light" series. This book and the entire series were written as a result of my search for the truth. Having grown up in a major protestant denomination since I was a small child, I had been steeped in doctrine which often times seemed to contradict the very words contained within the Scriptures. I always considered myself to be a Christian although I never took the time to research the origins of Christianity or to understand exactly what the term Christian meant. I simply grew up believing that Christianity was right and every other religion was wrong or deficient.

Now my beliefs were founded on more than simply blind faith. I had experienced a "living God," my life had been transformed by a loving Redeemer and I had been filled with a powerful Spirit. I knew that I was on the right track, regrettably I always felt something was lacking. I was certain that there was something more to this religion called Christianity; not in terms of a different God, but what composed this belief system that I subscribed to, and this label which I wore like a badge.

Throughout my Christian walk I experienced many highs and some lows, but along the way I never felt like I fully understood what my faith was all about. Sure, I knew that "Jesus died on the cross for my sins" and that I needed to believe in my heart and confess with my mouth in order

to "be saved." I "asked Jesus into my heart" when I was a child and sincerely believed in what I had done, but something always felt like it was missing. As I grew older, I found myself progressing through different denominations, each time learning and growing, always adding some pieces to the puzzle, but never seeing the entire picture.

College ministry brought me into contact with the baptism of the Holy Spirit and more charismatic assemblies yet, while these people seemed to practice a more complete faith than those in my previous denominations, many of my original questions remained unanswered and even more questions arose. It seemed that at each new step in my faith I added a new adjective to the already ambiguous label "Christian". I went from being a mere Christian to a Full Gospel, New Testament, Charismatic, Spirit Filled, Born Again Christian; although I could never get away from the lingering uneasiness that something was still missing.

For instance, when I read Matthew 7:21-23 I always felt uncomfortable. In that Scripture most English Bibles indicate that Jesus says: "*Not everyone who says to Me, Lord, Lord, will enter the kingdom of heaven, but he who does the will of My Father Who is in heaven. Many will say to Me on that day, Lord, Lord, have we not prophesied in Your name and driven out demons in Your name and done many mighty works in Your name? And then I will say to them openly (publicly), I never knew you; depart from Me, you who act wickedly [disregarding My commands].*" The Amplified Bible.

This passage of Scripture always bothered me because it sounded an awful lot like the modern day Christian Church, in particular, the charismatic churches which I had been attending where the gifts of the Spirit were operating. According to the Scripture passage it was

not the people who *believed* in the spiritual manifestations that were being rejected, it was those who were *actually doing* them. I would think that this would give every Christian pause for concern.

First of all "in that day" there are *many* people who will be calling Him "Lord." They will also be performing incredible spiritual acts in His Name. Ultimately though, the Messiah will openly and publicly tell them to depart from Him. He will tell them that He never knew them and specifically He defines them by their actions, which is the reason for their rejection; they acted wickedly or lawlessly. In short, they disobeyed His commandments. Also, it seems very possible that while they thought they were doing these things in His Name, they were not, because they may have never known His Name. In essence, they did not know Him and He did not know them.

I think that many Christians are haunted by this Scripture because they do not understand who it applies to or what it means and if they were truly honest they must admit that there is no other group on the face of the planet that it can refer to except for the "Christian Church." This series provides the answer to that question and should provide resolution for any who have suffered anxiety over this verse.

Ultimately, my search for answers brought me right back to the starting point of my faith. I was left with the question: "What is the origin and substance of this religion called Christianity?" I was forced to examine the very foundations of my faith and to examine many of the beliefs which I subscribed to and test them against the truth of the Scriptures.

What I found out was nothing short of earth

shattering. I experienced a parapettio which is a moment in Greek tragedies where the hero realizes that everything he knew was wrong. I discovered that many of the foundations of my faith were not rocks of truth, but rather the sands of lies, deception, corruption and paganism. I saw the Scripture in Jeremiah come true right before my eyes. In many translations, this passage reads: *"O LORD, my strength and my fortress, My refuge in the day of affliction, The Gentiles shall come to You from the ends of the earth and say, "Surely our fathers have inherited lies, worthlessness and unprofitable things. Will a man make gods for himself, which are not gods?"* Jeremiah 16:19-20 NKJV

I discovered that I had inherited lies and false doctrines from the fathers of my faith. I discovered that the faith which I had been steeped in had made gods which were not gods and I saw very clearly how many could say "Lord, Lord" and not really know the Messiah. I discovered that these lies were not just minor discrepancies but critical errors which could possibly have the effect of keeping me out of the New Jerusalem if I continued to practice them. (Revelation 21:27; 22:15).

While part of the problem stemmed from false doctrines that have crept into the Christian religion, it also had to do with anti-Semitism imbedded throughout the centuries and even translation errors in the very Scriptures that I was basing my beliefs upon. A good example is the next verse from the Prophet Jeremiah (Yirmeyahu) where most translations provide: *"Therefore behold, I will this once cause them to know, I will cause them to know My hand and My might; and they shall know that My Name is the LORD."* Yirmeyahu 16:21 NKJV.

Could our Heavenly Father really be telling us that

His Name is "The LORD"? This is a title, not a name and by the way, won't many people be crying out "Lord, Lord" and be told that He never knew them? It is obvious that you should know someone's name in order to have a relationship with them. How could you possibly say that you know someone if you do not even know their name. So then we must ask: "What is the Name of our Heavenly Father?" The answer to this seeming mystery lies just beneath the surface of the translated text. In fact, if most people took the time to read the translators notes in the front of their "Bible" they would easily discover the problem.

You see the Name of our Creator is found in the Scriptures almost 7,000 times. Long ago a false doctrine was perpetrated regarding speaking the Name. It was determined that the Name either could not, or should not, be pronounced and therefore it was replaced. Thus, over the centuries the Name of the Creator which was given to us so that we could know Him and be, not only His children, but also His friends, was suppressed and altered. You will now find people using descriptions, titles and variations to replace the Name such as: God, Lord, Adonai, Jehovah and Ha Shem ("The Name") in place of the actual Name which was given in Scriptures. What a tragedy and what a mistake!

One of the Ten Commandments, also known as the Ten Words, specifically instructs us not to take the Name of the Creator "in vain" and *"He will not hold him guiltless who takes His Name in vain."* (Exodus 20:7). Most Christians have been taught that this simply warns of using the Name lightly or in the context of swearing or in some other disrespectful manner. This certainly is one aspect of the

commandment, but if we look further into the Hebrew word for vain - שוא (pronounced shav) we find that it has a deeper meaning in the sense of "desolating, uselessness or naught."

Therefore, we have been warned not only to avoid using the Name lightly or disrespectfully, but also not to bring it to naught, which is exactly what has been done over the centuries. The Name of our Creator which we have the privilege of calling on and praising has been suppressed to the point where most Believers do not even know the Name, let alone use it.

This sounds like a conspiracy of cosmic proportions and it is. Anyone who believes in the Scriptures must understand that there is a battle between good and evil. There is an enemy, Ha Shatan, who understands very well the battle which has been raging since the creation of time. He will do anything to distract or destroy those searching for the truth and he is very good at what he does. As you read this book I hope that you will see how people have been deceived regarding the Scriptural Appointed Times.

My hope is that every reader has an eye opening experience and is forever changed. I sincerely believe that the truths which are contained in this book and the "Walk in the Light Series" are essential to avoid the great deception which is being perpetrated upon those who profess to believe in, and follow the Holy One of Yisrael.

This book, and the entire series, is intended to be read by anyone who is searching for the truth. Depending upon your particular religion, customs and traditions, you may find some of the information offensive, difficult to believe or contrary to the doctrines and teachings which you have read or heard throughout your life. This is to be

expected and is perfectly understandable, but please realize that none of the information is meant to criticize anyone or any faith, but merely to reveal truth.

The information contained in this book had better stir up some things or else there would be no reason to write it in the first place. The ultimate question is whether the contents align with the Scriptures and the will of the Creator. My goal is to strip away the layers of tradition which many of us have inherited and get to the core of the faith which is described in the Scriptures.

This book should challenge your thinking and your beliefs and hopefully aid you on your search for truth. May you be blessed in your journey of faith as you endeavor to Walk in the Light.

I

In the Beginning

The subject of time is one that everyone is familiar with to some extent. While we may share differing methods of measuring or quantifying time, one thing is certain, we are all presently subject to time. We all wake up, live our lives and go to sleep. We then repeat this familiar cycle until we die. Every person lives out a daily cycle. Regardless of our waking and sleeping hours, time moves relentlessly forward. Time does not sleep, it is a force that cannot be seen or felt, but it can be measured. In fact, time is actually a physical dimension.[1]

It has been described that time flows like a river, as indeed it does. Just as a great river flows and deposits its passengers from one point to another in a single direction, so too does time. All of mankind is caught in the same current. We are passengers in this river of time that is currently flowing from the beginning to the end. To what end is a mystery to many people.

This example falls short though, because time is not dimensionally restricted as is water. The waters of a river are held down by gravity. Their flow is directed and controlled by the shoreline until they spill into a larger body, such as a lake or an ocean. Maybe an even better analogy would be the currents in the ocean flowing in cycles around the planet, as time flows through the currents of space.[2] You cannot always see the actual particles of water that are in the current, but you can observe the physical effects of the flow.

While this text is not a treatise on physics or philosophy, in order to establish a context for this book it is important to explore the very important subject of time. We must acknowledge this invisible companion and try to understand this relentless reality that all must contend with. It is because we recognize the existence of this unseen thing, like gravity and sub-atomic matter, that we should endeavor to understand it and measure it.

Great men have pondered this subject and not all agree. Sir Isaac Newton, one of the greatest minds known to man described time as an absolute.  "Absolute, true and mathematical time, of itself, and from its own nature flows equably without regard to anything external, and by another name is called duration: relative, apparent and common time, is some sensible and external (whether accurate or unequable) measure of duration by the means of motion, which is commonly used instead of true time ..."[3]

While Newton saw time as an absolute, others understood time to be relative. When we understand time as a dimension we then see that it is linked with space. Einstein  postulated on this notion of spacetime. "Time has historically been closely related with space, the two together comprising spacetime in Einstein's special relativity and general relativity. According to these theories, the concept of time depends on the spatial reference frame of the observer, and the human perception as well as the measurement by instruments such as clocks are different for observers in relative motion. The past is the set of events that can send light signals to the observer; the future is the set of events to which the observer can send light signals."[4]

When we understand time as a physical dimension we

can begin to imagine all kinds of ideas such as time travel and parallel dimensions. In fact, the more you think about time, the more fascinating, and sometimes elusive, this subject becomes.

It is even more intriguing as we attempt to determine where we are in time, relative to the universe that we live in. There can be no doubt that time is a constant force in our particular spacetime perspective, so we look forward and backward in this current of time that we are flowing. We question whether there was a beginning of time, and whether there will be an end.

While scientists have relentlessly examined the former, the Hebrew prophets have been given the keys to both the beginning and end of time. It is those prophets who diligently searched to know the time throughout the ages. (See 1 Peter 1:10-11a). Ultimately, the question of beginnings leads to a clash between science and religion. These two camps were not always opposed, but with the passage of

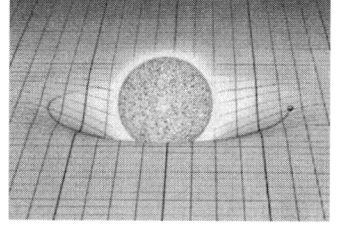

years we see a great divide continue to widen while both sides provide differing explanations for our physical existence, and thus the beginning of time. Science now attempts to find an explanation without the inclusion of a Creator, although quantum physicists skirt the issue through their notion of "The Ultimate Observer."

As a result of their quest for information, scientific speculation is continually evolving while those who rely on a Creator remain relatively fixed in their beliefs. Amazingly, the scientists who attempt to explain the complexities of our observable existence are acclaimed as brilliant and geniuses, despite the fact that they have more questions than answers. Meanwhile, those who rely on the historical record found in the Scriptures, attributing our existence to a Great Creator, are often deemed foolish and naïve.

Many in the scientific community believe that a mysterious "Big Bang" occurred billions of years ago which somehow resulted in enormously complex, and thus far, immeasurable, expanding and increasing galaxies that make up the cosmos. As a result of their faith in this scientific conjecture, they measure time from a hypothetical explosive event where matter and space mysteriously and miraculously appeared from nothing.

They actually gauge their measure of time on a year, which has traditionally been determined by the number of days that it takes the earth to revolve around the sun. A day was defined by the rotation of the earth and divided into 24 hours, each hour being subdivided into 60 minutes and each minute being further divided into 60 seconds.

Since their theory involves time when the earth and the sun did not necessarily exist, this was not a convenient method of reckoning time. In 1967 a second, at least in the scientific community, was defined as "the duration of 9,192,631,770 periods of the radiation corresponding to the transition between the two hyperfine levels of the ground state of the Caesium 133 atom."[5]

With this new measure of time, science is now capable of going as far back or forward in their examination of time assuming the constancy of an atom, another leap of faith considering that they are seeking constants out of chaos. Further, this measure of time now depends upon the existence of matter with no explanation of how or when that matter came into existence, thus creating quite a paradox.

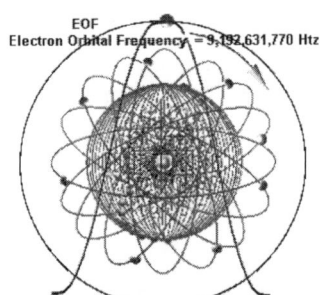

The "Big Bang Theory" relies heavily upon the hypothesis of evolution, which then explains the variety of living organisms that dwell upon and within the earth.

Because of the vast intricacies of the various species and all of the interrelated functions involved in living organisms, most of which we barely understand, evolutionists need a lot of time.

In fact, they need an incredible amount of time to support the notion that the amazingly complex systems that we witness today derived from billions of random and chaotic mutations which, over time, resulted in what some would describe as perfection; or perfection in a state of decline resulting from the introduction of entropy. Since their faith involves a hit and miss strategy of perpetual trial and error, which continually improves upon itself, they need as much time as they can justify.[6]

This is why we have witnessed scientists continually lengthen their estimate of the age of the universe, and the planet earth. Despite all of the time supposedly allotted for this grand evolutionary experiment, there is no fossil record showing any evidence of the remnants of this lengthy process.

Interestingly, this belief of order from chaos flies directly in the face of a simple and accepted law of thermodynamics involving entropy. You do not get order from disorder. For instance, no matter how many times I throw a stick of dynamite into a garbage heap I will not get a new car, ready to drive, nor will I ever get all of the parts ready to assemble that car. It will never happen! Likewise, the idea that the immeasurably complex systems found on our one planet, let alone the physical universe, came from chance or chaos is statistically impossible.[7]

As a result, those scientists, biased by their belief in evolution, have repeatedly adjusted the age of the expansive physical existence in order to accommodate their faith. Currently, they are running out of time as it is becoming increasingly clear that this present state of existence is finite. There was a beginning and we now know there is an end to the universe. If there was a "big bang" we can see the edge of the universe still moving away from the source of the beginning. We are actually encased within a finite physical container, albeit a large one, but nevertheless one with limits as to size.

Ultimately, the scientific notions and ideas concerning the Big Bang begin with randomness and chaos at a single point. This is in direct contravention to the belief that a Creator designed Creation and established order.

This is a very important distinction because we already mentioned that based upon entropy, it is a very difficult thing, highly unlikely, statistically improbable, and essentially impossible to get perfection from chaos. The First Law of Thermodynamics, also known as the Law of Conservation of Energy, would also hold that in our present physical state, energy cannot be created or destroyed. This would tend to support the notion that you cannot get something from nothing, vast cosmos from a speck of dense matter, without the intervention of some powerful outside intervening force.

Those who believe in the existence of a Creator can explain all of these mysteries, while evolutionary scientists desperately grapple to find new ways to describe creation without a Creator. These scientific explanations are more whimsical and outlandish than any described in the Scriptures, yet Scientists continue to laud one another as they stretch the bounds of logic or reason in an attempt to disprove the existence of God.

By doing this they tend to disregard another accepted notion known as Occam's razor often expressed in Latin as the *lex parsimoniae*, translating to law of parsimony, law of economy or law of succinctness.[8] Occam's razor "is a principle that generally recommends, when faced with competing hypotheses that are equal in other respects, selecting the one that makes the fewest new assumptions."[9]

Amazingly, when you get past the facade of genius presented by the scientific community to prop up their

science, which portends to explain our existence, you will find that it really only provides observation and speculation and seems determined to dispute and disprove the Scriptures at every turn.

So all of these "theories" are really "anti-theories" because they are more attuned to disprove Creation than they are to actually prove anything specific relative to how our present existence came into being. Time and time again the Scriptures win the battle of truth and there is no doubt, at least in my mind, that the Scriptures provide an authentic and reliable explanation of our existence.

Thankfully, science is not our only source for understanding and determining time. In fact, we have contained within the Scriptures a very old text, which vividly describes how life, as we know it, came into existence. It also tells us exactly how long the process took. The text known as Beresheet, is the source of our understanding of the physical and spiritual universe. It describes the Creator, referred to as Elohim, commonly called God.[10] It tells us that Elohim created everything in six days. That would include the planets, the stars and the cosmos – everything.

This text is bursting with information, much of it hidden within the depths of the ancient language in which it was originally written - waiting to be discovered. Beresheet, commonly called Genesis, was originally written in an Ancient Hebrew language rarely seen or used in this age.[11]

This is an important point to understand. The Ancient Hebrew language, as opposed to the modern Babylonian script, consists of pictographs with visually recognizable meanings. Therefore, each character had a meaning, which could be seen. Combining these symbols would result in concepts, not simply words. If we look at the first word in the text it might help the reader to better understand. The first word in the Hebrew text is translated as "In the beginning" in most modern English translations.

In ancient Hebrew we would see something like this:[12]

⨉⤳wⴱ⑨☐

We see what is known as the enlarged bet (☐), followed by the word "resheet" (⨉⤳wⴱ⑨). Grammatically, when the bet (☐) is found as a prefix it means "in." The word "resheet" is often translated as: "first" or "beginning." Therefore, the word beresheet or b'resheet is understood to mean: "in beginning." The phrase "in the beginning" is captured in one Hebrew word "beresheet."

Resheet literally means "first," so the first word of the Hebrew Scriptures is actually providing a point of reference – the beginning of time as we know it. There is much more to this "first" word than meets the eye when you look in the Hebrew language.

Again, the Ancient Hebrew language includes pictograms or ideograms. Essentially, each character represents a picture that expresses an idea. Therefore, instead of a character simply representing a letter which when combined with other characters spells a word, the Ancient Hebrew language combines pictures and ideas to describe concepts. The Hebrew language has changed over time and throughout this text we will look at various forms of the language.

With that understanding, we will often look at the Ancient Hebrew rendering of a word to help discern the concept being presented through the characters. Each character also has a numerical value. Known as Gematria, the study of those numbers can add an entirely new level of understanding.[13]

Sometimes the text offers other sources of valuable coded information through what are commonly referred to as "jots and tittles."[14] The first example of these codes is found in the first letter of the Scriptures. The fact that the bet is enlarged tells a story in and of itself. You see as previously stated, each symbol has an individual meaning.

The bet (☐) means "house," so we can safely assume

that a house is of great significance in the text. The rest of the characters literally symbolize "head", "ox", "teeth", "arm" and "mark." This is easier to see in the most ancient Script - ×⅃w 𐤉 𐤒𐤂.[15] A basic meaning that we could derive is "house, head, strength, cut, arm, covenant."

From this first word we can discern that "A great house will be built by the head man with the strength of his arm He will cut the covenant." When we look at the various combinations of the symbols we see even more in the text. We know that the focus is on the house due to the enlarged bet being the first character. We then see the word bar (𐤒𐤂), which means "head of house" or "son." This son, the head of the house, would be the first-born son.

Interestingly, the word for "son" connects the house with the "resheet" which is the first, sometimes referred to as the first fruit. This is a common agricultural term. So now we can see that the son is the "resheet" and the house is for the "resheet." With that introduction of "the beginning" we then have a context for everything else that follows.

It is important to understand that the beginning being described is the beginning of time itself – at least the beginning of a measurement of that time. Therefore, before the beginning there was no time, at least for the physical existence that we presently observe. In fact, it could be argued that this beginning was actually before time. Time was actually created along with everything else. This becomes evident as we continue to read the creation account in the text.

But first we will focus a bit on the first sentence of beresheet. Aside from the first word, which is a study in and of itself, the rest of the first sentence has more profound information. It actually reveals how this covenant house will be established, and it even provides a framework for time. Here is the entire sentence.

+𐤒𐤉𐤅 ×𐤉 ⅃ᵚ⅃ᵚw𐤅 ×𐤉 ⅃᷉𐤔𐤉𐤅 𐤉𐤒𐤂 ×⅃w𐤉𐤒𐤂

Now remember that Hebrew reads from right to left. That is why you see the first word Beresheet, all the way to the right. Phonetically the sentence reads as follows:

Beresheet bara Elohim et ha'shamayim v'et ha'eretz

→ 1　　2　　3　　4　　5　　6　　7

If you read it out loud, you just spoke Hebrew. There are seven words in this sentence, although only six are translated into English. This verse also contains two instances of the mysterious Aleph Taw (×Ⴒ). In the first instance we see the Aleph Taw (×Ⴒ) stand alone in position 4, untranslated but spoken. In the second instance it is in position 6, attached to a vav (Ꭵ) which represents a "peg" or a "nail." Again, in the second instance the Aleph Taw (×Ⴒ) is untranslated but spoken.

Some interpret this untranslated, but spoken Aleph Taw (×Ⴒ), as representing the Messiah revealed as the Word, sometimes referred to as the Memra.[16] If that is true then there are two instances of the Messiah, one being hidden, and the other attached to a "nail" which literally stands between the heavens (ᛗᒕᛗᚹᛉ) and the earth (ᛏᛞᚲᛉ). Of course, that fits in perfectly with the notion that Creation is all about a House for the first son, the Messiah, Who will be the head of the House filled with the firstfruits of His harvest. This concept will become clearer as we continue with this discussion.

It is commonly believed that this first sentence in the Scriptures begins a pattern of sevens that will be repeated throughout the Scriptures, providing seven millennium as the framework for time. This is very likely the case as we shall see further in the text. Obviously, that stands in stark contrast to the evolutionists mentioned previously in this chapter. Because of their belief in a Big Bang starting at one

point, they build in billions of years to account for everything at the edge of the universe to travel, or rather, expand from the explosion at the center of the universe.

When you consider the Scriptural account that everything was created and set in place at the same time during the creation event, and then essentially wound up like a clock, all of those required billions of years needed by the evolutionists simply vanish.

Therefore, if created time is encapsulated within the framework of seven millennium, then we should expect to see the Messiah around the 4th millennium, and between the 6th millennium and the 7th millennium.

This notion should give many pause for thought as Christianity claims that the Messiah did indeed come around the end of the 4th millennium, although He was hidden from many. We are now approaching the end of the 6th millennium, and there is currently a great Messianic expectation throughout the world.[7]

This makes understanding time even more important, and as we shall see, it could actually be an essential survival skill. It is not just acknowledging the existence of time as a physical dimension, but also understanding how to accurately calculate time so that we can discern where, in the framework of created time, we are presently located.

There can be no doubt that the pattern of seven established in the beginning was by design, and it continues throughout the Scriptures. In fact, the first verse provides an introduction and pattern for the rest of the Scriptures. If we continue to read, we see another pattern of sevens as we are provided more detail about time. So if we look at the beginning as a beginning of cycles, it will help us to better understand the rest of the Scriptures.

Many who are of the western mindset have learned to perceive time in a linear sense. (i.e. point A to infinity or infinity past to infinity present). My hope is to broaden your perception to a more ancient eastern mindset, which understands time as cyclical. All of Creation is filled with and operates in cycles. So learning to think in cycles helps us better understand Creation and the lives that we live.

Each individual lives within a daily pattern of sleep and awake time, although our own individual sleeping and waking routines are insufficient to provide a consistent gauge of time. While we gauge cycles of seconds into minutes and cycles of minutes into hours, the primary cycle of time that we operate within our physical existence is the day. Like it or not, our bodies must function within the daily cycle.

This makes perfect sense to anyone who recognizes that mankind was created by the same Creator that created the world within which we live. They were both designed for each other, to function in synchronicity. Essentially, people sleep at night and work during the day. People need darkness just as much as they need light. It is well established that the body undergoes various vital processes during the sleep cycle, and there are many important chemical functions that are triggered by, and rely upon the dark.[18]

Now we will return to the text in Beresheet. After the grand statement made about the beginning, we are told that the earth was without form and void. Darkness was on the face of the deep, and the Spirit of Elohim moved upon the face of the waters. (Beresheet 1:2). Interestingly, if we look at the Hebrew, we actually read that the Spirit or wind of Elohim was "making a vibrating (ⵝⵣⵀⵯⵈⵯ) to be over the face of the waters." There is much information contained within the text which is a lesson in physics, and reveals how the Creator actually created.[19]

For the purpose of this book we are particularly interested in the next verses. Here is the account that follows:

> "*3 And Elohim said, Let there be light: and there was light. 4 And Elohim saw ⵝⵣ -the light, that it was good: and Elohim divided the light from the darkness. 5 And Elohim called the light Day, and*

*the darkness He called Night. And the evening and
the morning were the first day."* Beresheet 1:3-5.

Now it is important to understand that this light was
not the light emitted from the sun. The sun was not created
until the fourth day. (see Beresheet 1:14). We will be
discussing that in much detail further in this book. So this
light was not the light we typically associate with photons
emitted from the sun. In the Hebrew it is called "owr"
(𐤀𐤅𐤓).

Other Scripture passages actually provide hints
regarding this mysterious light. In fact, the Proverbs describe
the Torah (𐤕𐤅𐤓𐤄) as light (𐤀𐤅𐤓). (Proverbs 6:23). This
would make sense since the Torah is the instruction of
Elohim, which provides distinctions and often separates right
from wrong, righteousness from evil, the way of light from
the way of darkness. The Torah reveals the way of the
Creator and establishes the rules of His Kingdom reflected
through creation.

Therefore, this light was spoken into the very fabric
of creation. It is interesting to examine these words in the
original Hebrew describing the bringing forth of light.
Essentially, we read that the Creator said: "Let it be" and "it
was". In each case the word describing the existence of light
is yihey (𐤉𐤄𐤉). The word includes two yuds (𐤉), which
symbolize arms as can plainly be seen in the Ancient Hebrew
Script.

The two arms surround a hey (𐤄) which often is
understood to represent spirit, breath or wind, but in the
Ancient Hebrew Script is more representative of a man.
There is something very interesting about this light, and in
the passage there are two representations of this "spirit man".
This word is closely linked with the description and Name of
the Creator revealed as 𐤄𐤅𐤄𐤉, often depicted as YHWH in
English. (See Shemot 3:14-15).[20]

So, if we look at this text in Hebrew we will see some

important details and connections that are not properly conveyed in translated "Bibles."[21] Translations do not always effectively convey the complete meaning of the text, and it is very helpful to review and amplify the text using the original language.[22]

If we read further we start to learn more about this light. Here is what we see in the Hebrew text:

ᚥᛁᚥᚢ-ᚷᚥ ᛘᚱᚢᚵᚱᚥ ᚢᚱᚱᚹᛏ

Literally this reads: "and saw Elohim et-the light". The et is the Aleph Taw (ᚷᚥ) which is actually connected with the light. Again, we already mentioned the Messianic significance of the Aleph Taw (ᚷᚥ), and in the text we see the Aleph Taw (ᚷᚥ) actually connected to the light. It is specifically described as "good". This essentially reveals that the Messiah was that Light. Of course, this makes perfect sense when we understand that all of Creation was made to be a House for the Head Son - the First Son - the Messiah.

Elohim then divided the light from the darkness. In Hebrew the word divided is "yabadal" (ᚱᚢᚷᚱ). It is translated as "severed" and literally means: "hand house door staff." This division has "the door to the house" at the center and again, we recall from the enlarged bet (ᚷ) that this Creation is all about a house from the beginning. Note the order of the letters as the hand (ᚱ) and the shepherds staff (ᚱ) surround "the door to the house" - (ᚢᚷ).

Since this is the first mention of light we should take particular note of what is going on. Originally, "in the beginning" there was darkness, which is choshech (ᚻᚹᚻ).[23] The darkness is not merely the absence of light, it too was created. We can see from the Hebrew that there is a "fence" or "wall" on each side of the word (ᚻ) with "cutting" or

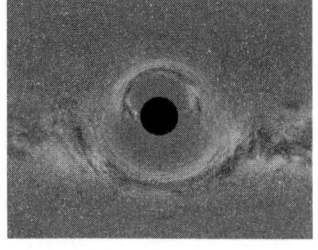

"consume" (w) on the inside. Since Hebrew is a cyclical language this almost appears to describe a black hole. A black hole is considered to be a region of spacetime where nothing, not even light can escape. The primary way to detect a black hole is based upon the effect that it has upon light.[24]

Interestingly, scientists have very recently discovered the existence of "dark matter" and "dark energy." Dark matter cannot be seen, but apparently has up to six times the mass of other known matter. Through a technique known as gravitational lensing, scientists have been able to detect dark matter.

It is speculated that dark matter actually holds the entire universe together through a network of filaments making up a giant cosmic web that is invisible to the eye. While dark matter binds things together, dark energy conversely pushes things apart. It appears that science is finally catching up with the knowledge contained within the Scriptures by recognizing that darkness is the underpinning of the universal superstructure.

There then came a time when Elohim spoke light into existence, and light was then divided from the darkness to help delineate time. The light was called day, which is "yom" (ᵐ⌐⌐) in Hebrew. The darkness was called night, which is "lilah" (ᵡ⌐⌐⌐) in Hebrew. What comes next is critical to our understanding of time. A common translation reads:

> *"And the evening and the morning the first day."*
> (Beresheet 1:5).

We can see here that the concept of a day began in the evening. This is consistent with the pattern of Creation as Creation started in darkness, and then there was light added to Creation.

Interestingly, many translations miss what really went on here. During this event we see a separation and then a unification, which resulted in the creation of a day. Elohim actually took darkness and light and united them together as a day. We know this from the very Hebrew text which literally states: "And the evening and the morning the unified (echad) day." The text includes the word echad (ᵀⱧⱵ) which can mean: "one or unified".

If the text simply wanted to mention the "first" day as in order, it likely would have used "rishon." Yom Rishon means first day of the week, and rishon shares the same root as resheet – "first." While echad can be used in the cardinal or ordinal sense, the use of the word echad versus the word rishon in this text has profound implications. The unifying aspect of the word adds an entirely different flavor, and we can see that something started here. The fact that the Scriptures state "Yom Echad" points to something special, more than just the order of appearance.[25]

Through this unification Elohim actually created a day, which would progress in a cycle from evening to night to morning to day. The two divided and separate concepts of night and day, darkness and light, were essentially stitched together at evening and morning to form a cycle.

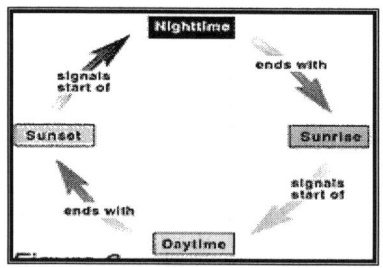

And of course the reason YHWH used "Yom Echad" or "Day 1," instead of "Yom Rishon" or "First Day," was to signal to His creation the day from which they should begin the count until the restoration of all things. For the beginning of every 7 day cycle begins with "Yom Rishon," but only the 7 day cycle began on "Yom Echad."

The word for "evening" in Hebrew is ereb (ᴰⱵᴼ), and the word for "morning" is boker (Ⱶᴼᴰ). These words, although apparent opposites are very much alike. Both transition the day and the night, although in opposite sides of the cycle. The word ereb literally means "see the head of the house" while boker literally means "house back head." Both include the head and the house.

We know that the "ereb" is a time of encroaching darkness when the sun has set. With this fading of light we begin a new day. As darkness sets in it becomes harder to see without the light of the sun. "Boker," on the other hand, is a time when things become discernable. It is the time when the sun starts to come forth again at the dawn.

These two times are very important, and the ereb includes a time often referred to as "twilight." This special time will receive more attention as the discussion progresses. The boker includes a time known as "the dawning of the day," which also has great significance.

As we shall see, this newly created concept of time, known as the day, is full of patterns and it is gauged from evening through morning to the following evening. That is what constitutes a day, known as "yom" in Hebrew.[26] The Messiah asked the question: "Are there not 12 hours on a day?" (Yahanan 11:9). According to this understanding it is generally understood that each yom contains 12 hours of night and 12 hours of day. The division points that we currently use are sunrise and sunset, but for the first three days the sun did not exist, or emanate light.

From this we must conclude that the Creator likely operated on a calculation. This is a clue to how He ultimately keeps track of time. While Elohim gives us visible markers to help us gauge His time, He clearly has His own clock that keeps "ticking" whether or not we realize or recognize that undeniable truth.

Every day is essentially a reminder of Creation and the patterns imbedded therein – the Creation Code if you will. Elohim is all about unity. He divides and then He unifies. By doing so He multiplies. These are the mathematics of the Creator.

As the creation account unfolds we are presented with another important cycle and pattern - the cycle of seven repeating days that constitute a week. It is within this period of time that the pattern for all of Creation is contained, and it is within the first 6 days that everything was created.

So then we have an account of creation occurring within 144 hours followed by a period of 24 hour rest.[27] Interestingly, while each of the first six days ends with the phrase *"and there was evening and there was morning"*, it is absent on the seventh day.

> *"[2] By the seventh day Elohim had finished the work He had been doing; so on the seventh day He rested from all His work. [3] And Elohim blessed the seventh day and made it set apart, because on it He rested from all the work of creating that He had done."* Beresheet 2:2-3.

This passage begs the question: Did the Creator really need to rest on the seventh day? Likely not, but by doing so He made a very compelling point. By resting Himself, He set an example for all created living beings. Now there is speculation that the rest day is the daylight yom, and not the entire 24 hour yom. Some believe that He was still creating in the evening, and it was not until the light that He rested.

The Scriptures are not clear, but there is no reason to believe that this yom was reckoned any different than the others in terms of duration, although there is an aspect of the eternal associated with this day. It is as if the Sabbath day were a gateway to another dimension, which transcends time – on a weekly basis. Since it is generally understood to be a day to commune with the Creator Who is outside of time, this makes perfect sense.

The seventh day was blessed, and set apart from the other days. It was clearly a unique and special day. It was even given a name – Shabbat. So the seventh day Shabbat completes the pattern of seven, although the seventh day was mysteriously left open ended.

The cycle of seven days that was established "in the beginning" continues to this day. This cycle is a simple seven day count, and relies on nothing other than the elapse of seven yom cycles.

From this Creation account we can see there were things that went on before the time presented in the text. There is a back-story, which is not provided at this point, although there are hints throughout the Scriptures. There was a creation and existence of the spiritual realm before the creation of this physical age. There was also a desolation before this present age. (see Isaiah 34:11, Jeremiah 4:23).

As a result, there were things that occurred in the spiritual realm, outside of the time of our present physical existence. Therefore, everything that occurred after Beresheet 1:1, the beginning, occurred in the physical universe, within our present understanding of time. Time, as we know it, was created on day one. It is finite. In other words, it has a beginning and an end. While the Creator provides us with a reckoning of days divided into four general units, evening, night, morning and day, men have attempted to further dissect a day.

Beyond the hours which make up a yom, man has broken down time into smaller units of measurement known as minutes and even seconds. It would appear that you could continually divide these units of time into ever smaller units but that is not the case. It has been discovered that there is a limit to the division of time units. It has been determined that the smallest measurable unit of time, known as Plank Time, is 10^{-43} seconds.[28] Thus time is a measurable physical property that has its limits in size and scale.

Within the framework of the first six days of Creation, Elohim established a mechanism for reckoning other durations of time greater than a week. He established units of time that are known as months and years which are determined by the sun and the moon.

In the midst of the seven day cycle we are told about the Creation of the sun and the moon and the stars on day four.

"*14 And Elohim said, 'Let there be lights in the expanse of the sky to separate the day from the night, and <u>let them serve for signs and for seasons (moadim) and days and years,</u> 15 and let them be lights in the expanse of the sky to give light on the earth.' And it was so. 16 Elohim made two great lights - the greater light to govern the day and the lesser light to govern the night. He also made the stars. 17 Elohim set them in the expanse of the sky to give light on the earth, 18 to govern the day and the night, and to separate light from darkness. And Elohim saw that it was good. 19 And there was evening, and there was morning - the fourth day.*"
Beresheet 1:14-19*

Again, it is important to note that the day count existed before the sun and the moon were created on day four. The sun and the moon were later created to separate between the newly created periods of time called the day and the night. The sun was the greater light and the moon was the lesser light. We read the word "separate" once again as we previously saw the separation between the light and the darkness.

These were two different and unique separations. Even the Hebrew word for "separate" on the fourth day is a bit different than that of the first. The root word in Hebrew for "separate" or "partition" is bedel (ٱﬥﬞ). If we look at the Hebrew text for the fourth day we see ﬥٱﬦﬠﬞ.

Notice how this word is surrounded by the shepherd's staff (ﬠ), and even the root (ﬥٱﬠ) is slightly different than the prior separation (ﬠٱﬦ) on the first day. In each case there is a yud added to the word. Remember, that the yud (ﬦ) represents an arm as can be clearly seen in the ancient script.

When the division between light and darkness occurred on the first day, the hand was in front of the house, represented by the bet (□). When the division between day and night occurs on the fourth day the hand is found after the door, represented by the dalet (▽) and before the staff, represented by the lamed (٦).

Often when there is a difference in spelling, it is meant to draw our attention as a hint toward a deeper meaning. Some refer to this as remez.[29] In this example we can see the arm moving from within the house, through the door and outside where it takes the shepherds staff.

We should then be looking for the Arm or Hand of the Creator to act as a Shepherd within the context and framework of created time. In fact, it is very significant that this second separation occurred at the midpoint in the seven day cycle of days.[30]

So we have the cycle of days, determined by the passage of evening and morning – two parts. The sun and the moon were created on the fourth day to mark the passage of days on this particular planet. The way we calculate time is unique to our environment. We then have the cycle of weeks, which consists of seven days ending with a special day named Shabbat, also known as the Sabbath. The sun and the moon were also created to mark cycles of months and years.

It is important to note, the weekly count is distinctive and independent of the month and the year. This is very important to understand as we continue to study time. There are cycles within cycles. So here we have these two related, but separate reckonings of time occurring simultaneously.

While the weekly cycle has remained and exists to this day, the correct observation of years, months and days has been lost, and today is the subject of much confusion. In the Second Temple period, when the Levitical priesthood was operating in Yisrael, there was no confusion about years, months and days. The nation of Yahudah observed these cycles in the proper manner.

In fact, in the New Testament we read about Zechariah and Elizabeth, who were both considered to be righteous before Elohim. The text details that they walked in all the commandments and ordinances of YHWH blamelessly. (Luke 1:6). Therefore, they would have had to know when the year, month and day began. This is especially true, since Zechariah was a priest serving in the Temple in Jerusalem, which operated around the Calendar of the Creator.

Although there is evidence that the Qumran sect followed a sectarian calendar, the nation of Yahudah, as a whole, reckoned time correctly. It was not until 359 CE, when Hillel II invented the Rabbinic calendar under Julian the Apostate, that times and laws were changed to fulfill Daniel's prophecy. (see Daniel 7:25).

Today, some attempt to construe that the stars are involved in telling time. The text is quite clear that the greater light and the lesser light are for determining time. They are the hands on the clock. It just so happens that the stars were also made on the fourth day, that is why they are mentioned, but not in the context of reckoning time.

Due to the procession of the equinoxes, the constellations are continually "moving." In other words, they are not in regular, fixed positions that provide a constant and continuous cycle which would allow us to mark days, months and years - that is left to the greater light and the lesser light. The stars are for signs, but the greater light and the lesser light are made for telling time in months and years. This is confirmed through the Psalms (Tehillim): *"He appointed the moon for seasons (moadim): the sun knoweth his going down."* Tehillim 104:19.

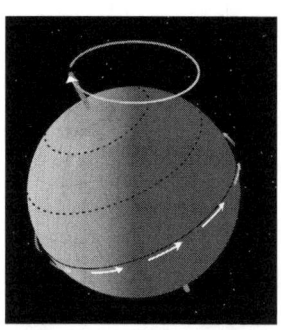

You may have noticed the word "moadim" in parenthesis in the passage quoted above as well as with Beresheet 1:14. That is the actual Hebrew word found in the

text, and it does not mean seasons. While it is true, to a certain extent, that the sun and the moon traverse a yearly cycle which can be divided into four discernable seasons, that is not what the text is referring to.

The Hebrew word "tequfah" means "turn or circuit" and there are four tequfahs each year described as equinoxes and solstices. Each solar year is divided into four tequfahs, or rather "turns" and they are intimately tied with the four seasons. Now the Scriptures really only describe two seasons – summer and winter. As a result, some argue that there are only two tequfahs known as the vernal (spring) equinox and the autumnal (fall) equinox. Each equinox is a point, or turn, when the day and night are equal. Therefore, it could be argued that the autumnal equinox marks the end of summer and the beginning of winter while the vernal equinox marks the end of winter and the beginning of summer.

There are two other distinct points in this grand yearly cycle. Not only were the sun and the moon created to mark time, but the earth is obviously integral to the process of reckoning time. It is constantly revolving on a tilted access, and both of these factors are critical for life to exist on the planet, and for providing markers for the year. The tilting results in a constant change in the amount of sunlight that strikes various points on the planet. It is this tilting that results in the four general demarcation points, or turns, in the cycle.

While the equinoxes mark the two points when day and night are the longest, there are two remaining tequfahs called the solstices. The summer solstice is the turn when the day is longest and the night is shortest. The final tequfah is the winter solstice, when the day is the shortest and the night is the longest. The winter solstice is likely the most well recognized and celebrated due to the

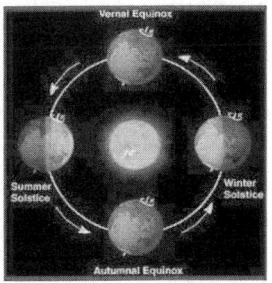

fact that it used to fall on December 25. That date is infamous as the source of many pagan traditions revolving around sun god worship. Since the days start to get longer, the pagans who worshipped the sun saw it as a "rebirth" of the sun as the days grew longer.[31]

Christianity found it convenient for conversion purposes to adopt this pagan date as the "birth" date for their christ.[32] Due to the procession of the equinoxes, the winter solstice now falls on December 21. Christians continue to revere the past solstice date of December 25, due to the pagan traditions adopted into the religion centuries ago.

Pagans actually ascribe sacred meaning to all of the tequfahs. As a result, many truth seekers view them as "unholy" or unscriptural, although nothing could be further from the truth. They are absolutely Scriptural and part of the elegant design of our universe. The tequfahs are easily recognizable and determinable events built right into creation. They mark time on the Creator's clock, and if you fail to recognize that truth, you will continually struggle to understand His time.

The first stated purpose in Beresheet 1:14 for the creation of the sun and the moon was for signs. The signs referred to here are solar and lunar eclipses. Eclipses occur every year, and when a historical record was made that referred to an eclipse, it became an important piece of evidence for the reconstruction of history. The second stated purpose for the sun and the moon was for "seasons" (moadim). The third stated purpose for the sun and the moon was for days, and the fourth purpose was for years. The fact that Elohim states in His word that the sun and moon were created to determine years has obviously not been contemplated by many, but should not be ignored.

Now that is all interesting background information, but it is important to reiterate that the Hebrew text in Beresheet 1:14, regarding the second purpose for the creation of the sun and the moon, does not actually say "seasons."

Again, in the Hebrew we read the word "moadim" which is commonly translated as Appointed Times. This begs the question of what exactly are the moadim that the sun and the moon were set in the heavens to mark. That is the subject of the next chapter, and the rest of this book.

2

Moadim

The name of this Chapter might seem strange to many who are used to reading an English Bible, and rely solely upon the work of translators. We have already seen that it is a Hebrew word, often hidden behind the word "seasons." The word "moadim" is a very unique and special word. It might have looked something like this  in the most ancient Hebrew script. It is understood to mean "appointed times" which are the prescribed times of YHWH. These times, at least in a traditional sense, are familiar to a person of Jewish[33] descent, but probably foreign to most other people, including Christians.

Interestingly, the text of Beresheet does not provide any more details concerning these Appointed Times, despite the fact that the sun and the moon have been set in their courses to mark these events. This stands out as a great mystery from the beginning.

In fact, this first mention of the word "moadim," in the plural sense, is the only time the word can be found in the entire text of Beresheet. It is specially located and stands out in many ways to draw our attention to its significance.[34] The only other usage in Beresheet is in the singular sense. Three times the word moad is found involving the birth of Isaac (Beresheet 17:21; 18:14; 21:2).[35]

The word itself is quite mysterious. It begins and ends with men () which represents "water." At the heart of the word we see ayin-dalet (), which literally means: "see the door." Therefore, if we interpret this word using the ancient symbols as a guide we would see the following concept: "as we pass through the waters (ᴹ), held back in their place (Ɂ) we see the door by the arm (ᴗ) of YHWH. The door, of course is the door to the House of YHWH that was alluded to at the beginning.

When I look at this word in the Ancient Script I immediately see a picture of the children of Yisrael[36] passing through the waters of the Red Sea, and the Jordan River. Of

course, as we shall see, these moadim are for Yisrael – the people in Covenant with YHWH.[37] Just as the Yisraelites once passed through the waters on their way to the Promised Land, the Covenant people "pass through" these Appointed Times as they progress toward the House of YHWH.

We see this concept right at the beginning on the sixth day when Elohim created man. The word for man in Hebrew is Adam (ᴹ∪ɣ). Notice the dalet (∪) which means: "door." The door is located at the center of this word surrounded by the word am (ᴹɣ) which means: "assembly or people." Interestingly, both the Rea Sea crossing and the Jordan crossing occurred at harvest times, and as we shall see, the moadim are intimately connected with the harvest in the Covenant Land.[38]

The common definition of moadim is "Appointed Times," and time is a very important aspect of the moadim. That is why we looked at the concept of time in the previous chapter. If we are going to concern ourselves with the times appointed by the Creator, then we should understand how He reckons time.

The word moadim does not only involve time though. There is another dimension that we must consider – space.

The very idea of an appointment involves being at a set place at a set time. It also involves meeting with someone for a purpose.

In the case of the moadim, at the heart of the word is "ad" (ⅤꙨ) which is translated: "witness" or "testimony." Remember that in the ancient symbols it would mean "see the door" so we can equate seeing the door with the witness or testimony. We will see this notion of the witness and the testimony take on physicality through the Ark of the Covenant and the Tabernacle, which actually becomes an important focal point of the moadim.

In fact, the singular form of the word is "moad" and it actually means: "place of assembly." So through the moadim we see times where we assemble at a place. As previously mentioned, each letter in the Hebrew language has a numeric value. This provides a very interesting study often referred to as Gematria. By looking at the numerical values of certain words we can find intriguing connections and enhanced meaning. The numeric value for the word moad (ⅤꙨꟾᛘ) is 120 (ᛘ = 40, ꟾ = 6, Ꙩ = 70, Ⅴ = 4).[39] This will become more significant as we examine the flow of the moadim through the cycles of time.[40]

Interestingly, we are not specifically provided a list of the moadim until much later in the text. It is not until we read about Yisrael that we are provided a detailed list of all of the moadim. They clearly existed from the beginning, and you can actually see them throughout the text, even when they are not specifically mentioned.

For instance, not long after we read about the creation of man and woman the Scriptures describe a disturbing story telling how Qayin (Cain)[41] killed his brother Hebel (Abel).[42] We are told of an incident when they both presented offerings to YHWH *"at the conclusion of days"* or *"in the process of time."* Here is an account of what happened.

"² Now Hebel was a keeper of sheep, but Qayin was a

tiller of the ground. ³ And at the conclusion of days (in the process of time) it came to pass that Qayin brought an offering of the fruit of the ground to YHWH. ⁴ Hebel also brought of the firstborn of his flock and of their fat. And YHWH respected Hebel and his offering, ⁵ but He did not respect Qayin and his offering. And Qayin was very angry, and his countenance fell." Beresheet 4:2-5.

We can safely deduce that this was a moad. The brothers knew that they were supposed to bring offerings to YHWH at this particular time, and they both presented their offerings at the same place. The offering of Qayin was not looked upon favorably by YHWH. This passage reveals that there was an established time and method of worship which was known from the beginning. There was a right way and a wrong way to come before YHWH with gifts – Hebel did it properly while Qayin did not.

This is particularly significant since Qayin is the firstborn son, which is bakar (𐤒𐤔𐤁) in Hebrew. Adam was the firstborn of all creation, and thus he bore the responsibility as priest for all mankind. It is interesting that Adam was not present in this instance, but as the firstborn son, Qayin would have born the responsibility of priest in the absence of his father. As such, he should have known how to properly present offerings before YHWH.

The major clue to our linking this event with an Appointed Time is the phrase *"in the process of time"* which is "m'qetz yomim" in Hebrew (𐤌𐤉𐤌𐤉 𐤒𐤒𐤌). The word "m'qetz" means: "to chop or cut off." The word "yomim" is literally spelled yom yom, or "day day" and is translated as "days."

The phrase is understood to mean: "end of days" or a time when the days were ended or cut off. Interestingly, chopping and cutting is intimately connected with harvesting something. So this was not just any day that they chose to

present offerings before YHWH, it was likely when the days of harvesting had ended. It is also a day of future significance as we will soon explore the connection with the Jubilee.

This was a very specific and important day, and it is within this context that we must view the sacrifices which were rendered by these two brothers. Not only were they expected to be some place at a particular time, but they were also supposed to bring something and do something. There was a right way and a wrong way and YHWH's reaction was determined by each individual's actions.

This event reveals a pattern that is repeated in the Scriptures, and shows us behavior that is pleasing and that which is displeasing to YHWH. The Scriptures reveal that Qayin brought an offering of the fruit of the ground to YHWH, and Hebel also brought the firstborn of his flock and their fat. It is possible that Hebel brought an offering of the fruit of the ground to YHWH, and also brought the firstborn of his flock. The Hebrew word used for flock is tsone (𐤑𐤍𐤀𐤕) which implies a goat or a lamb.

So Hebel knew what YHWH required and he complied. He brought the firstborn - the bakar (𐤁𐤒𐤓) of his flock. This was pleasing to YHWH. Qayin must have also known what pleased YHWH. Indeed, I believe that the Torah and the patterns found within the Appointed Times go back to the beginning. Adam surely was given this information when he received the instructions from YHWH, and transmitted the Torah to his sons. In fact, we are told that YHWH has declared the end from the beginning.[43]

His patterns and His ways go back to the beginning, and they are revealed through cycles – one of those cycles being harvests. Throughout the Scriptures we see the terms "in the beginning" (beresheet) referring to the beginning of a harvest or the firsts of a harvest, and the term "in the end of days" (miqetz yomim) would therefore bring us to the end of that harvest.

Many interpret this passage with Qayin and Hebel as

if to show that raising animals was better than tilling the ground, but this is not the relevant point. We see that Hebel offered his firstfruits, while there was no mention of this for Qayin. Also note that the offering of Hebel involved blood, while the offering of Qayin did not. Thus, the offering of Qayin was not acceptable – it did not include blood, and he did not receive atonement. As a result, he was overtaken by sin and he ultimately did shed blood – the blood of his brother. This provides us with a very important pattern, as we see further in the discussion.

The event reveals to us that there was a time and a place as well as a right way and a wrong way to meet with YHWH at the moadim. Those Ways were later written down in what is known as the Torah, but they were certainly known by all who walked with YHWH before that time. Since the sun and the moon were set in their courses to mark these times then we know that they existed from the beginning, and were essentially built into the fabric of creation.

The reason why the moadim were specifically delineated for the Yisraelites is because Yisrael was the Community of people who were committed to follow the ways of YHWH. Again, YHWH made a Covenant using the day and the night and those celestial bodies that were created to mark the day and the night as well as the Appointed Times. Accordingly, it makes perfect sense that the Appointed Times are then made to draw people into a Covenant relationship with the Creator.

We first read a formal listing of these Appointed Times in the Wilderness, detailed to the people in Covenant with YHWH known as Yisrael.[44] They were written by a man named Mosheh and given in the Torah.

The instructions, known as the Torah, were known by mankind from the beginning. They were created and established in the beginning. It is the framework for all of creation. As a result, those instructions belong to no man or

group of people. They belong to the One Who Created them – YHWH. This is clearly provided in the Scriptures.

The Appointed Times were described within the context of a Covenant, to a Covenant Community. Therefore, in order to better understand the Appointed Times we must first examine that Covenant.

3

The Covenant

There are many who believe that a Covenant existed with man in the Garden. Although there is no specific mention of a covenant in the text, the first word, beresheet (Xᵧ-ᴡ ᵟ ᵠ⬜) holds many mysteries, as we have already seen. In fact, that word contains many words, one of which is "brit" (Xᵧ-ᵠ⬜), the Hebrew word for Covenant, which surrounds another word – "aish" (ᴡᵟ) which means: "fire".

Therefore, while this first word emphasizes a house, through the enlarged bet (⬜), it also emphasizes a covenant from the beginning.[45] At the center of that Covenant is fire, a source of light.

Indeed, the Prophet Jeremiah, better known as Yirmeyahu,[46] makes reference to a covenant with the day and the night. It appears that YHWH actually made a Covenant on day one – yom echad.[47] Therefore, one could certainly make the case that mankind dwelling in the garden represented the House, and that relationship was essentially a Covenant involving man and Elohim. In fact, that was likely the essence, or ideal, of the Covenant.

We know that man was given a purpose. He was to tend and guard the Garden. He was also given instructions, and was told what to eat and what not to eat. It is interesting that the first recorded commandment given to man involved his diet. The man and the woman disobeyed the dietary instructions. Their punishment involved banishment from the House, and ultimately death. Their disobedience impacted all of mankind and creation. Amazingly, there are those who currently claim to follow the Creator, yet they continue to disregard and ignore His dietary instructions.[48]

After the man and the woman were expelled, blood was shed, and they were covered with animal skin. This provided a pattern that blood must be shed to cover sin until the problem of sin was ultimately dealt with. That first blood-shedding event did not resolve the disobedience. The man and the woman were still punished, and they still died. The blood of the animal provided a temporary atonement, or rather covering.

We know that things did not go well with Creation after sin was introduced. It spread like a disease. Qayin killed his brother Hebel, whose blood cried out from the ground. Things continued to deteriorate to the point where YHWH was forced to intervene.

After the passage of ten (10) generations, the Scriptures record the condition of Creation during the life of a man named Noah. "[5] *And Elohim saw that the wickedness of man was great in the earth, and that every imagination of the thoughts of his heart was only evil continually . . .* [11] *The earth also was corrupt before Elohim, and the earth was filled with violence.* [12] *And Elohim looked upon the earth, and, behold, it was corrupt; for all flesh had corrupted his way upon the earth.*" Beresheet 6:5, 11-12.

We read an interesting passage as YHWH looks upon the Earth and actually repented for having made man. "*And YHWH said, My Spirit shall not strive with man forever (olam), for that he also is flesh: yet his days shall be an hundred and twenty years.*" Beresheet 6:3. Now on its face, the text appears to indicate that mankind had another 120 years until they would be wiped out. In fact, the Book of Yasher specifically interprets the prophecy in this manner. However, not all flesh was destroyed in the flood so this passage must have a deeper meaning. In fact, it could also be read to put a limit on time itself. YHWH actually stated that He will not strive with man forever - olam (𐤏𐤋𐤌).

Olam is a very mysterious word, often misunderstood

to mean "eternity." It actually can be translated as "until the most remote time." Instead of the abstract notion of "eternity," the word "olam" is meant to express a range between the "remotest time and perpetuity." (See Jenni-Westermann Theological Lexicon.) So "olam" could be interpreted as meaning: "until the end of the age." It is very important to understand the concept of ages when dealing with creation and time. Time has limits, and it has been divided into ages, which include cycles. This becomes evident as we further explore the text of Beresheet 6:3.

The word translated as "years" is "shanah" (ΨᐱW). While "shanah" is commonly translated as "year," it essentially means a revolution or cycle of time. It is commonly understood to mean a year, but it can mean a whole age. (See Strong's Hebrew Concordance # 8141). Therefore, on another level of understanding, one could interpret the text to describe 120 "cycles."

We already referred to the cycle of the Jubilee, which is a 50 year cycle. As a result, YHWH may have been placing a limit on the time that He would strive with mortal man as being 120 Jubilee cycles or 6,000 years. This makes sense when one understands that a thousand years is commonly linked to a day for Elohim. Thus, 6,000 years is like 6 days to YHWH.[49] This fits perfectly within the 6 day pattern established at creation, followed by a 1 day Sabbath.

So then we must make a distinction between time in general, and time associated with our present physical existence. The Scriptures seem to be indicating that the time that mankind exists in corruptible bodies on the Earth will be a total of 6,000 years, followed by a millennial Sabbath where YHWH will reign for 1,000 years. We therefore understand that the end of 6,000 years will be the end of an age and the beginning of another age that will last 1,000 years with the redeemed of mankind.

It is within this time frame, up through "the end of this age" (olam), that we see the plan of YHWH develop through His Covenants. He desires to fellowship with mankind intimately in paradise. This is what we saw in the Garden. Eden actually means: "paradise." The Creator wants the best for His Creation, but through the disobedience of man, that ideal was disrupted.

Ever since then, YHWH has sought for those who would be obedient to work out His restoration plan. He found such a man in Noah. The Scriptures proclaim that *"Noah was a just man and perfect in his generations, and Noah walked with Elohim."* Beresheet 6:9. The Hebrew provides more insight into the character of Noah. The word for "just" is "tzedek" (𐤑𐤃𐤒), and it refers to "righteous conduct toward Elohim." The word for "perfect" is "tamiym" (𐤕𐤌𐤉𐤌), which means "upright, undefiled, clean." So we have a picture of Noah as one who walked according to the ways of YHWH.

Noah obviously knew the way that YHWH had established for men to live. The commands that were given in the Garden were surely transmitted by Adam through his descendants. As a result, Noah walked with YHWH and was righteous. That meant he followed the instructions of YHWH and was obedient. This provides us with some interesting insight into who YHWH decides to establish His Covenant with.

We have already discussed the "cutting" aspect of the word "brit," and we shall continue to see that throughout the text. The word "brit" also derives from the word "bara" (𐤁𐤓𐤀) which means to "select" or "create." Thus the party included in a covenant with YHWH must be selected or "chosen." So in the Scriptural sense, when we talk about a "chosen people" or a "chosen generation" we are talking about those who are in a Covenant relationship with YHWH, and as such, those who walk according to His ways.

Noah was chosen by YHWH to enter into a Covenant relationship. He was told about the Covenant that YHWH would establish with him. *"¹⁷ I am going to bring floodwaters on the earth to destroy all life under the heavens, every creature that has the breath of life in it. Everything on earth will perish. [18] But I will establish ✕𝒰 My Covenant with you, and you will enter the Ark - you and your sons and your wife and your sons' wives with you. [19] You are to bring into the Ark two of all living creatures, male and female, to keep them alive with you. [20] Two of every kind of bird, of every kind of animal and of every kind of creature that moves along the ground will come to you to be kept alive. [21] You are to take every kind of food that is to be eaten and store it away as food for you and for them. [22] Noah did everything just as Elohim commanded him."* Beresheet 6:17-22.

YHWH informed Noah that He was going to wipe out life on the planet by a global flood. YHWH would establish His Covenant with Noah. The word "establish" derives from the Hebrew word "quwm" (ᴍꟼ) which means "to stand" or "raise up." The Aleph Taw (✕𝒰) is an integral element in "establishing" the Covenant, which specifically belonged to YHWH. He chose Noah to enter into His Covenant relationship.

As a result, Noah would be saved along with his family and some select creatures. While this was certainly good news for Noah, it was only the beginning of the Covenant process. It was simply a promise that came with conditions. Noah was required to perform his part - he had to build the vessel of his deliverance, which would protect him from the judgment of YHWH. It was also incumbent upon him to store all of the food required for the Ark's passengers. This was a lot of hard work.

If Noah did not build the Ark, he would have been killed along with the rest of mankind. Instead, Noah believed the promise, and his actions were consistent with his belief. Thus, through the obedience of Noah we see the continuation of man and animals. Noah was, in essence, like Adam. He was the father of all of mankind, and because of his obedience, men would continue their physical existence.

When Adam disobeyed, mankind experienced a separation from YHWH and separation from the Tree of

Life, the life-giving source of YHWH on planet Earth. The expulsion from the Garden exposed mankind to both physical death and spiritual death. Due to the deterioration of the inhabitants of the planet, YHWH was prepared to wipe them out. Because of the obedience of Noah, mankind would be spared annihilation, and all subsequent generations owe their existence to the mercy of YHWH and the obedience of Noah.

Because of his walk, Noah found favor in the eyes of YHWH, and he and his family would be spared from the flood. Noah was not an arbitrary choice. He was chosen, because of his walk, to build an Ark - a vessel that would save a portion of creation.

The word "ark" in the modern Hebrew text is "tebah" (תבה). It is a very curious and unique word. In fact, if you look at most Hebrew dictionaries you will find that the origin of the word is at question. Some actually believe that it is borrowed from Egyptian or Arabic where similar sounding words refer to a "chest" or a "coffin." Essentially the word has been given its meaning from the context of the passage, not necessarily because of the root meaning.

In cases like this it is often helpful to look at the ancient language, and in the case of "tebah" (ᵞ⬚X) we see the taw (X), the bet (⬚) and the hey (ᵞ). Once again, the taw (X) is a mark which means "covenant." The bet (⬚) means "house" and the hey (ᵞ) represents a "window." In the most ancient Hebrew pictographic texts the hey (ᵞ) appears as a man with his arms upstretched which means: "behold." It shows that something important is being revealed.

This word "tebah" (ᵞ⬚X) seems to be describing much more than a boat, it is pointing us to something important. A literal definition from the ancient script could mean: "behold the covenant house." It is demonstrating that if we follow the instructions of YHWH, and remain in Covenant with Him, we can enter into His House, where there is protection from judgment.

There was a window, so this was not a coffin, as many liken the word. In this protected place man could see and be seen – it was a place of safety meant for the living. It was not a place for the dead. It was a place separated and apart from judgment and death. Death was on the outside, and life was on the inside.

After YHWH gave the promise, there came a time when He commanded Noah to actually build the Ark. According to the Dead Sea Scrolls, a messenger told Noah that a flood would occur after a certain number of Shemitah cycles. Most people are unfamiliar with the concept of Shemitah cycles, but it is a most important pattern established on the first week of creation – the pattern of sevens. In the case of the Shemitah cycle, it is a pattern of seven years.

As discussed previously, every seventh year in the count is a Shemitah year or a Sabbath year – a year of rest. These Shemitah years are then counted seven times and after the seventh Shemitah year is a Jubilee year. (Vayiqra 25:8-10). This is how the Creator gauges time, and it is this calculation of time which is imbedded within the Covenant relationship with YHWH.

Therefore, every Jubilee cycle contains seven Shemitah cycles each consisting of seven years. The seven Shemitah cycles, totaling 49 years, are followed by one Jubilee Year. These 50 years form a Jubilee cycle. You might be wondering why this is important when talking about the story of the flood. The reason why it is mentioned again here is because, according to the Dead Sea Scrolls 1 QapGen Col. 6, the flood was to occur in the year that followed a Shemitah cycle.[50]

The point is that YHWH had Noah counting Shemitah cycles. The importance of the Shemitah count is extremely significant when examining creation, time and the future.[51] This is especially true in light of the fact that through the Jubilee cycles we can discern that mortal man was given a finite amount of time upon the earth - namely 6,000 years.

The Scriptures record that: *"Noah did everything just as Elohim commanded him."* Beresheet 6:22. As a result, the Ark was ready to deliver him and his family when the floodwaters came. *"¹ YHWH then said to Noah, 'Go into the Ark, you and your whole family, because I*  *have found you righteous in this generation. ²* <u>*Take with you seven (7) of every kind of clean animal, a male and its mate, and two (2) of every kind of unclean animal, a male*</u> *and its mate, ³ and also seven (7) of every kind of bird, male and female, to keep their various kinds alive throughout the earth. ⁴ Seven (7) days from now I will send rain on the earth for forty (40) days and forty (40) nights, and I will wipe from the face of the earth every living creature I have made."* Beresheet 7:1-4.

The Scriptures then specifically report the fact that: *"Noah did all that YHWH commanded him."* Beresheet 7:5. The point is quite clear; Noah obeyed the instructions of YHWH. Notice that Noah was commanded to take seven (7) pairs of clean animals. Previously we read about two (2) of each animal and now we read about seven (7) clean animals. It is important to understand that there is, and always was, a distinction between clean and unclean, righteousness and sin. We currently find those instructions written in the Torah, but they were ever present before mankind.[52]

Noah knew those distinctions and we already discussed that he was literally described as "righteous" and "clean." The instructions of YHWH were no doubt handed down by Adam although, by this time, very few were actually following them.

Besides these distinctions, it is also interesting to look at the significance of numbers in the text. Numbers are very prominent and significant in the account of the flood. The Scriptures specifically provide that Noah was six hundred

(600) years old when the floodwaters came. The number six (6) is closely tied with man, and we saw that six thousand (6,000) is the number of years given to man.

It is striking to note that Noah lived for 600 years before the flood, which is equivalent to the span of time covered by twelve (12) Jubilee cycles. As we shall see, the Jubilee is intimately connected with restoration, as is the number twelve (12). This will become even more significant when we examine the role of Yisrael in the restoration of Creation.

There is another number that stands out in the story of Noah. The Scriptures record that Noah obeyed YHWH. As a result, he and his wife along with their three sons and their wives were saved from a flood that destroyed the inhabitants of the Earth. The number of people on board the ark was (8) eight.

This number is significant because eight means: "new beginnings." This was to be a new beginning for mankind. We see this in the patterns of seven (7) provided through the Scriptures, so the number eight (8) is essentially the "beginning" of a new cycle, after seven (7). The eighth letter in the Hebrew Aleph Bet is het (ᛞ), which means: "fence." This can clearly be seen in the Ancient Hebrew pictograph, which actually looks like a fence. The number eight is closely linked with covenants, and a special final Appointed Time that will be discussed further in the text.

When all preparations were completed, YHWH closed the door of the Ark, sealing the eight (8) beings along with the animals inside the "House of the Covenant."

The rains began to fall: "*¹⁷ For forty (40) days the flood kept coming on the earth, and as the waters increased they lifted the Ark high above the earth. ¹⁸ The waters rose and increased greatly on the earth, and the Ark floated on the surface of the water. ¹⁹ They rose greatly on the earth, and all the high mountains under the entire heavens were covered. ²⁰ The waters rose and covered the mountains to a depth of more than twenty feet. ²¹ Every living thing that moved on the earth perished - birds,* livestock, wild animals, all the creatures that swarm over the earth, and all mankind. ²² Everything on dry land that had the breath of life in its nostrils died. ²³ Every living thing on the face of the earth was wiped out; men and animals and the creatures that move along the ground and the birds of the air were wiped from the earth. Only Noah was left, and those with him in the Ark. ²⁴ The waters flooded the earth for a hundred and fifty (150) days. ⁸:¹ But Elohim remembered Noah and all the wild animals and the livestock that were with him in the Ark, and He sent a wind over the earth, and the waters receded. ² Now the springs of the deep and the floodgates of the heavens had been closed, and the rain had stopped falling from the sky. ³ The water receded steadily from the earth. At the end of the hundred and fifty (150) days the water had gone down, ⁴ and on the seventeenth day of the seventh month the ark came to rest on the mountains of Ararat. ⁵ The waters continued to recede until the tenth month, and on the first day of the tenth month the tops of the mountains became visible. ⁶ After forty (40) days Noah opened the window he had made in the ark ⁷ and sent out a raven . . ." Beresheet 7:17-8:7.

One will notice from reading this account that Noah knew exactly how to reckon days, months and years from all the specific dates that are given – even when the entire earth was flooded by water. As Noah was a righteous man, he would have had to know how to reckon time. He used the sun and the moon to reckon days, months and years. This is an important point to appreciate when some today are promoting adherence to man-made calendars, or calendars that determine months and years based upon factors that are not prescribed by the Scriptures.

The floodwaters receded and Noah, along with the occupants, exited the Ark safely. It is then that we are told of a Covenant established by Elohim. "⁸ Then Elohim spoke to Noah and to his sons with him, saying: ⁹ 'And as for Me, behold, I establish My Covenant with you and with your descendants after you, ¹⁰ and with every living creature that is with you: the birds, the cattle, and every beast of the earth with you, of all that go out of the ark, every beast of the earth. ¹¹ Thus I establish My

Covenant with you: Never again shall all flesh be cut off by the waters of the flood; never again shall there be a flood to destroy the earth.' ¹² And Elohim said: 'This is the sign of the Covenant which I make between Me and you, and every living creature that is with you, for perpetual generations: ¹³ I set My rainbow in the cloud, and it shall be for the sign of the Covenant between Me and the earth. ¹⁴ It shall be, when I bring a cloud over the earth, that the rainbow shall be seen in the cloud; ¹⁵ and <u>I will remember My Covenant which is between Me and you and every living creature of all flesh; the waters shall never again become a flood to destroy all flesh.</u> ¹⁶ The rainbow shall be in the cloud, and I will look on it to remember the everlasting Covenant between Elohim and every living creature of all flesh that is on the earth.' ¹⁷ And Elohim said to Noah, 'This is the sign of the Covenant which I have established between Me and all flesh that is on the earth.'" Beresheet 9:8-17.

It is important, once again, to note that YHWH repeatedly refers to the Covenant as "My Covenant." In other words, it belongs to Him and none else. This Covenant is an everlasting Covenant. It went beyond the life of Noah, or his immediate descendants for that matter. YHWH promised that He would never again cut off all flesh by a flood, and never again would He use a flood to destroy the whole earth.

There was no corresponding duty or obligation required from man or the animals. It was a promise accompanied by a sign – the bow. So the ultimate blessing associated with this Covenant was without any conditions. There was no further obligation from mankind. Noah had done the work to get them to the point of the Covenant. He had paid the price, and now the rest of mankind and creation would reap the reward, which is "sakar" (𐤔𐤊𐤓) in Hebrew. Interestingly, "sakar" is the root

of "Issachar" which is the Tribe of Yisrael responsible for the calendar according to I Chronicles 12:32. No doubt there are great rewards associated with knowing the times of YHWH, as we shall see.

The fact that there was a sign attached to the Covenant is significant. The Hebrew word for sign is "owt," spelled (אות) in the Babylonian derived modern Hebrew Script, and (𐤀𐤅𐤕) in ancient Hebrew. It can mean a "mark" or a "token," and is intended to be a visible sign or reminder of the Covenant. We shall see that YHWH often attaches these marks or signs to His Covenants. In the case of the Covenant with Noah and creation, we see the bow as the sign of that particular Covenant. It was a sign placed in the sky visible to all creation.

The word for bow in modern Hebrew is "qesheth" (קשת). It is interesting that the bow consists of seven colors which correlate to the seven Spirits described by the Prophet Isaiah (Yeshayahu)[53] in Chapter 11 and verse 2 of the text attributed to him. As we shall see, the number 7 is not only an important representation of the Spirit of YHWH, it is also an integral aspect of creation and time. Indeed, this sign of colors is also the same bow described as being in the Throne Room of Heaven.[54]

In fact, from Elohim's perspective from His Throne in the heavens, the bow was held backward. This was an ancient sign by which warriors often indicated that a battle was over.[55] We can still see the bow to this day. It is a reminder of His Covenant, which is essentially a demonstration of His mercy and restraint.

While we continue to see floods on the Earth, we have never seen the entire planet judged by water since the time of Noah – a promise kept. The Earth is full of sin, which cries out for judgment. This cry is heard in the Throne Room of YHWH, which is colored by the sign of the promise as a continual reminder. As a result, YHWH remembers His Covenant, and keeps His promise by not judging the Earth

by a total flood.

There is a pattern established here. As YHWH makes Covenant with His creation He uses a man as the mediator. In this instance, Noah represented mankind and creation. Part of this Covenant process also involved the shedding of blood.

A literal rendering of the Scriptures provides that: *"²⁰ Noah built an altar to YHWH, and took of every clean animal and of every clean bird, and offered burnt offerings on the altar. ²¹ And smelled YHWH ✕ﬠ a soothing aroma. Then YHWH said in His heart, 'I will never again curse ✕ﬠ the ground for man's sake, although the imagination of man's heart is evil from his youth; nor will I again destroy ✕ﬠ every living thing as I have done.'"* Beresheet 8:20-21.

Noah had already been saved, but the future promise was sealed by the shedding of blood. So the Covenant with Noah was essentially two fold. First, Noah had to obey and act in faith in order to be in a place where he and his family, along with the animals, could be saved. Second, YHWH promised that He would never again destroy the planet by a flood.

This was an everlasting Covenant made for all of mankind as Elohim had done with Adam, except that this Covenant was unconditional. It is a unilateral or unconditional Covenant made between YHWH and mankind. Only YHWH has to keep the Covenant, and He gave a continuing sign of this Covenant for all future generations to see.

Man could not save himself from judgment, and the only way to life was through obedience. Ultimately, it was YHWH Who provided the salvation. To emphasize this point, there are three instances of the un-translated Aleph Taw (✕ﬠ) in Beresheet 8:21 when the burnt offerings were being made to YHWH. There are also three instances of the Aleph Taw (✕ﬠ) when YHWH declares that He will make a Covenant. (Beresheet 9:9-10).⁵⁶

YHWH did not have to enter into this Covenant

with man. He could have easily stated, "If you continue to sin I will flood the planet again until you learn your lesson." On the contrary, He unilaterally stated that He would never do such a thing again. This is very telling.

It must have grieved the Creator to destroy His creation through the flood. As bad as things had deteriorated, it was still His creation. It was a very difficult decision, and He waited a long time before He finally rendered judgment, which demonstrates His patience. The fact that He made this Covenant with man immediately after the judgment by water is a demonstration that YHWH is a merciful Elohim. He made this Covenant as part of His plan to restore His creation, which reveals His mercy and love.

When Adam and Hawah transgressed His commandments, YHWH could have killed them and annihilated all of Creation. Likewise when the planet was corrupted during the age of Noah, He could have destroyed everything. Instead He continued to work with certain men to bring about a restoration.

This is the repeating theme that we shall see throughout the Scriptures - the Covenants are specifically designed to bring about "the restoration of all things." YHWH always preserves a righteous line through which He operates His Covenant promises. Thanks to the mercy of the Almighty and the obedience of Noah we are alive today to participate in this process.

The phrase "the restoration of all things," is associated with two concepts in Hebraic thought. It is ultimately linked with the restoration of earth to paradise in the seventh millennium. However, it is also linked with the idea of the Jubilee year, which was the year of the restitution of all things in Ancient Yisrael, when the Jubilee was being counted and its specific laws observed. Both concepts are the subject of the prophecy in Acts 3:21, which indicates that the heavens will release the Messiah in a Jubilee Year to bring about the Kingdom of Elohim in the Sabbath millennia.

"19 Repent therefore and be converted, that your sins may be blotted out, so that times of refreshing may come from the presence of YHWH, 20 and that He may send Yahushua Messiah, Who was preached to you before, 21 Whom heaven must receive until the times of restoration of all things, which Elohim has spoken by the mouth of all His set apart prophets since the world began." Acts 3:19-21.

There are some who teach that through this Covenant, YHWH established what are commonly referred to as The 7 Noahic Laws. This is an erroneous doctrine, which creates division between Jews and non-Jews. It teaches that Gentiles are only required to obey 7 laws to be deemed righteous. Those who believe and teach this lie discourage the Nations from obeying the commandments of YHWH. They profess that only Jews are required, or permitted, to obey the Commandments of YHWH outlined in the Torah.

Those who teach and believe this doctrine believe that the world is essentially divided into two categories: 1) Jews, and 2) non-Jews – called Gentiles. This is simply preposterous and is not supported by the Scriptures.[57]

The label "gentile" is actually equivalent in meaning to the word "heathen." It means "the nations" and refers to those who are not in Covenant with YHWH. A fundamental teaching in the Scriptures is that righteousness is determined by the heart, and is demonstrated through a person's conduct – whether they obey the instructions of YHWH.

The Scriptures specifically and repeatedly teach that YHWH Elohim is NOT a respecter of persons.[58] This concept is difficult for people entrapped in religion to grasp, but it is critical to understand. YHWH is only in covenant with those who believe, and therefore obey Him. YHWH does not make allowances for disobedience toward Him based on race, ethnicity, wealth or religious affiliation. This was a revelation to certain Judeans 2,000 years ago, but has been true since the beginning.

John (Yahanan) warns against being deceived on this very issue: *"7 Little children, let no one deceive you. He who practices righteousness is righteous, just as He is righteous. 8 He* who sins is of the devil, for the devil has sinned from the beginning. For this purpose the Son of Elohim was manifested, that He might destroy the works of the devil. ⁹ Whoever has been born of Elohim does not sin, for His seed remains in him; and he cannot sin, because he has been born of Elohim." I Yahanan 3:7-9.

As we shall see, there is no special provision made for Gentiles. There was no such thing as a Jew or even a Hebrew, when Noah participated in this Covenant. In fact, the first Hebrew would not arrive on the scene for another ten (10) generations through Noah's son Shem. That man was named Abram, and his name was later changed to Abraham after he too was chosen by YHWH and entered into Covenant with YHWH.

Sadly, even after this worldwide deluge and the promise of YHWH, mankind rebelled again. The Scriptures briefly describe an incident at Babylon. We know from history that it was at Babylon where mankind developed a religious system that focused on the creation, rather than the Creator.

Babylon is the source of sun worship, and the myriad of derivative religious systems that we see throughout history up to the present. As a result of Nimrod's sin in building the Tower of Babel, the people were disbursed and the languages were confused. The dispersion at the Tower of Babel happened during the days of Peleg when the earth was divided according to Beresheet 10:25, when Abram was 48 years old.[59] Mankind was divided in such a way that they were prohibited from unifying and continuing the activities begun in ancient times. It would be centuries later that Babylon would develop into a world power sometimes referred to as neo-Babylon.

As a result of that scattering the world population developed into different cultures, which developed their own variations in telling time. While mankind developed different calendars, YHWH never changed the one created at the beginning. As in the days of Noah, He sought a man that

He could enter into Covenant with.

Out of all of the chaos He found a man named Abram. YHWH eventually brought this man named Abram out of the region of Babylon and made a Covenant with him. Through his journey and life we can glean an understanding of the path of restoration.

The life of this man must be examined from the perspective of a Covenant with YHWH. When we do so, we see the Plan of YHWH unfold. First we see him brought out of the source of sun worship. He came out of Babylon with his wife and some family and servants.

He journeyed to the land of Canaan and was promised that land. He later went to Egypt where his bride, Sarai, was taken captive by Pharaoh. Pharaoh was plagued and his bride was released. Abram then left Egypt with great riches and another woman named Hagar (𐤄𐤂𐤓), who would eventually bear him a son. Interestingly, her name literally means: "the stranger" in Hebrew.

Abram later returned to the land of promise, and was told that he would have descendants as numerous as the stars. Abram believed the promise and his belief was counted as righteousness. We can see a common trait in these Covenant men chosen by YHWH. They are given promises and they act on those promises. They express belief by their actions and YHWH looks upon them as righteous.

Abram asked for proof of the promises. Thus far, he had gone through a lot, but he still did not have a son and he was getting concerned that he had no heir to fulfill the promise. The Scriptures then provide a description of a very elaborate covenant ceremony. Abram slaughtered five animals and arranged eight pieces parallel to one another.

Traditionally, the parties entering into a blood covenant would both pass between the pieces and walk through the blood. This would indicate that they were both subject to the penalty of death if they broke the Covenant. With Abram, this would not be the case. Abram was placed into a deep sleep, a sort of symbolic death. We are then shown that while Abram is "dead," that fire and smoke, representing YHWH, passed through the pieces. After passing through the pieces, the Scriptures then record YHWH entering into a Covenant with Abram. The borders of a very large land grant are described, from the Nile to the Euphrates. (Beresheet 15:18-21).

This event indicated that YHWH alone would suffer the penalty for the Covenant with Abram being broken. So this large land grant was essentially unconditional, but YHWH was going to have to pay the price, and since this was a blood covenant, that price was death.

Now it is important to understand that Abram was uncircumcised at the time of this covenant. He was described as a Hebrew, but he had not yet been circumcised. That would come later, but as was already stated, the life of Abram is a pattern of the walk of faith which is the Covenant path.

Those who are uncircumcised are typically called the Nations or the Gentiles. In this case we have a picture of YHWH entering into Covenant with the nations. In fact, YHWH actually told Abram that, *"in you all of the families of the Earth will be blessed."* (Beresheet 12:3).

This uncircumcised Hebrew then walked away from this event and had a son with Hagar. Hagar actually means "ha ger" – the stranger. It appeared that the promise would now be fulfilled through this son named Yishmael. But this was not to be.

Thirteen years later, YHWH appeared to Abram and instructed him that He was not finished. When Abram was 99 years old, he was instructed to walk perfect before YHWH. He was told that he would be the father of many nations – nations and kings would come out of him. Sarai was 90 years and barren.

YHWH told Abram that his name was changed to Abraham, and he was instructed to circumcise himself and his household. This act was now a requirement of the

Covenant which would be marked in the flesh of all who were in the Covenant. At that time, the name of Sarai was changed to Sarah. Both Abram and Sarai had a hey (ﬦ) added to their names. They were like a new Adam and Hawah with the breath of YHWH added to them. From this union would come the promised son who would be named Yitshaq.

Yitshaq would be the first covenant son who would be circumcised on the 8th day. This blood letting event on the 8th day connects with the previous blood covenant involving the 8 pieces. The picture was made complete later in the life of Yitshaq when Abraham is told to slaughter his "only son."

Abraham was told that the Covenant would pass to Yitshaq and not Yishmael. For the purposes of this discussion it is also significant to note that YHWH told Abraham that Yitshaq would be born at the Appointed Time, the moad next year. So this promise involved a child being born at an Appointed Time the following year. (Beresheet 18:14).

This is important to recognize, because these words were spoken immediately prior to the judgment that was about to befall Sodom and Gomorrah. Since we are provided some hints that Lot was eating unleavened bread (Beresheet 19:3), this event likely occurred at the time that we now refer to as Passover.

As we shall see, just as the righteous were delivered from Egypt hundreds of years later, Lot and his family were delivered from judgment during this important time. Thus, *the Appointed Time next year*" in which Yitshaq was born would have likely been Passover. Passover will be discussed at length throughout this text.

After Yitshaq was born and grown, Elohim said to Abraham: "*Take your son, your only son, Yitshaq, whom you love, and go to the region of Moriah. Sacrifice him there as a burnt offering on one of the mountains I will tell you about.*" Beresheet 22:2.

Imagine! This promised son was a miracle child who

was given to Abraham and Sarah in their old age in order to fulfill the promises of great multitudes of descendants. YHWH was now telling Abraham to sacrifice him as a burnt offering. This would involve slaughtering him, by shedding his blood and then burning him by fire.

I doubt that Abraham told Sarah. Instead, early the next morning he arose and took Yitshaq and two servants. On the third day[60] they arrived in the land of Moriah. Abraham told the two servants, "stay here with the donkey, the young man and I will go yonder and worship, and we will come back to you." Abraham placed the wood of the sacrifice on the shoulders of Yitshaq. Abraham took the fire for the burnt offering and a knife.

Yitshaq must have known that something was amiss. Abraham was probably not himself as he struggled to obey this difficult command. They typically would have brought their sacrifice with them, leading Yitshaq to ask the question: *"We have the fire and the wood. Where is the lamb?"* Abraham's response was: *"Elohim Himself will provide the lamb for the burnt offering, my son."* Beresheet 22:8. A direct translation from the Hebrew reads: *"Elohim will provide Himself a lamb."* This passage is often thought to mean that Elohim would be the One providing the lamb, which is true.

Another reading which has deeper meaning could mean that Elohim would provide Himself *as the* Lamb. Now this makes perfect sense when we recall who exactly passed through the cuttings of the Covenant and Who would bear the penalty of the Covenant. The Covenant with Abraham and this event would reveal how Elohim would provide the Lamb and provide Himself as the Lamb

When they came to the place where YHWH had said to make the offering, Abraham built an altar and laid out the wood on the altar. He then bound Yitshaq and laid him on the altar to sacrifice

him. It is important to note that there is nothing to indicate that Yitshaq struggled or protested. He was a grown man while Abraham was quite old. According to the Book of Yasher, Yitshaq was 37 years old, so he obviously could have escaped, but it appears that he willingly laid down his life. (Yasher 22:41, 53).[61]

As Abraham was about to slaughter his son he was stopped by the Messenger of YHWH and told not to touch his son. The Messenger then went on to state: *"Now I know that you fear Elohim, because you have not withheld from me your son, your only son."*

There was a sacrifice made that day, only it was not Yitshaq. It was a ram caught in a thicket by his horns. This ram in the thicket was then slaughtered and offered as a burnt offering by fire. This was the provision of YHWH, and the entire event provided a picture of how the Covenant with Abraham would culminate. Abraham called the place YHWH Yireh. Some translations indicate that the meaning is: "In the Mountain of YHWH it shall be provided." While there certainly was provision, the word "yireh" (ᵞᵞᵞ) comes from the root "ra'ah" which means: "to see, to consider, to discern." The question any reader should ask is: What shall be seen?

This moment was revealing how YHWH would provide the redemption and restoration of Creation through the Covenant with Abraham. It actually brings us back to the former Covenant, and makes the connection between the Word of YHWH and the Lamb of Elohim. This picture of the restoration provided by YHWH repeatedly emphasizes "your son, your only son." Obviously, Abram had a son named Yishmael, but Abraham had only one son – Yitshaq. This distinction is critical.

There is so much more going on in this passage than we can possibly see by simply reading the English. On the surface we see a great promise that "the seed" of Abraham will be incredibly numerous and powerful and all the nations

of the earth would be blessed because of the seed.

As with many Scripture passages we can only understand the profound depth of the text by reading and studying the original Hebrew. For instance, this entire passage is filled with the Aleph Taw (ΧΖ), which is a clear indication that it is a Messianic reference.

There are three times when Abraham is given directions regarding *"your son, your only son,"* or Yitshaq. In each of those three references there are three occurrences of the untranslated Aleph Taw (ΧΖ). In Beresheet 22:9, the passage where it describes Abraham as laying the wood on the altar and binding Yitshaq, there are three occurrences of the untranslated Aleph Taw (ΧΖ). Also in the following passage when Abraham was preparing to slay Yitshaq, there are three occurrences of the untranslated Aleph Taw (ΧΖ).

This event, often referred to as "the Akeda," was a shadow picture of the fact that Elohim would provide a Lamb, His only Son. Some believe that Abraham simply obeyed and was willing to kill his son out of pure obedience – in a robotic fashion.

This is neither a fair nor a complete understanding of the faith and righteousness expressed by Abraham. For as Abraham told his servants who had accompanied him to stay with the donkey until he and his son returned, it is absolutely clear that Abraham believed his "only son" would be resurrected. Since the Covenant was promised to pass through the son, it was imperative that this "only son" live, even if he was offered as a sacrifice.

Therefore, the faith of Abraham was not so much that he was willing to kill his promised son, as pagans regularly offered their children to their gods. The faith of Abraham was more fully expressed by his belief in the resurrection of his son. He specifically told the servants "we will come back to you." He fully expected Yitshaq to live <u>after</u> being slaughtered.

The Lamb of Elohim would be slain and the promise

to Abraham that *"all nations would be blessed"* would extend through this Lamb. This is powerful information and it can only fully be seen in the Hebrew text.[62]

Many fail to recognize the Messianic significance of this Covenant made with Abraham, which was proclaimed immediately after he offered his son. A substitute sacrifice was made, just as had been done for Adam and Hawah. YHWH had provided His Lamb in place of the Covenant Son.

"[15] The messenger of YHWH called to Abraham from heaven a second time [16] and said, "I swear by Myself, declares YHWH, that because you have done ×ל this thing ×ל and have not withheld your son, ×ל your only son, [17] that in blessing I will bless and in multiplying I will multiply your ×ל seed as numerous as the stars in the heavens and as the sand on the seashore, and shall possess, your seed, ×ל the gates of their enemies, [18] and through your seed all nations on earth will be blessed, because you have obeyed Me." Beresheet 22:15-18.

The message could not be any clearer. The Covenant Son, born at the Appointed Time, would receive atonement by the shed blood of the Lamb of Elohim. To confirm this point, in this passage of Scripture, the word "son" is couched between two instances of the untranslated Aleph Taw (×ל). Likewise, when the Messenger refers to the seed, there are two occasions when the untranslated Aleph Taw (×ל) is right next to the word "seed."

This is, no doubt, a Messianic reference and it is interesting to note that the word "seed" (○ᚼᚱ) is a singular subject noun, it is not plural. While the seed of Abraham is often interpreted to mean his descendants, the text can also refer to one Seed. This is the same Seed described in Beresheet 3:15 as the promised Seed of Hawah that would crush the head of the nachash – or "shining one."[63]

So we see from this example in the Covenant with Abraham that YHWH would offer up the Lamb of Elohim - His only Son. This offering would be specifically related to the Covenant. That is why Abraham called the place

YHWH Yireh, because "*On the mountain of YHWH it will be seen.*" Beresheet 22:14. On the mountain of YHWH it would be seen how the Lamb of Elohim would be provided.

While tradition holds that this is the same location that the House of YHWH was later erected by Solomon, it is also very possible that this was on the Mount of Olives, on what is called the Miphkad Altar.[64] The location provided in the Scriptures is the general location "in the land of Moriah," not Mount Moriah specifically. It is also highly likely that the Binding of Yitshaq occurred at the same Appointed Time that Yitshaq was born – Passover.

"In the Jewish tradition, the Binding of [Yitshaq] is also remembered on Passover. The *Akeda* is interpreted as a historical precedent with regard to the miracles associated with the holiday. Because [Yitshaq] was Abraham's first-born son, it is believed that [Elohim] spared the first-born Israelites over the first-born Egyptians because he remembered the Binding of [Yitshaq]. Similarly, there is an idea that the reason the blood of the lamb was spread over the door was to remember that just as the ram was sacrificed in the place of [Yitshaq], the lamb is being sacrificed to save the first-born Israelites. This idea comes from the *Mekhilta of Rabbi Ishmael*, which said 'And when I see the blood, I will pass over you. I see the blood of the Binding of [Yitshaq].'"[65]

After Abraham had offered the ram, in place of Yitshaq, we read the following: "*[15] The Messenger of YHWH called to Abraham from heaven a second time [16] and said, I swear by Myself, declares YHWH, that because you have done this and have not withheld your son, your only son, [17] I will surely bless you and make your descendants as numerous as the stars in the sky and as the sand on the seashore. Your descendants will take possession of the cities of their enemies, [18] and through your offspring all nations on earth will be blessed, because you have obeyed Me. [19] Then Abraham returned to his servants, and they set off together for Beersheba. And Abraham stayed in Beersheba.*" Beresheet 22:15-19.

This was a merging of the Covenants made with

Abram and Abraham. Previously, YHWH had promised seed as numerous as the dust of the Earth, prior to Abram entering into the Land. Later, when YHWH entered into Covenant with Abram, He promised seed as numerous as the stars of the heavens. Now after offering up His only son, the promise was elevated to include numbers as great as the stars in the heavens <u>and</u> the sand on the seashore.

So through this event where Abraham was to bring his only son and kill him, we see how YHWH intended to pay the price of the Covenant made with Abram. YHWH would provide Himself a Lamb. This did not simply mean that YHWH would find His own lamb, it meant that YHWH Himself would be the lamb sacrifice symbolized by the ram.

YHWH would allow the blood of His only Son to be shed which is how all of the families of the earth would be blessed. It is through the Covenant process that YHWH would rectify the problem that plagued mankind since the garden. He would provide new land, a new garden, which the unclean families of the earth would be allowed to enter through the Covenant path lived through the life of Abram through Abraham and his seed.

His life was a rehearsal and we can infer that his life revolved around the Appointed Times, once we understand the intimate relationship between the Covenant and the Times. Through the two Covenants made with this one man, YHWH provided a framework for His plan of Restoration.

The Covenant of Circumcision passed through Yitshaq to Yaakob. Yaakob led a very interesting life, and a common thread that we see in his life is deception. He left the land after deceiving Yitshaq and receiving the birthright over his brother Esau. It is ironic that despite the fact that he obtained the birthright, he essentially became a fugitive. Like Abram he had a promise, but would have to wait for the fulfillment.

On his way to his Uncle Laban's he had an encounter

with YHWH at Beth El and anointed a pillar. He was later welcomed by his uncle, but was repeatedly deceived by him. Yaakob eventually married two daughters of Laban, Rachel and Leah, and had twelve children – 11 sons and 1 daughter. He also obtained great wealth and possessions while living as a virtual slave in his uncle's home.

After twenty years, YHWH instructed Yaakob to leave, and he stealthily took his family and returned to the Land of his inheritance. After three days, Laban discovered that Yaakob had left. Laban gave chase and confronted Yaakob. As it turns out, the favored wife of Yaakob named Rachel, the mother of Joseph, had stolen Laban's idols. She then lied about it and almost died because of her thievery. These idols ended up becoming a problem that Yaakob needed to deal with. He made a covenant with Laban and proceeded on his journey home.

Before crossing over into the Land, he wrestled with a mysterious man until the "dawning of the day." As a result of that encounter he experienced a name change to "am Yisrael." Not only would he be called Yisrael, but he would become a people or community (am) called Yisrael. Upon crossing over into the Land of Promise he camped at a place called Succot. It is important to take note of this place because it appears again, later in the history of Yisrael's descendants and eventually becomes an important Appointed Time.

Yisrael had one more son named Benjamin, who was the only child actually born in the Promised Land. His mother Rachel died giving childbirth. Rachel was also the mother of Joseph. The children grew, and it became very apparent that Joseph was the favored son of Yisrael.

In fact, Joseph actually had dreams that he was elevated above his brothers, and his parents. He dreamed that the sun, the moon and the eleven stars paid homage to him. These celestial bodies, given for signs, apparently represented his family. He also dreamed that he and his family were binding sheaves in the field. All of their sheaves stood up and

bowed to Joseph's sheave. Take special note that this would have occurred during the harvest, and both of these dreams have deep prophetic significance. (Beresheet 37).

As a result of all the favor shown to Joseph, his brothers became very jealous and sold him into slavery. He was taken to Egypt and went from a slave, to a prisoner, to the Viceroy of Egypt. He was set up to save the people from a devastating famine which lasted 7 years. He prepared for the 7 years of famine during the 7 years of plenty, and those preparations revolved around the harvests. After some very dramatic events during the famine, Joseph was revealed at the Appointed Time.

He was reconciled with his family and prepared for  them to move to Egypt. The clan eventually moved out of the land of Canaan and into Egypt. The Scriptures record 70 "souls" or "beings" that came out of the loins of Yaakov and presumably went into Egypt with him.

Interestingly, these 70 beings moved into a region in Egypt called Goshen, which actually fell within the Covenant boundaries described to Abram. The number 70 has very significant meaning. It is typically associated with "the Nations" based upon the number of descendants from Noah.[66]

Essentially this is being linked with a repopulation event within a Covenant, just as we saw with Noah. It reinforces the fact that that the Covenant with Abram was intended to draw the Nations into the Covenant. As we shall see, the number 70 is also intimately linked with time.[67] It was while the man Yisrael was in Egypt, before his death, that he gave an interesting prophecy over the children of Joseph. In particular, he declared that the youngest son Ephraim would become "a multitude of nations." (Beresheet

48:19). This is critical to understand as we continue to examine the unique role that Joseph plays in the Covenant and the Appointed Times.

While in Egypt, the descendants of Yisrael were eventually afflicted and oppressed, just as foretold to Abram during the Covenant process. When this period of captivity was concluded, YHWH chose another man named Moses (Mosheh)[68] to help deliver them out of bondage.

The irony is that Mosheh was raised in the household of Pharaoh. Just as Joseph had been grafted into the Egyptian power structure to bring Yisrael into Egypt, now Mosheh was grafted in to lead them out. This was accomplished in a very unique and interesting fashion.

The Scriptures describe a time when the Pharaoh of Egypt instructed two Hebrew midwives to kill males that were born to Hebrew women. The midwives refused to obey. They revered Elohim over Pharaoh and they were blessed while the Yisraelites prospered. Later the Scriptures record: *"So Pharaoh commanded all his people, saying, 'Every son who is born you shall cast into the river, and every daughter you shall save alive.'"* Shemot 1:22.

A reasonable person might question why Pharaoh would do such a thing. Maybe he was cognizant of the fact that someone important was about to be born. Could it be that he was aware of the promise made to Abraham? After all, Abraham had contacts with Egypt.

Apparently, Pharaoh saw the Hebrews as a threat and sought to weaken them by killing their male offspring. There was a reason that Pharaoh had the children thrown into the Nile River. These children were an offering to the river god Hapi. Therefore, it was by no coincidence that YHWH sent a deliverer from those very waters.

Here is the account from the Scriptures. *"¹ And a man of the house of Levi went and took ×ץ a daughter of Levi. ² So the* woman conceived and bore a son. And when she saw ✗℧ that he was a beautiful child, she hid him three months. [3] But when she could no longer hide him, she took an ark of bulrushes for him, daubed it with asphalt and pitch, put therein ✗℧ the child, and laid it in the reeds by the river's bank." Shemot 2:1-3. Interestingly, in this passage which first describes the baby, there are three instances of the untranslated Aleph Taw (✗℧).

The Scriptures proceed to describe how this child was spared from the death sentence issued by Pharaoh. "[5] Then the daughter of Pharaoh came down to bathe at the river. And her maidens walked along the riverside; and when she saw ✗℧ the ark among the reeds, she sent ✗℧ her maid to get it. [6] And when she opened it, she saw ✗℧ the child, and behold, the baby wept. So she had compassion on him, and said, 'This is one of the Hebrews' children.'" Shemot 2:5-6.

This passage also includes three instances of the untranslated Aleph Taw (✗℧), so by now, a person reading the Hebrew text would begin to realize that this baby was quite special. There are many others that follow in the subsequent text as it describes how Pharaoh's daughter proceeds to adopt the child and name him Mosheh.

It was truly a miracle that this child was saved and adopted by the same family that was set to kill him. Pharaoh's daughter instantly knew that he was one of the Hebrews, because he was circumcised – he was a son of the Covenant.

There are two important questions that anyone would reasonably ask. First, Why did the mother of Mosheh choose this method of getting her child into the hands of Egyptian royalty? The second is: Why would the daughter of Pharaoh adopt a slave baby that was supposed to be killed?

The answer to both questions is better understood when you realize why Pharaoh's daughter was likely bathing in the Nile. We are talking about a River that is generally heavy laden with silt and filled with crocodiles. Not a very inviting place to take a bath. The princess could surely have had a nice, clean relaxing bath in the safety and security of

the palace.

Some speculate that she was not taking a bath, but rather she was immersing herself in the sacred River because she was barren. She was immersing herself in the hope that Hapi, the fertility god, would give her a child. Under these circumstances, you can imagine that the baby would have been considered to be an answer to prayer – a miracle child straight from the gods.

It is possible that Mosheh's mother was hoping for just that response. Any other way would have likely led to Mosheh being killed, along with the other Hebrew babies. How ironic since the method of disposing of the Hebrew children was to throw them into the Nile as an offering. Mosheh's mother surely knew the story of Noah being protected from the waters of judgment. Therefore, she made an ark for her son to escape Pharaoh's judgment.

Interestingly, according to Hebrew tradition in Sotah 12B, Mosheh was placed in the basket on the Appointed Time of Shabuot. The Book of Jubilees 47:4 says that Mosheh remained in the ark for seven days at which time he was discovered by Pharaoh's daughter.

As with Noah – this Ark was intimately connected with the Covenant. It pointed to the fact that the man in this "Covenant House" would be used by YHWH as a mediator for His Covenant plan. This child was a son of the Covenant – circumcised on the 8th day no doubt. He was being prepared to lead the seed of Abraham into their inheritance. The two Ark events are essentially book ends to a process leading up to the gathering of a Covenant people called Yisrael.

4

Yisrael

This is where we begin to see some of the patterns come together. Remember, it was Abram who was told that his seed would go into bondage. When that Covenant was made Abram was uncircumcised, and he did not pass through the cuttings. It would be through their captivity in Egypt that the seed of Abraham would mix with the nations, the uncircumcised, and an incredible pattern will emerge. Through this promise, the nations would be brought out of Egypt and gathered to YHWH.[69]

In order for this to occur, YHWH would raise up a deliverer to represent Him through the process. So we see this child, Mosheh, who was born to a Hebrew slave from the Tribe of Levi, and then placed into an Ark. He was put into the Nile River, the very place where the other Hebrew children were being thrown to their death. He survived Pharaoh's judgment and was adopted into the royal family of Egypt.

Mosheh was actually a prince of Egypt. He was apparently adopted by Sobekhotep IV Khaneferre, of the 13th Dynasty, whose wife was named 'Merris' according to ancient Jewish historian Artapanus.[70] Other texts describe the daughter of Pharaoh as Bathia or Bithia.[71]

After murdering an Egyptian, Mosheh fled Egypt, and eventually arrived in Midian where he met Zipporah at the well. While in Midian he returned to the heritage of his ancestors and became a shepherd of flocks. This life in

Midian was quite different than in Egypt. It must have been a humbling experience since shepherding was a lowly profession in Egyptian society. This was important training as Mosheh was preparing to lead the flock of Yisrael.

When he was about 77 years old, Mosheh saw a bush that burned with fire, but was not consumed. Seder Olam 5 says the episode of the burning bush took place on Day 15 of Month 1, the first day of another significant Appointed Time called the Feast of Unleavened Bread. It is important to note that this event occurred on Mt. Horeb, described as the Mountain of Elohim. The Messenger of YHWH appeared in "a flame of fire" out of the midst of a bush. (Shemot 3:1-2). In Hebrew "a flame of fire" is "b'labat ash" (ש א ×□٦□).

Also, the Hebrew for bush is "senah" (ΨЛ‡), which means "thorn, prick or bramble." Remember that Abraham took the ram from the thicket or thorn bush. He specifically said: "It shall be seen on the Mountain of YHWH." Was this what he was talking about?

Here we have fire - fire in a thorn bush. This was the same fire that passed through the pieces when Abram was "dead" during the Covenant process. Now this fire was in a thorn bush, just as the ram provided by YHWH was in a thorn bush. The connection between the fire and the ram is clear. This should immediately make us think about the Covenant, and this event is all about the Covenant with Abraham.

Mosheh then proclaimed: "*I will turn aside now and see* ×ʊ *this great appearance (phenomenon).*" Shemot 3:3. Mosheh turned to see the Aleph Taw (×ʊ), which also is connected with the fire and the ram. The implication is that Mosheh actually met with the Messiah, the Messenger of YHWH. The Scriptures record that YHWH saw him turn aside, and Elohim called from the bush. We now see a direct connection between Elohim, the fire, the ram and the Messiah in this event. Mosheh was told to take off his sandals for where he stood was holy – set apart – because the presence of YHWH was manifested in that space.

"[2] *Elohim also said to Mosheh, 'I Am YHWH.* [3] *I appeared to Abraham, to Yitshaq and to Yaakob as El Shaddai, but by My Name I was not known to them.* [4] *I also established* ✕Ƴ *My Covenant with them to give them* ✕Ƴ *the Land of Canaan,* ✕Ƴ *where they lived as aliens.* [5] *Moreover, I have heard* ✕Ƴ *the groaning of the Yisraelites, whom the Egyptians are enslaving, and I have remembered* ✕Ƴ *My Covenant.* [6] *Therefore, say to the Yisraelites: 'I Am YHWH, and I will bring you out from under the yoke of the Egyptians. I will free you from being slaves to them, and I will redeem you with an outstretched arm and with mighty acts of judgment.* [7] *I will take you as My own people, and I will be your Elohim. Then you will know that I Am YHWH your Elohim, who brought you out from under the yoke of the Egyptians.* [8] *And I will bring you to the Land I swore with uplifted hand to give to Abraham, to Yitshaq and to Yaakob. I will give it to you as a possession. I Am YHWH.'"* Shemot 6:2-8.

Mosheh was told that YHWH saw the suffering of the Yisraelites. YHWH then charged Mosheh to return to Egypt and deliver His people and gather His sheep out of bondage. This encounter was directly linked to the Covenant with Abraham and the Land of Canaan. YHWH remembered His Covenant with the offspring of Abraham and was ready to fulfill His promise. In that passage we see numerous instances of the Aleph Taw (✕Ƴ).

There is an interesting distinction made which deserves comment. YHWH specifically states that He appeared to Abraham, Yitshaq and Yaakob as El Shaddai, but by His Name He did not make Himself known. Does this mean that they did not know the Name of YHWH? Likely not since men were calling on the Name of YHWH since the time of Seth. (Beresheet 4:26).

We are looking at the distinction between a title and an actual name. While Abraham, Yitshaq and Yaakob knew YHWH and were in Covenant with Him, their relationship had not yet reached the level where they were on a "first name basis." We are dealing with intimacy here, YHWH was about to reveal the intimacy associated with the seed of Abraham through the Covenant of Circumcision, which was only alluded to in the flesh. While Abraham was a friend of YHWH, the plan was for a deeper relationship – Marriage.

In fact, YHWH said He would "take" the Yisraelites to be His own people and He would be their Elohim. The Hebrew word for "take" is "laqach" (ﬡﬠﬡ) which can mean: "to take in marriage." This relationship language, repeated throughout the Scriptures, describing YHWH as their Elohim and Yisrael as His people, refers to the marital relationship accomplished through the Marriage Covenant.

Mosheh was apparently overwhelmed with the great task assigned to him. He immediately begged YHWH not to make him speak as he was instructed. He indicated that he was slow of speech and tongue. Amazingly, this prince of Egypt, personally chosen by YHWH Himself, was shy and afraid. This once strong and bold man was now unsure of himself and his ability to speak, so YHWH instructed Mosheh to use his brother Aaron (Aharon).[72]

Mosheh and Aharon approached Pharaoh and attempted to obtain his permission to let the Yisraelites go into the desert to hold a festival to YHWH. The Scriptures detail the confrontation: "*¹ Afterward Mosheh and Aharon went to Pharaoh and said, This is what YHWH, the Elohim of Yisrael, says: 'Let My people go, so that they may hold a festival to Me in the desert.' ² Pharaoh said, 'Who is YHWH, that I should obey Him and let Yisrael go? I do not know YHWH and I will not let Yisrael go.' ³ Then they said, 'The Elohim of the Hebrews has met with us. Now let us take a three-day journey into the desert to offer sacrifices to YHWH our Elohim, or He may strike us with plagues or with the sword.'*" Shemot 5:1-3.

It is quite interesting to note that Pharaoh, the ruler of a large portion of the civilized world, did not know the Name of the Elohim of a large part of his population. That was about to change, because YHWH prepared a great deliverance for His people so that the whole world would thereafter know his Name.

These people, who were in Covenant with YHWH, were known as Hebrews and they were part of an assembly called Yisrael. While there was a tribe called Yahudah, members of which were later referred to as Jews, the Covenant people were Hebrews and YHWH is the Elohim of the Hebrews.

"*13 Then YHWH said to Mosheh, Get up early in the morning, confront Pharaoh and say to him, This is what YHWH, the Elohim of the Hebrews, says: Let My people go, so that they may worship Me, 14 or this time I will send the full force of My plagues against you and against your officials and your people, so you may know that there is no one like Me in all the earth. 15 For by now I could have stretched out My Hand and struck you and your people with a plague that would have wiped you off the earth. 16 But I have raised you up for this very purpose, that I might show you My power and that My Name might be proclaimed in all the earth.*" Shemot 9:13-17.

Notice again that YHWH identified Himself as "The Elohim of the Hebrews." Abram, being the first person called a Hebrew, represented a people who followed YHWH. In the Paleo script the word "Hebrew" is depicted as ↵ ૧▢◔. A mechanical translation is "eye – house – head – hand." Could it be that a Hebrew is one who sees the house and knows and does the commandments? There are many possible expansions and translations of this very important word, and Abram is the model for this word. We actually look to his life for the definition, and it did not stop with Abram.

Abram was later circumcised and his name was changed to Abraham. So a Hebrew is one who enters into the household of YHWH by hearing and obeying – Shema. A Hebrew then enters into the blood Covenant and becomes transformed into a new being. The Covenant of Circumcision leads one into the community of Yisrael (ૌ૪ ૧w↵). When you take the mark of circumcision, you are acknowledging that you belong to the royal family of El, that you walk straight in His path and He is your head. Therefore, Yisrael is essentially a community of Hebrews.

The household of Abram, and later Abraham, consisted of many people who were not his direct offspring. If they lived under his tent – they too were Hebrews if they followed his Elohim - YHWH.

YHWH called the first Hebrew out of Babylon and brought him to the Promised Land. Now YHWH was calling a "multitude" of Hebrews out of Egypt to the Covenant Land. This is a pattern that will be repeated again in the future.

Therefore, it was YHWH, the Elohim of the Hebrews, Who had sent a representative to collect His people. It was now time for the Name of YHWH to be proclaimed in all the earth. Pharaoh resisted and YHWH decimated this powerful nation through a series of plagues. Again, this was the pattern previously revealed through Abram.

YHWH eventually killed all of the firstborn of Egypt, who were not covered by the blood of the lamb, during the Passover, known as Pesach (ﬤﬤﬡ). This was in direct retaliation for what a Pharaoh had previously done to the Hebrew sons.

It is important to note that the Yisraelites were not harmed by those plagues, because they were set apart from the Egyptians. The Passover was specifically orchestrated to provide them protection from the final plague – death of the firstborn. Those who obeyed the instructions were spared from death, while those who did not obey received the final plague.

Now we do not know precisely who obeyed and who did not obey. There was clearly a distinction made between Yisrael and Egypt on that night. The Yisraelites were those who obeyed the instructions of YHWH delivered through Mosheh and Aharon, and the Egyptians were those who did not obey.

The primary distinction was not the land where you were born, they were all born in Egypt – thus they were technically all Egyptians by birth. The real question was

whether or not they were in Covenant with YHWH. Those who are in Covenant with YHWH become citizens of the Kingdom of YHWH.

All the males who obeyed were circumcised, and every one who was part of Yisrael ate of the lamb. (Shemot 12:43-49). All had to be within the Covenant of Circumcision which involved, not only the act of circumcision, but also belief in the promises of YHWH.

Every individual had to demonstrate their belief by following the instructions, called the Torah. YHWH was very specific about the fact that: "*the same Torah applies to the native-born and to the alien living among you.*" Shemot 12:49. There were not different rules for different people. Just as with the tents of Abraham, if you wanted to dwell within the Covenant, you obeyed the same rules of the house – no exceptions and no differences.

As a result, everyone who participated in the Passover was in "am Yisrael" - the people of Yisrael. It was the firstborn of "am Yisrael" who were delivered from death, while the firstborn of the Egyptians were killed.[73] The households of all who obeyed - all that were protected by the blood of the lamb - were delivered from death. But there was more to the promise than mere salvation from physical death of the firstborn. This was just the beginning of their journey of deliverance. There was still much more to be completed at the Mountain of YHWH and it would all revolve around the Appointed Times.

Just as Adam was connected to YHWH and that connection was broken through disobedience, YHWH had plans to reconnect that relationship through the union of marriage with those who obeyed. This pattern was seen through the life of Abraham.

After the Passover meal at the beginning of Day 14 of Month 1, and the night of death, the Children of Yisrael plundered the Egyptians. They departed in a calm and organized fashion on Day 15 of Month 1, loaded with gold and

silver. These people had become free and rich overnight!

It is critical to point out that the children of Yisrael were miraculously delivered from Egypt, not by themselves, but along with a mixed multitude of people. According to Shemot 12:37-38: "*37 The children of Yisrael journeyed from Ramses to Succot, about six hundred thousand men on foot, besides children. 38 A mixed multitude went up with them also, and flocks and herds - a great deal of livestock.*"

This is very important and often overlooked. Remember that as a result of Joseph and his leadership Egypt owned much land and possessions. People had come from all over the world seeking food and many sold themselves into servitude. The children of Yisrael were probably not the only slaves in Mitsrayim. This is how the unique Covenants made with Abram and Abraham would be combined. It is a pattern of how the nations would be joined, through the shedding of blood, with Yisrael.

I imagine that if you were a slave, and just witnessed your master wiped out by a Mighty Elohim, you would probably leave if you had the chance. This is not to say that everyone that went with Yisrael was a slave. There were likely a variety of people from every level of Egyptian society. This mixed multitude consisted of a diversity of people from a range of cultures and languages.

It was the children of Yisrael, along with this mixed multitude, who were redeemed. It is at this point in the Scriptures that we begin to see the redemption plan of YHWH unfold. In ancient days the process of redemption typically involved purchasing something that used to belong to you or a kinsman. It might be land, property or even a person.

The Exodus from Egypt was an act of redemption, and this concept of redemption is essential to understand. It implies either ownership, right or title to something or someone. It was because of this relationship, through the Covenant established with Abraham, that the Hebrews were

redeemed and the price of redemption was the blood of the Lamb which was demonstrated through the Passover. This redemption was for a reason higher than merely freeing slaves. The redemption was meant to restore that which had been lost in Eden.

After this great troop of people marched out of Ramses as a conquering army, the Scriptures record that they camped at a place called Succot. It is no coincidence that the first place that they camped was Succot, just as their father Yisrael had first camped at Succot when he returned to the Land.[74] These were not the same physical locations, but they obviously are meant to tell us something. Succot, as it turns out, is more than just a place – it is also a time. It is a very important Appointed Time that we will read about further on in the discussion.

After leaving Succot, the Yisraelites then proceeded to different camps led by YHWH Who appeared as "a pillar of fire" by night and "a pillar of cloud" by day. This imagery should continue to remind the reader of when the smoking furnace and the lamp of fire passed through the cuttings of the Covenant made with Abram. This fire and cloud was YHWH fulfilling His promise. This was a Covenant procession.

Again, notice that just as the household of Abraham had originally contained numerous individuals who were not his physical descendants, so too this great assembly included the physical offspring of Yisrael as well as a mixed multitude of people.

The Scriptures record that the assembly was led to the edge of the Red Sea where they found themselves trapped between water and the army of Pharaoh. *"Then Mosheh stretched out* ×ʏ *his hand over the sea; and YHWH caused* ×ʏ *the sea to go back by a strong east wind all that night, and made* ×ʏ *the sea into dry land, and the waters were divided."* Shemot 14:21. In this passage there are three instances of the Aleph Taw (×ʏ) related directly to the waters of the sea.

The waters have always symbolized judgment and cleansing. When YHWH previously flooded the planet He was judging the people for their sin while cleansing the planet from that sin. When the Yisraelites passed through the parted waters of the Red Sea, they literally passed through judgment and were cleansed. The very same waters that were used to cleanse this people were later used to judge Egypt. This act of passing through the waters was symbolic immersion or "mikvah."[75]

At this point in their journey the Scriptures provide a very interesting time reference. *"[40] Now the sojourning of the children of Yisrael, who dwelt in Egypt, was four hundred and thirty years. [41] And it came to pass at the end of the four hundred and thirty years, even the selfsame day it came to pass, that all the hosts of YHWH went out from the land of Egypt. [42] It is a night to be much observed unto YHWH for bringing them out from the land of Egypt: this is that night of YHWH to be observed of all the children of Yisrael in their generations."* Shemot 12:40-42.

Notice the reference to the "selfsame day." Some erroneously construe this text to mean that they left the same night of the Passover. That is not a correct understanding. They did not even begin to leave Egypt until Day 15 of Month 1. They camped in several locations on their journey out of Egypt. They started at Ramses and travelled to Succot. They then travelled to Etham, on the edge of the wilderness. Pharaoh's heart was hardened and he gave chase with all of his horses and chariots. He found Yisrael camped by the Sea at Pihahiroth, which is on the eastern shore of the Sinai Peninsula, presently called Nuweiba.

So this was not just some arbitrary day that they left Egypt, it was the seventh day of Unleavened Bread – Day 21 of Month 1. This is a well accepted Hebrew tradition from Seder Olam 5, Sotah 12B, Megillah 31A, Rashi Shemot 14.5. It is also a tradition that even carries into Rabbinic Judaism, when they sing the Song of Mosheh on Day 21 of Month 1, although on a false calendar. (Shemot 15:1).

Also note the emphasis on the night. It is a night to be

observed - that night of YHWH as they crossed through the Red Sea. It was in the morning of the seventh day of Unleavened Bread, on Day 21 of Month 1, that the Yisraelites, after having "crossed over" to the other side, witnessed the destruction of Pharaoh's army. (Shemot 14:30). Interestingly, this day is an "atzeret" - one of 2 days when Yisrael is commanded to assemble.

Although Yisrael left the city of Ramses on Day 15 of Month 1 according to Bemidbar 33:3, their journey out of Egypt took them seven days to complete. They only left the borders of the nation of Egypt when they crossed the Red Sea on Day 21 of Month 1 according to Shemot 12:41-42.

Now we also read the first specific reference to an Appointed Time, the time of Passover and Unleavened Bread. "*3 And Mosheh said unto the people, 'Remember this day, in which you came out from Egypt, out of the house of bondage; for by strength of hand YHWH brought you out from this place: there shall no leavened bread be eaten. 4 This day came you out in the month of the abib. . . . 8 And you shall show your son in that day, saying, This is done because of that which YHWH did unto me when I came forth out of Egypt. 9 And it shall be for a sign unto you upon your hand, and for a memorial between your eyes, that the Torah of YHWH may be in your mouth: for with a strong hand has YHWH brought you out of Egypt. 10 You shall therefore keep this ordinance at its Appointed Time from year to year.*" Shemot 13:3-4, 8-10.

So here we have a specific command to observe these times as Appointed Times. The story is to be told and it will be "a sign upon your hand and for a memorial between your eyes." Anyone unfamiliar with the Shema would find this language to be quite strange. This is actually linking the observance of Passover with the Shema.[76] As previously mentioned, the word for "sign" is "owt" (×ℸⴟ), and it is the same word used for the various signs, or marks of the Covenant. Notice the Aleph Taw (×ⴟ) surrounding the vav (ℸ), which is a "nail" or "stake." The word for "memorial" is "zikrone" (ꜜℸ ⴑ⅏ℸ), which also means: "remember."

The children of Yisrael were to remember they were on their way to the Land promised to Abraham. These people were like a bride preparing to be married to YHWH. Their journey was symbolic of the preparations for a wedding. As the Bride of YHWH, they first needed to be separated from the abominations of the Egyptians and then they needed to be cleansed. Once this occurred, they needed to prepare themselves for the wedding ceremony.

Prior to a Hebrew wedding, a bride will immerse herself representing that she is pure for her husband. This was the purpose of the waters of the Red Sea. The mixed multitude received cleansing through these divided waters while the Egyptians received judgment. The symbolism with the Covenant established with Abram is profound. The fire was there protecting the Hebrews, as a shield. The waters of this "red" sea actually symbolized the blood of the Covenant.

The interesting thing that must be pointed out is that within this dual Covenant, there is individual responsibility and community responsibility. The people must obey individually, and they must obey as a community. They were washed as a community, but they would still need to cleanse themselves individually.

The Scriptures record that the Children of Yisrael were led into the Desert of Shur. For three days they travelled without finding water and they grumbled against Mosheh. They had just been passed over from death, freed from slavery, given great wealth and miraculously saved from the army of Pharaoh, and it only took them three days to start complaining.

Mosheh cried out to YHWH and YHWH showed him a piece of wood that, when thrown into the water, made it sweet. The people were being tested and they were given a very specific and powerful promise. *"If you listen carefully to the voice of YHWH your Elohim and do what is right in His eyes, if you pay attention to His commands and keep all His decrees, I will not bring on you any of the diseases I brought on the Egyptians, for I AM YHWH who heals you."* Shemot 15:26.

Just as He instructed Abraham to walk perfect before Him, YHWH was telling these people to do the same. In other words, in order to avoid the judgments that the Egyptians had just experienced – walk perfect before Elohim. This perfect walk then led them to a veritable oasis called Elim which contained twelve (12) springs and seventy (70) palm trees. One cannot ignore the significance of these numbers.[77]

After leaving Elim, they travelled to the desert of Sin. On Day 15 of Month 2 the whole community grumbled against Mosheh and Aharon. This time they were complaining about the food. They alleged that Mosheh and Aharon brought them out into the wilderness to starve to death. Notwithstanding the fact that they came out of Egypt with their cattle, YHWH provided them with quail in the evening and manna in the morning. They were not to keep any manna overnight. They were to gather it for six days, but not the seventh, which was the Sabbath.

YHWH, once again, gave them very specific instructions to test them. He wanted to see if they would diligently obey His commandments. Many would not. When they left Sin they journeyed to Rephidim where there was no water. Again, they were being tested and they quarreled with Mosheh. This time Mosheh was instructed to take some of the elders along with the rod which he used to strike the Nile. He struck the rock at Horeb at the place he called Massah and Meribah. Water poured forth from the rock for all the people to drink.

Sadly, the people had been tested and they failed. They still had a slave mentality and needed a serious attitude adjustment. In order to be Covenant people, they needed to trust the One Who they were in Covenant with. They needed to believe as their father Abraham believed.

Later, when they fought the Amalekites, they were victorious as long as Mosheh kept his arms raised to YHWH. The point was crystal clear – look to YHWH and give Him worship and praise and He will provide for their every need. He would even fight with them in their battles.

The people eventually moved on from Rephidim to the desert of Sinai where they camped in front of Mount Sinai. When they arrived at the mountain we read the following passage. "*³ Then Mosheh went up to Elohim, and YHWH called to him from the mountain and said, This is what you are to say to the house of Yaakob and what you are to tell the people of Yisrael: ⁴ You yourselves have seen what I did to Egypt, and how I carried you on eagles' wings and brought you to Myself. ⁵ Now if you obey Me fully and keep My Covenant, then out of all nations you will be My treasured possession. Although the whole earth is mine, ⁶ you will be for Me a kingdom of priests and a set apart nation. These are the words you are to speak to the Yisraelites.*" Shemot 19:3-6.

Notice the distinction between "the house of Yaakob" and "the people of Yisrael." The house of Yaakob was referring to all of the direct descendants of Yaakob and the people of Yisrael were all those in Covenant with YHWH. Yaakob was the name of Yisrael before he entered into the fullness of the Covenant, before He fully became a Covenant people dwelling in the Land. Yisrael is the name representing the people in Covenant with YHWH.

Your genetics do not dictate your Covenant status – it is your heart. We shall soon see that the Covenant of Circumcision, which began in the male organ, will ultimately extend to the heart. Our willingness to obey is often a good representation of our hearts.

Here is the mandate for these people – keep (shamar) the Covenant. Guard it and protect it, just as Adam was to have done and as Abraham had done. They

needed to obey YHWH fully, not partially or half-heartedly. If they did this, they would be a kingdom of priests - set apart from all other nations.

This was essentially a marriage proposal that Mosheh then brought to the elders and the people. Their response was unequivocal – "We will do everything YHWH has said." In other words – "I do." They accepted the proposal and were all told to get cleaned up for the ceremony. Even though they were part of a community, as individuals they all had to wash their clothes, wash their bodies – consecrate themselves like a bride preparing for her wedding. The ceremony would take place "on the third day." Then YHWH would come down from the mountain in the sight of all the people.

YHWH was now completing the marriage Covenant aspect of the Abrahamic Covenant. Included within that Covenant were those who dwelled together in the community known as Yisrael. They would not know YHWH simply as El Shaddai – a title. They would now know Him by Name. The instructions, known as the Torah, remained at the center of the Covenant - like a Ketubah or a written marriage contract between a husband and a wife.[78]

When a Hebrew bride and groom enter into their marriage relationship, they traditionally stand underneath a huppa, which consists of the four-cornered garment of the husband, known as a tallit. This symbolizes the protection or the covering of YHWH over the relationship. When YHWH prepared to marry Yisrael, His Huppa of smoke descended over them. They then camped at the base of Mount Sinai and preparations were made for the wedding ceremony.

Remember, this was the Mountain of YHWH where Mosheh originally received instructions from the fire in the thicket bush. This is where the fullness of the Covenant was going to be revealed to the seed of Abraham.

As YHWH began to speak the terms of the Covenant, the people began to experience the awesome presence of YHWH and became afraid. *"[18] Now all the people saw ×ϑ the thunderings and ×ϑ the lightning flashes and ×ϑ the voice (sound) of the shofar, and ×ϑ the mountain smoking; and when the people saw it, they trembled and stood afar off. [19] Then they said to Mosheh, You speak with us, and we will hear; but let not Elohim speak with us, lest we die."* Shemot 20:18-19.

After Elohim had spoken what are referred to as the ten commandments, or ten words, the people could not take anymore. They were afraid of what they saw, they even "saw the sound." They asked Mosheh to listen to the commandments, and then relay them to the people. This is very important, because they actually asked Mosheh to represent YHWH in their marital relationship. They asked a man to stand between them in their relationship with YHWH.

YHWH agreed to this request. So Mosheh, as the mediator of the Covenant, drew near the thick darkness where Elohim was. He then transmitted the Words to the people.

While the instructions had been revealed to mankind from the beginning, something different was happening at Mount Sinai - just like something different happened with Abraham. Something was being birthed at Sinai. We read that Mosheh was on the Mountain 40 days and 40 nights and the use of the number 40 is no coincidence.

Remember how Noah and the Covenant family were protected from the waters which rained 40 days and 40 nights. The Hebrew letter mem (ᴹᴹ) has the numerical equivalence of 40. Mem (ᴹᴹ) means "water" and is linked to the water of a womb. Just as that Covenant family protected in the Ark, the Covenant house, were birthing a new beginning for mankind on Earth, we can see the same happening here. The number 40 always carries with it the meaning of a probationary period. This theme readily reveals

itself throughout the entire Scriptures.

This group of people, lead through the waters of the Red Sea by the man Mosheh whose name literally means: "out of water," were in the midst of another birthing process. It was another step in the process of restoring mankind with the Creator. It was another phase in the Covenant cycle. At this time, the Torah was written and incorporated into a Covenant with these redeemed people called Yisrael.

YHWH had told Abram that his seed would be afflicted for 400 years.[79] When the time was up, at the Appointed Time, the promise was fulfilled through the seed of Abraham that passed through Yitshaq to Yaakob - whose name was changed to Yisrael.

At Sinai, YHWH was consummating the marriage Covenant, and included within that Covenant were those who dwelled with Yisrael. An important part of this Covenant involved the Moadim, which were specifically outlined for the people. In fact, this would be the first time that the Appointed Times are fully detailed in the Scriptures. These are to this day the Appointments between YHWH and His Covenant people Yisrael.

5

Appointments

Before the Children of Yisrael left Egypt YHWH gave Mosheh and Aharon a lesson in time. *"¹ And YHWH spoke unto Mosheh and Aharon in the land of Egypt, saying, ² This month shall be unto you the beginning of months: it shall be the first month of the year to you."* Shemot 12:1-2.

The Hebrew word for month is "chodesh" (wᴜᴴ). It actually means: "to bring back, to make anew." There is no definite period of time established for a month other than the cycle of the moon. Unlike a week, which consists of seven full days, the months are not based upon a specific day count cycle. The months are intimately connected with the cycle of the moon.

The moon travels around the earth in 29.53059 days *on average*, which is called a synodic month. A synodic month is 29 days, 7 hours, 44 minutes, 2.8 seconds on average as measured from one astronomical new moon to another. An astronomical new moon is defined as occurring when the moon has the same ecliptic longitude as the sun, as seen from the center of the earth. In other words, it is when the sun, the moon and the earth are almost in one line. This is the modern measure of a new moon that is published in newspapers and used by the astronomical community in general.

However, as precise as man has become in understanding the science of celestial mechanics, the new moon used for reckoning time on the Creation Calendar of YHWH is the first visible crescent moon. A Hebrew month is defined as the moment of sunset the evening the moon's crescent first becomes potentially visible to the naked eye in Jerusalem, assuming ideal sighting conditions without smog, haze or clouds. The ancients always looked for the visible crescent moon which was an owt (ﬡﬡﬡ) or "sign" to them. (Encyclopedia Judaica, Vol. 12, p. 1039). The ancients called the new moon "rosh chodesh" - literally "head of the renewal" or "head of the month."

The text in Shemot 12 is specifically referencing a "renewed moon" which would occur when the first sliver of the moon is seen, marking the beginning of a month.[80] So we have YHWH, telling Mosheh and Aharon that "this new moon" shall be the beginning of new moons – it shall be the first new moon of the year or cycle (shanah).

Some who desire to follow Torah erroneously hold to the astronomical view of the new moon. They believe that the moon is renewed when it is in conjunction with the sun and the earth. While the conjunction actually only lasts for a few minutes, the moon will not be visible for as many as 3 days. Astrology actually refers to this as the "dead" moon. There is no historical support for the conjunction position being used by Yisrael, and it actually flies in the face of the entire context of the passage.

There is a mathematical aspect to the calendar, the greater light - shemesh (ﬡﬡﬡ) and the lesser light - yerach (ﬡﬡﬡ), were set in the sky to serve as markers so that we can discern the time, like hands on a clock. The Scriptural Calendar is thus described as luni-solar. Both the sun and the moon are integral in determining the length of a year.

Remember that the moon is made for a sign, and that sign is intimately related to the passage of a month. (Beresheet 1:14). It could be argued that this is the primary purpose of the moon. A sign is meant to be seen, not calculated. It is quite absurd to think that Mosheh and Aharon were looking up at nothing.

In fact, you can almost picture Mosheh and Aharon standing in Egypt looking up at the sliver of the new moon as

YHWH gave them the instructions in Shemot 12:2. Further, the concept of bringing back and making anew is consistent with something that can be seen. The renewal of light from darkness has very deep significance.

When YHWH instructed Mosheh and Aharon to reckon the month of the Exodus as "the head of the months" (Rosh Chodeshim) in Shemot 12:2, He was apparently asking Yisrael to change their paradigm about how to reckon a year. The physical universe was created in the fall in Month 7 as a result of the fall of satan. Therefore, mankind from Adam to Mosheh apparently reckoned a year from the fall – ie. Month 7 to Month 7. This is the reckoning for the Civil Year and the physical universe.

As YHWH wanted Yisrael to be a renewed spiritual nation walking in the light of truth, He instructed Mosheh and Aharon to reckon a year from the spring – ie. Month 1 to Month 1. This is the reckoning for the Spiritual Year and the spiritual universe. Just as the spiritual universe preceded the physical universe by 6 months,* so the Spiritual Year precedes the Civil Year by 6 months. This overlap between the Spiritual Year and the Civil Year are the warp and woof of all things spiritual and temporal.

Paradigm Shift to Spiritual Reckoning

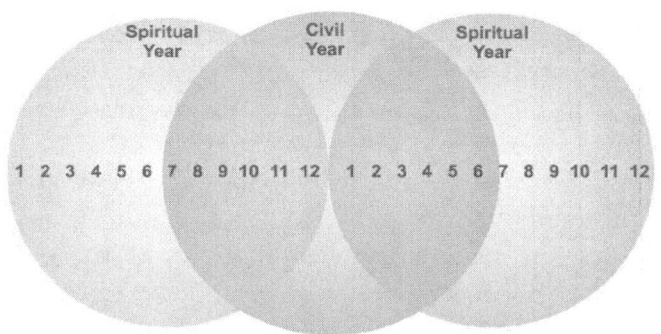

Shemot 12:2

This interplay between the Spiritual year and the Civil year makes even more sense when we examine the timing of all of the Moadim, and their corresponding parallels. When viewed in the context of this inter-locking relationship, we can see the same pattern emerge in the Appointed Times of YHWH. There is a 7 day Festival in month 1 as well as month 7.

Those who properly keep the Appointed Times of YHWH naturally come to recognize the existence and connection between the Spiritual Calendar and the Civil Calendar. For instance, there is a very special and unique Appointed Time on Day 1 of Month 7, while Day 1 of Month 1 was the Day that Mosheh erected the Tabernacle in the wilderness – an act that symbolized the marriage of YHWH to Yisrael. This is but one example, and we will examine that interrelationship repeatedly throughout this discussion.

We know that Yisrael observed the Passover on day 14 of month 1. They then departed from Ramses on day 15 and eventually crossed the Red Sea on Day 21. This seven day trek out of the land of Egypt occurred during a special Appointed Time called the Feast of Unleavened Bread. Yisrael was on the move for this seven day period, and did not have time for their bread to rise. How interesting that this event is commemorated by food. As we shall see, bread is symbolic of sustenance, and is a very important part of the Appointed Times.

After the Yisraelites were miraculously delivered from Egypt through the parting of the Red Sea, they were directed to the mountain where they would prepare themselves to enter into Covenant with YHWH. Throughout their trek to the mountain we are provided specific information concerning time, and we can discern when they eventually stood terrified at the base of Mount Sinai in Arabia, and heard the voice of YHWH proclaim the Ten Words.[81]

This day was no ordinary day. It was a very specific and special day. It was another Appointed Time, when YHWH spoke the Ten Words to Yisrael. Often referred to as the Ten Commandments, these Words stand apart from all others because they were spoken by YHWH to all of Yisrael. The children of Yisrael could not bear to hear the Voice of YHWH and requested that Mosheh be their mediator. (Shemot 20:19).

The people remained at a distance while Mosheh drew near to the thick darkness where Elohim was located. There he heard the words of YHWH. It was there in the thick darkness that YHWH gave the instructions to Yisrael regarding how they should live. This was essentially the instruction manual for a group of people taken out of a pagan civilization and chosen to dwell with the Creator of the Universe. These were the instructions for a Covenant people.

YHWH gave instructions on how to live with one another and how to deal fairly with people, including aliens and slaves. These were instructions for righteous and just living. YHWH ended with great promises concerning the Land that was previously promised to Abraham's seed. Interestingly, couched between the general list of instructions and the promise of the Land, they were given a schedule of appointments that they were supposed to keep.

Specifically, the Yisraelites were reminded of the Sabbath. They had already been instructed that the seventh day was set apart. It was a day when no work was done. They were also given three annual appointments when all of the men were to appear before YHWH.

"*14* Three times a year you shall celebrate a feast (hagag) unto Me. *15* ΧΥ-the Feast of Unleavened Bread (hag hamatzot) you shall keep (shamar) seven days: eat unleavened bread (matza) as I commanded you, in the appointed time (moad) the month (chodesh) of the abib; for in it you came out from Egypt: and none shall appear before Me empty: *16* And the Feast of the cutting (haqatsiyr), the firstfruits (bikkuri) of your labors, which you have sown in the field: and the Feast of Ingathering (awseef), which is in the end of the year, when you have gathered in your labors out of the field *17* Three times in the year all your males shall appear before the Master YHWH." Shemot 23:14-17.*

I included some transliteration of various Hebrew words so that you can see how much information is packed into this short verse. All three of these times are called Feasts, which is "hag" (ᴧᕼ) in Hebrew. It means: "festival" or "gathering."

Interestingly, no specific dates are provided, except for the reference of unleavened bread to be kept as they were already commanded. The Feast of Ingathering was at the "end" of the year, and the Feast of the cutting of the harvest was to occur somewhere in between the others.

Notice that the three times are preceded by the ᙭ᕘ which is literally connected with the Feast of Unleavened Bread. In fact, it immediately precedes the Feast, which is when the Passover occurs. So we have a powerful connection between the Messiah and the Passover.

We are told that Mosheh spoke all the Words that YHWH had given him, and also wrote down all the Words. (Shemot 24:3-4). These Words were the instructions for a Covenant people to live with the Creator. After the golden calf incident, they obviously needed some parameters. They clearly did not instinctively know how to please YHWH, so they were given very specific and straight forward instructions.

The people agreed to obey all of the Words and those instructions were not too difficult for the Yisraelites to obey as specifically indicated by Mosheh. (Debarim 30:11-14). For some reason, many people believe that YHWH gave Yisrael a burdensome set of rules and regulations that essentially put them into bondage. There are those who refer to Yisrael as being placed "under the law" as if YHWH delivered them from slavery in Egypt simply to make them His slaves.

Nothing could be further from the truth, and those who hold that view had better rethink their opinion of YHWH. He is not a cruel slave master as some would dare to portray Him. The Torah was a gift to Yisrael, and was meant to provide them with abundant blessings. It was a treasure because it unlocked some of the mysteries of the universe. It showed them the way to abundant blessing and life. It showed them the Covenant path back to the Garden.

The Children of Yisrael entered into Covenant with YHWH. This Covenant was confirmed by blood, half of the blood was sprinkled on the altar and half was sprinkled on the people. (Shemot 24). Mosheh, Aharon, Nadab and Abihu, along with seventy elders of Yisrael then went up and "*saw the Elohim of Yisrael.*" (Shemot 24:10). They ate and drank with Him in a very special place.

A very interesting event, shrouded with much mystery, then occurs. The Scriptures describe that Mosheh and his assistant Yahushua (Joshua) rose up, and Mosheh went up to the Mountain of Elohim.

"*15 And Mosheh went up into the mount, and a cloud covered the mount. 16 And the glory of YHWH abode upon Mount Sinai, and the cloud covered it six days: and the seventh day He called unto Mosheh out of the midst of the cloud. 17 And the sight of the glory of YHWH was like devouring fire on the top of the mount in the eyes of the children of Yisrael. 18 And Mosheh went into the midst of the cloud, and he went up into the mount, and Mosheh was in the mount forty (40) days and forty (40) nights.*" Shemot 24:15-18. It was on the seventh day that YHWH called out to Mosheh from the midst of the cloud, and this was the seventh day of the week.

Thereafter, YHWH gave Mosheh instructions concerning building His House, known as the Tabernacle, as well as all of the furnishings. He was also given the instructions for those who would serve in the House. When all of the instructions concerning the House were given, YHWH ended with this final instruction:

"*12 And YHWH spoke to Mosheh, saying, 13 Speak thou also unto the children of Yisrael, saying, Verily My Sabbaths you shall keep: for it is a sign between Me and you throughout your generations; that you may know that I am YHWH that does set you apart. 14 You shall keep the Sabbath therefore; for it is set apart*

unto you: every one that defileth it shall surely be put to death: for whosoever does any work therein, that soul shall be cut off from among his people. *[15]* Six days may work be done; but in the seventh is the Sabbath of rest, set apart to YHWH: whosoever doeth any work in the Sabbath day, he shall surely be put to death. *[16]* Wherefore the children of Yisrael shall keep the Sabbath, to observe the Sabbath throughout their generations, for a perpetual Covenant. *[17]* It is a sign between Me and the children of Yisrael throughout the ages: for in six days YHWH made heaven and earth, and on the seventh day He rested, and was refreshed. *[18]* And He gave unto Mosheh, when He had made an end of communing with him upon Mount Sinai, two tables of testimony, tables of stone, written with the finger of Elohim." Shemot 31:12-18.

So the Sabbath cycle was referred to as a perpetual Covenant. The Sabbath was actually woven into the thread of Yisrael. Interestingly, the word Sabbath is mentioned six times, which is a number attributed to man. So we see that the Sabbath was actually made for man. We also see the creation of two tablets of testimony written on both sides with the finger of Elohim. (Shemot 32:15-16). Prior to that time Mosheh had spoken the words, and written them on a Scroll. Now the Words of the Covenant were etched in stone.

This was a great moment. The Covenant relationship was sealed. It should have been a happy ending, but sadly, while Mosheh was on the mountain working out the Covenant, the Yisraelites were down below fornicating. When Mosheh saw what the Yisraelites were doing he broke the tablets. The Covenant had been broken.

While the Yisraelites had entered into a relationship with YHWH and reaped the rewards of deliverance, they committed idolatry, which was similar to adultery. They were unfaithful in their relationship with YHWH. They were running around naked, fornicating with Egyptian gods, which obviously made YHWH incensed.

It is no different than a man walking in on his fiancé while she is in the midst of an orgy. It was an unimaginably repulsive act of unfaithfulness. The deal was off. YHWH had no obligation to continue with the relationship, and who would blame Him if He simply smote the Yisraelites for their

unfaithfulness. They had made gods of gold in direct contravention to the commandments of YHWH.

They had made sacrifices to their calf, but that was not the only blood that was shed that day. Three thousand died at the hands of the Levites. That day the Levites acted as the Hand of YHWH, and as a result, they were blessed and set apart. They would stand in the place of the firstborn of Yisrael. They would be substitutes that would serve in the House of YHWH in place of the firstborn. This was a very significant event that will be discussed further in the text.

Mosheh thereafter returned to YHWH, and confessed the sins of Yisrael. He interceded and offered himself to be blotted out of the Scroll YHWH has written.[82] Mosheh essentially offered himself as an atonement for their sins. YHWH agreed to continue with the promises, but He assured Mosheh that those who sinned would be punished. YHWH struck Yisrael with a plague because of the calf Aharon made.

Things were different now. YHWH would fulfill His Word. He would allow them to go into the Land, but He said, "*I will not go with you, because you are a stiff necked people and I might destroy you on the way.*" Shemot 33:3. The party was over. The people were told to take off their ornaments, and YHWH would decide what to do with them. Mosheh spoke with YHWH and requested that the presence of YHWH be with them. YHWH replied "*My presence will go with you, and I will give you rest.*" Shemot 33:14.

Probably the most critical point in this entire process is the fact that the Yisraelites were given a second chance. Since the Covenant was broken, it needed to be renewed. This time, the man who mediated had to cut the stones and carry them up the mountain. Mosheh cut the new set of tablets and once again ascended the mountain. YHWH again inscribed the commandments, the same words that were inscribed upon the first tablets.

"[1] And YHWH said unto Mosheh, Hew thee two tables of stone like unto the first: and I will write upon these tables the words that were in the first tables, which thou brakest. [2] And be ready in the morning, and come up in the morning unto mount Sinai, and present thyself there to Me in the top of the Mount. [3] And no man shall come up with thee, neither let any man be seen throughout all the Mount; neither let the flocks nor herds feed before that mount. [4] And he hewed two tables of stone like unto the first; and Mosheh rose up early in the morning, and went up unto mount Sinai, as YHWH had commanded him, and took in his hand the two tables of stone." Shemot 34:1-4.

Mosheh was once again on the mountain for 40 days and 40 nights. This time the Scriptures specifically record that he was fasting. As the mediator of this renewed Covenant, he was now becoming the suffering servant, a role that would become increasingly important in a future renewal.

Interestingly, during this renewal process YHWH once again reiterated the three Appointed Times mentioned previously. These times are obviously significant to receive so much attention.

"[18] The Feast of Unleavened Bread shalt thou keep. Seven days thou shalt eat unleavened bread, as I commanded thee, in the time of the month the abib: for in the month of the abib you came out from Egypt. [19] All that opens the matrix is mine; and every firstling among your cattle, whether ox or sheep, that is male. [20] But the firstling of an ass you shalt redeem with a lamb: and if you redeem him not, then shalt thou break his neck. All the firstborn of your sons you shall redeem. And none shall appear before Me empty. [21]

Six days you shall work, but on the seventh day you shall rest: in earing time and in harvest you shall rest. [22] *And you shall observe the Feast of Weeks, of the firstfruits of wheat harvest, and the Feast of Ingathering at the year's end.* [23] *Three times in the year shall all your men children appear before the Master YHWH, the Elohi of Yisrael.* [24] *For I will cast out the nations before thee, and enlarge your borders: neither shall any man desire your land, when you shall go up to appear before YHWH your Elohim three times in the year."* Shemot 34:18-24.

We are given a little more information relative to the three appointments. We already knew that the Feast of Unleavened Bread would occur during the month of the abib. Abib refers to "fresh, young ears of barley." It is a seven day Feast, and only unleavened bread is to be eaten during the entire period of time. We previously read the instruction that none were to appear empty handed and that point was reiterated. While there is no mention of the Passover in this passage, it is alluded to in the reference to the male firstborns belonging to YHWH. Passover on Day 14 of Month 1 was the day the firstborn were redeemed.

This also marks the beginning of the harvest, and the Yisraelites are reminded to work six days and rest on the seventh, even during the harvest. We then read about the Feast of Weeks, previously referred to as the Feast of cutting. This Feast was directly linked with the firstfruits of the wheat harvest, but we are not given a specific time when to celebrate that Feast. Finally, we read a very terse reference to the Feast of Ingathering. This Feast is to occur at year's end, which is "tequfot hashanah" in Hebrew – the turn or circuit of the year.

After 40 days and 40 nights Mosheh descended from the mountain. His face actually radiated so that he needed to wear a veil over his face.[83] All tolled, there were three different times when Mosheh went up the mountain for 40 days and 40 nights.[84] Remember the significance of 40 with the letter mem (ᴍ). These three times on the Mountain meeting with YHWH are mirrored in the three times each

year that we are to "appear before YHWH."

These 3 annual appointments are an intimate part of the Covenant process just as the 3 meetings between Mosheh and YHWH were critical to the Covenant process. Something is birthed during these 3 annual times. So we can see that an important part of the Covenant process involved appointments that they needed to keep with YHWH. Just as a pregnant woman attends regular checkups with her doctor prior to giving birth, so these Covenant people must keep their spiritual appointments with YHWH.

After descending from the Mountain, Mosheh then went on to gather the offerings of materials to build the House, but first he reiterated the command concerning the Sabbath. He reminded them that it was a set apart day – qadosh (ⲱⵡⵤⴼ).

The first mention of an appointment was actually spoken by YHWH when He proclaimed the Ten Words. Commonly referred to as the Fourth Commandment it was given as follows: "*[8] Remember the Sabbath day, to keep it set apart. [9] Six days shall you labor, and do all your work: [10] But the seventh day is the Sabbath of YHWH your Elohim, in it you shall not do any work, you, nor your son, nor your daughter, your manservant, nor your maidservant, nor your cattle, nor your stranger that is within thy gates: [11] For in six days YHWH made heaven and earth, the sea, and all that in them is, and rested the seventh day: wherefore YHWH blessed the Sabbath day, and set it apart.*" Shemot 20:8-11.

Notice that it is the Sabbath of YHWH. It belongs to Him. It was not newly established for Yisrael on that day. It was created at the beginning. This was not the first time that the Yisraelites were told about the Sabbath. Earlier in the journey out of Egypt, when they were given the promise of manna, they were also instructed to rest on the seventh day. (See Shemot 16:23). YHWH also ended His instructions with the Sabbath as seen in Shemot 31:12-17, so the Sabbath was firmly established as a very significant time.

So before Yisrael could begin building the House of

YHWH, they needed to be reminded of the Sabbath. As YHWH rested after building all of Creation, they were to rest while building His House. They then went about building the House of YHWH. At the conclusion of the Book of Shemot we read that they set up the House on Day 1 of Month 1. There was not a complete explanation of this place, often called the Tabernacle. It literally means the tent of appointment. This was to be the place that they would meet with YHWH for their 3 appointments - their 3 annual Feasts.

Once it was built, they knew the place of the appointment, but the other key was to be able to determine the right time. We currently see many different opinions about how to calculate the calendar of YHWH in order to determine when to keep the appointments – more than at any other time in history.

Since these Appointed Times are critical to the Covenant, it is important to know when they occur. To do this we must know how to reckon time, and in particular we must be able to figure out when the first Feast occurs. Since the first Feast mentioned, Unleavened Bread, occurs in the first month we must know how to determine the year.

6

The Year

In order to determine when a year begins we must understand how the Creator reckons time. This is not something that many people think about. In fact, other than a scant newspaper article or brief radio segment on January 1, most people would not even imagine that this is even a subject to question or debate. That is because most of us have grown up and lived within a society that operates under a solar based calendar called the Gregorian Calendar.

Developed by Pope Gregory XIII and decreed on February 24, 1582 by papal bull, it was intended to correct some of the errors found within the Julian Calendar, promoted by its namesake, Julius Caesar in 45 BC. The Julian Calendar was actually an attempt to reform the Roman Calendar which had numerous variations and obvious flaws.[85]

"The motivation for the Gregorian reform was that the Julian calendar assumes that the time between vernal equinoxes is 365.25 days, when in fact it is presently almost exactly 11 minutes shorter. The error between these values accumulated at the rate of about three days every four centuries, resulting in the equinox occurring on March 11 (an accumulated error of about 10 days) and moving steadily earlier in the Julian calendar at the time of the Gregorian reform. Since the Spring equinox was tied to the celebration of Easter, the Roman Catholic Church considered that this steady movement in the date of the equinox was undesirable."[86]

There are numerous other calendars used by different cultures throughout the centuries, and there are a variety of different calendars in existence today. This is important to understand, because they all represent man's desire to keep track of time for their own unique purposes. Unless they synchronize with the Creator's Calendar, they are all flawed. These flaws are recognized as cultures attempt to divide the 365 day solar year by 12 months, which mathematically does not result in a whole number, so there is a leftover fraction of a day.

As a result, some attempt to resolve these discrepancies by inserting or intercalating days and months, but over time these calendars tend to drift one way or another. This, of course, should be expected if you simply rely upon the sun. As we already discussed, the Scriptures tell us that the sun and the moon were created to mark time.

Since both of these celestial bodies were created to help the inhabitants of this planet mark time, it would only make sense to use them both if you want to understand the Creator's Calendar. Many of the problems that we see with the solar based calendars are that they do not synchronize with the markers. Therefore, they are not in synchronicity with the Creator.

While they may appear to calculate a solar year, if they do not properly account for the Appointed Times they are useless in understanding the Covenant path and the Covenant Appointments. In fact, they are often more of a distraction than they are a help. Any attempt to understand Scriptural dating or prophetic events is destined to fail if it is reliant upon a man made calendar system which is out of synch with Creation.

Now it is important to understand that there is nothing specifically telling us when there are 12 or 13 months in a year. We do know that 12 months would constitute a typical year according to the ancient Gezer stone as well as 1 Chronicles 27:2-15. So the question arises as to how we

determine the length of a year, and specifically when do we add a month 13? We are given some very important clues within the commandments concerning the Appointed Times which guide us to an answer.

We know that there is a month 1, a beginning of months when the Feast of Unleavened Bread occurs around the time of the abib or "green ears of grain." This refers to a condition when barley is not yet ripe. We also know that there is another Feast called the Feast of Ingathering that occurs at the end, or turn of the year. All of the Appointed Times must occur within a complete year.

The Covenant people were provided with this Calendar information so that they could keep their appointments. Since the appointments were with the Creator, we can safely assume that He is keeping the same calendar.

With that having been established, we must remember that all of Creation is mathematics powered by the fuel of YHWH. Scientists rely upon these preexisting mathematical equations, that they are in the process of discovering, to better understand the universe. These mathematics were built into everything at the beginning, and mathematics are at the center of the calendar. The mathematics relating to the calendar were meant to be seen and observed through the signs of the sun and the moon. Again, the Scripture Calendar is luni-solar.

Let us consider an analog clock as an example. The clock has a face with hands and numbers which, depending upon their positions, tell us what time it is. Inside the clock are mechanisms carrying out mathematical functions under power. The same holds true with the Scriptural Calendar. The sun and the moon show us the time, but behind these "hands" lie the mathematics that control them.

The clock example falls short when examining the Creator's Calendar, because it operates in only two dimensions. It usually has a spring to be wound or is powered by batteries, and it requires setting. If it is not set properly, it will never give you accurate time. Further, if you move from one side of the earth to the other, your clock will be wrong. It must be reset if moved because the mathematics do not allow it to adapt. Newer digital clocks with GPS capabilities can account for this movement but they too have their limitations.

Another problem with the clock example is that it is usually limited to seconds, minutes and hours. These are calculations of times that are not mentioned at the beginning. Remember that the first day was reckoned by evening and morning – night and day. The Scriptural calendar primarily consists of days, weeks, months and years.[87]

This was the ancient reckoning of Yisrael, but things changed with history. There came a time when the 12 Tribes of Yisrael eventually entered the Covenant Land, but things did not go well for them. They repeatedly departed from the ways of the Covenant and fell into idolatry. After King Solomon (Shlomo) died, the Kingdom of Yisrael was divided into two parts, the House of Yisrael in the North, and the House of Yahudah in the South.

The House of Yisrael toyed with the calendar and the Appointed Times, which ultimately led to their demise. The first king of the House of Yisrael was Jeroboam I, and he actually ordained a festival in month 8 exactly one month after the Festival ordained by YHWH in month 7. According to 1 Kings 12:32-33, he also set up golden calves and sacrificed to them on Day 15 of Month 8 at an altar that he made at Bethel.

The House of Yisrael continued 209 years until they were completely removed from the Land by the Assyrians through 5 successive captivities spanning between 723 BCE and 714 BCE.* They have been in exile ever since that time.[88]

The House of Yahudah also fell

away from YHWH. After lasting 324 years, they were partially removed from the Land by the Babylonians through 7 successive captivities spanning between 618 BCE and 595 BCE.* They were exiled to Babylon for a period of seventy years. While in Babylon, the House of Yahudah developed many traditions and even came out with a new language.[89] They gave names to each month – something YHWH never commanded them to do. They even named the fourth month Tammuz! For those unfamiliar with pagan traditions, Tammuz was the son of Nimrod and Semaramis. He is part of trinitarian sun worship and because of that fact, it is highly inappropriate and even blasphemous to give the fourth Scriptural month that name.[90]

Those from the House of Yahudah who returned from Babylon came to represent all of Yisrael, since the House of Yisrael remained in exile and had essentially "disappeared."[91] Yahudah became fractured into various sects, but established a ruling body called the Sanhedrin. Within that ruling body they operated a Calendar Court which made decisions regarding the calendar.[92] So the Calendar of the Creator had fallen into the hands of men who faithfully implemented its rules for a time, but that was about to change.[93]

We currently see the religion of Rabbinic Judaism, consisting primarily of those individuals from the House of Yahudah. Over the centuries, this religion has adopted many different traditions and beliefs, although it derived from the Pharisaic sect which came to dominate the Yahudim after the destruction of Jerusalem in 70 CE. Judaism now primarily follows a mathematical calendar generally attributed to Hillel II, although there are sects such as the Karaites that have their own unique traditions concerning the calendar.

"In the fourth century, Hillel II established a fixed calendar based on mathematical and astronomical calculations. This calendar, still in use, standardized the length of months and the addition of months over the course of a 19 year cycle, so that the lunar calendar realigns with the solar years. Adar I is added in the 3rd, 6th, 8th, 11th, 14th, 17th and 19th years of the cycle."[94]

This calendar was not based upon a perfect mathematical calculation, and only very rarely coincides with the Creator's Calendar. The Rabbinic calendar arbitrarily predetermines the month lengths in advance, just as the Julian or Gregorian calendar does. It also operates under certain rules of postponement, contrary to what Mosheh commanded the Covenant community Yisrael in Debarim 5:32.

The error of this calendar can easily be seen when it provides for a new moon when one does not exist, or has already passed. Amazingly, many people today still follow the invented Rabbinic calendar rather than the observable sign in the sky. This shows the power of tradition, which often has a stronger hold than truth over people.

While mainstream Judaism has essentially adopted the calculated calendar attributed to Hillel II, the Karaite sect has adopted their own reckoning systems which do not conform to the Torah and Beresheet 1:14. One particular Kariate teaching hinges upon the notion that the first month is named Abib, so there must be a "sufficient" amount of abib barley in the land of Israel prior to the sighting of the new moon in order to make a declaration of the first month.

This method of reckoning is flawed on many levels. First, the Scriptures do not name the first month "Abib." They simply call month 1 "the month of the abib." In other words, month 1 is the month when the barley will be abib. The Karaite tradition fails to acknowledge that abib barley is simply a marker that will occur within the first month. The barley does not control the month, nor does abib barley need to exist prior to the first month. That is simply a tradition. The first month will be a month when the barley is green, and there is no need from Scripture to have green barley before the first month begins.

There is also a problem with requiring "sufficient amounts" of abib barley prior to the sighting of the new moon. This belief is solely based upon tradition, and is not supported by the Scriptures. According to Beresheet 1:14, the sun and the moon determine time. Just exactly what constitutes "abib" barley, and what are "sufficient amounts" of abib barley prior to the sighting of the new moon, and at "what" geographical locations in the land, are all man-made, subjective determinations.

Once again, men are attempting to take hold of the Creator's perfectly mathematical calendar, and modify it with their own traditions. All of these man-made determinations have at various times been different than the Creator's true reckoning of time, so those practicing this tradition have essentially "changed" the times and taught others to do so. They are on extremely dangerous ground by doing so. (See Daniel 7:25).

This would have had catastrophic results in the original exodus from Egypt, when keeping Passover on the correct day meant life of death for some. We shall see that it is also critical as we approach the end of days, when the cost of "not watching" and not observing the Appointed Times as YHWH has instructed, will definitely result in missing an important event. (see Mattityahu 25:1-13).

While those in the religion of Judaism may choose to deviate from the Torah, that is their prerogative, but it is not something that the Covenant people of Yisrael do. Therefore, anyone who enters into the Covenant and belongs to the Covenant assembly "am Yisrael" should simply follow the instructions and number the months according to the count provided by YHWH.

By naming the months, Judaism has also created confusion, particularly regarding the first month which they named Abib. The first month was never named Abib, it was simply referred to as the month of the abib. This gave us an agricultural clue as to when it should occur.

Remember that the first of the three Pilgrimage Feasts, the Feast of Unleavened Bread occurred in the first month, the month of the abib. The third Feast occurred at the end of the year – the tequfah. The tequfah's are the marks or turns, which are built right into the Creator's clock. Therefore, it is safe to assume that if the Feast at the end of the year occurred at or around a tequfah, then the Feast at the beginning of the year should also occur at or around a tequfah.

So it is misleading to name the first month, and essentially attach it to a barley crop, when it is more likely associated with the tequfah. The Scriptural years, months and days of the week are supposed to be identified simply with numbers, not with names. As can be seen time and again, whenever man deviates from the simple and specific commands of YHWH, things get problematic.

There is a much more reliable and constant method of determining the beginning of a year which is built into creation by the Creator. Not only does it take men and their subjective opinions out of the equation, but it also makes absolute sense that the Creator, Who made this entire Creation based upon mathematics, would operate His Calendar mathematically, including those very elements that He said would determine time – the sun and the moon.

Now if the issue were as simple as having 12 months, each beginning with the sighting of the new moon, there would likely be little dispute. The problem, as we already discussed, is that there are 365 days in a solar cycle and there are an average of 29.53 days in a lunar cycle. Multiplied by 12 months this amounts to 354.36 days in 12 lunar months. This shortfall requires the occasional insertion of a 13th month, known as intercalation.

If you do not intercalate then you eventually end up celebrating winter in summer and vice versa. This actually happens to the Muslims who operate strictly on a 12 month lunar calendar. That system does not synchronize each year

with the harvests in the Covenant Land.

The primary purpose of intercalation is to prevent the drift found in most man-made calendars. For the purposes of the Appointed Times, it is to keep the harvest festivals in their correct seasons. For it was YHWH Who instructed Yisrael to keep the Feast of Unleavened Bread *"in its season (moad) from year to year."* Shemot 13:10. And if the Feast of Unleavened Bread is kept in its correct "season" in month 1, it is a simple matter to keep the subsequent Appointed Times in their "season."

Intercalation is essentially a reset button that occurs to keep the calendar correct. This is where much of the confusion and debate rests – when do you intercalate and add a thirteenth month? This, of course, will have a direct impact on determining the first month, and therefore all of the Appointed Times for the entire year.

We have discussed some of the different methods and traditions developed by men, but our discussion has by no means been exhaustive.[95] I find that most people are oblivious to the underlying debate, and simply want to look on a calendar and have someone tell them what time it is. It amazes me how people are so willing to follow tradition like a bunch of drones. When asked why they celebrate on a certain day the response is: Because the calendar says so. There is no inquiry into who developed the calendar or what it is based upon. They just follow the calendar that somebody has told them to follow.

Now remember, we are talking about meeting with the Creator of the Universe here! This is not something to be taken lightly. In fact, it should be one of the most important issues on any person's mind who really wants a relationship with the Creator.

The Creation Calendar, and the Appointed Times which occur on it, were conceived by the Creator. The Scriptural Calendar is not something that men can change or control. The celestial orbs of the earth around the sun, the moon around the earth and the earth on it's axis, move in the courses established for them from the beginning, and the calendar continues from the beginning. Creation is very mathematical, and the solar system works like a finely tuned clock.

As shown in the beginning, the Creation was made to be in synchronicity with the Calendar. The sun and the moon were set in their places to gauge time. Their movement can be calculated as the calendar is a mathematical calculation. If we look to ancient records we can see that it is controlled exactly as the Scriptures indicate, by the sun and the moon.

Often referred to as the Rule of the Equinox, this ancient calculation used the tequfah to determine the beginning of the year. As a result, it is absolutely in line with Scriptures by using the sun and the moon to determine time.

Simply stated, the Rule of the Equinox "always places Day 15 of Month 1 *on or after* the Hebrew Day in which the spring equinox occurs. If at the moment of sunset at the end of Month 12, on the evening of the first crescent moon at Jerusalem, there are 15 Hebrew Days or less until the spring equinox, then Month 1 is declared. If there are 16 Hebrew Days or more until the spring equinox, then Month 13 is declared. The spring equinox is defined as the time when the apparent geocentric longitude of the sun (that is, calculated by including the effects of aberration and nutation) is zero degrees."[96]

The Rule of the Equinox is an ancient reckoning understood and used in the past by Yisrael. This has been historically documented.[97] Calculating the year based upon the Rule of the Equinox has been proven to be accurate and valid.[98] It insures that all of the Appointed Times occur within one complete year. Most importantly, it is also confirmed by Scriptures.[99]

This is an incredible truth that has profound implications. It takes men and their subjective

determinations out of the equation and places it back where it belongs – the Creator and His Creation. Another reason why this is so incredible is because once you understand that the Calendar is mathematical, time opens up to you, because now we can go forward and backward in time, like a veritable time machine.

Once you realize the method for calculating the beginning of the year through the Rule of the Equinox, there is one more thing to determine – the first day. We have already mentioned that the month begins at the Rosh Chodesh which literally means "head of the month" or "beginning of the renewal."

The overwhelming evidence is that this was determined at the first sighting of the crescent moon, typically when the moon is at 2 to 3 percent illumination. This is sometimes made difficult with the existence of atmospheric pollution and was likely easier in the past. Interestingly though, we now have technological advances that can tell us precisely the illumination of the moon at any given moment.

The point is to see the light. Again, the tradition and spiritual implications of looking up and seeing the visible sign in the sky are overwhelming. Just like evening and morning can be observed so the renewed moon can be observed. While there are those who hold to the astronomical conjunction dark moon theory, it is simply not supported by the evidence.[100]

Once you properly understand how to calculate the new year, you are then ready to "keep" the Feasts.

7

Keeping the Times

Before we proceed any further it is important to understand the relevance, and significance of the appointments. It has already been mentioned, but bears repeating. These were not simply legalistic exercises that the Yisraelites were made to follow every year. They were Appointments with the Creator with incredible purposes that we shall examine through the remaining portion of this text.

There are those who believe that since they are found in the "Old" Testament that they are outdated, irrelevant and done away with. This is largely in part to the Christian notion that the Church has replaced Yisrael or that the Torah has been done away with. Both of these are untrue and false doctrines.[101]

While some see the significance in the Appointed Times, they believe that we can no longer "keep" the Feasts, since there is no Temple in Jerusalem. Actually, we are commanded repeatedly to "keep" the commandments of YHWH, not just the Appointed Times. The word "keep" is shamar (𐤔𐤌𐤅) in Hebrew and it means: "to hedge about, to guard, to protect, to attend, to observe, to preserve, to regard, to watch."[102]

The existence or non-existence of a Temple does not affect the Torah, or time for that matter. The planets did not stop their courses simply because YHWH allowed His House in Jerusalem to be destroyed. It was never meant to be there permanently, at least not one built by the hands of man.

So the commandments, including those concerning the Appointed Times, are not contingent upon the existence of a structure.

While there are certain rituals and sacrifices that cannot be carried out because there is not an altar or an operating priesthood, it is important to point out that those sacrifices and ceremonies were not originally mentioned with the Appointed Times. Thus, the Appointments are still occurring whether you choose to recognize them or not. The point of this text is to show the Times as well as their significance and meaning – not only in the past, but also in the future.

The Appointed Times are mentioned throughout the "New" Testament, and were repeatedly validated by the Messiah.[103] There are still others who believe that these are exclusively Jewish Holidays. As we continue to examine the Appointed Times, all of these notions should be easily dispelled, and the importance and relevance of these Times should be abundantly clear.

These Times belong to YHWH and no other. They are Times for a Covenant people to observe as we saw at Sinai. This was later reiterated by Mosheh to Yisrael. We find a very interesting list in the Book of Vayiqra which continues the trend of revelation and details regarding these important Times.

"*[1] And YHWH spoke unto Mosheh, saying, [2] Speak unto the children of Yisrael, and say unto them, Concerning the Appointed Times (moadi) of YHWH, which you shall proclaim to be holy convocations, even these are My Appointed Times (moadi). [3] Six days shall work be done: but the seventh day is the Sabbath of rest, a holy convocation; you shall do no work therein: it is the Sabbath of YHWH in all your dwellings. [4] These are the Appointed Times (moadi) of YHWH, even holy convocations, which you shall proclaim in their Appointed Times (moadim).*"* Vayiqra 23:1-4.

There are a couple of things that should jump right off the page. First, within the first 4 sentences, the Appointed

Times are mentioned 4 times, divided into two parts. In each instance where the Appointed Times are mentioned twice, they are also called "holy convocations," and it is clearly stated that these times belong to YHWH. Finally, these two references essentially bracket the Sabbath, which is also called a "holy convocation" and is at the very center of the brackets.

It would appear that at the center of the Appointed Times is the Sabbath. This Sabbath is the seventh day Sabbath. It is being set apart and distinguished from the other Appointed Times, which are mentioned later and also include Sabbaths. The reason for this separation and distinction is because they are calculated differently. The seventh day Sabbath is on a seven day cycle which started at Creation. The other Appointed Times are calculated by the sun and the moon annually.

So the first moad that we read about in the comprehensive listing of the moadim is the seventh day Sabbath. The Sabbath is the first moad mentioned in the Scriptures, and it was the first to occur in time – the seventh day. It is connected to the weekly day count which is not tied to both the sun and the moon as are the annual Moadim.

The Sabbath is clearly special and unique as we have already pointed out on several occasions. It is separate and set apart from the other Appointed Times. Since it is on a different cycle than the other times, it is reckoned differently. You do not need to know anything other than the passage of days, and the ability to count to seven.

Just as we saw the creation week on a seven day cycle, beginning with the first week of creation, separate from the monthly and yearly cycle, we see the same here. So while it is clearly an Appointed Time, it is weekly and it is not dependent upon the sun and the moon.[104] Because it is so unique and special, the Sabbath is dealt with in a separate text.[105]

The Appointed Times are described as "holy

convocations" which is "qadosh miqra" (ᛑ ᛈ ᛈᛘ ᚹᚢᛈ) in Hebrew. A better translation is "set apart gatherings." The word qadosh (ᚹᚢᛈ) is often defined as "holy," but is better described as being "set apart." It describes something not common, or profane. It is usually something meant for YHWH - something acceptable for His presence. The word miqra (ᛑ ᛈ ᛈᛘ) is defined as: "a summons or assembly, a reading or recitation." It is also defined as a rehearsal. So on these special days YHWH calls us to essentially read and rehearse something special for Him - something set apart. They can literally be called set apart rehearsals. We read about those times, we learn about them and we act accordingly. These times are likened to rehearsals for a future event. They are set apart because they specifically belong to YHWH.

Sadly, they have been obscured from most of the world because they are mislabeled "Jewish Holidays." While it is true that most in the religion of Judaism recognize the moadim as special days, they have their own traditions and calendar for conducting their celebrations which do not always align with the Scriptures. Just because those in Judaism recognize the significance of these Times does not give them exclusive rights to these Times.

The Moadim are for all those who are in Covenant with the Creator. Since Yisrael, not the religion of Judaism or Christianity, represents the Covenant people, the Appointed Times were detailed to them. Therefore, those who belong to Yisrael are expected to meet with YHWH at His times.[106]

So, if you want a relationship with YHWH, you must enter into Covenant with Him, and part of that Covenant relationship involves meeting with Him at His Appointments.[107]

The passage in Vayiqra continues by providing the most comprehensive list of the Appointed Times that can be found in the Scriptures. It also provides more information relative to the timing. There is some debate about how some of the text is translated, but for the time being we will look at a basic translation, and later delve into individual passages and their unique issues.

"*4 These are the Appointed Times (Moadi) of YHWH, set apart rehearsals which you shall proclaim at their Appointed Times (Moadim). 5 On the fourteenth day of the first month at twilight is YHWH's Passover. 6 And on the fifteenth day of the same month is the Feast of Unleavened Bread to YHWH; seven days you must eat unleavened bread. 7 On the first day you shall have a set apart rehearsal; you shall do no customary work on it. 8 But you shall offer an offering made by fire to YHWH for seven days. The seventh day shall be a set apart rehearsal; you shall do no customary work on it. 9 And YHWH spoke to Mosheh, saying, 10 Speak to the children of Yisrael, and say to them: When you come into the Land which I give to you, and reap its harvest, then you shall bring ✗𝔶 a sheaf of the firsts (resheet) of your harvest to the priest. 11 He shall wave the sheaf before YHWH, to be accepted on your behalf; on the day after the Sabbath the priest shall wave it. 12 And you shall offer on that day, when you wave ✗𝔶 the sheaf, a male lamb of the first (ben) year, without blemish, as a burnt offering to YHWH. 13 Its grain offering shall be two-tenths of an ephah of fine flour mixed with oil, an offering made by fire to YHWH, for a sweet aroma; and its drink offering shall be of wine, one-fourth of a hin. 14 You shall eat neither bread nor parched grain nor fresh grain until the same day that you have brought an offering to your Elohim; it shall be a statute throughout the ages (olam), throughout your generations in all your dwellings. 15 'And you shall count for yourselves from the day after the Sabbath, from the day that you brought*

$\times \mho$ the sheaf of the wave offering: seven complete Sabbaths. [16] Count fifty days to the day after the seventh Sabbath; then you shall offer a new grain offering to YHWH. [17] You shall bring from your dwellings two wave loaves of two-tenths of an ephah. They shall be of fine flour; they shall be baked with leaven. They are the firstfruits to YHWH. [18] And you shall offer with the bread seven lambs of the first year, without blemish, one young bull, and two rams. They shall be as a burnt offering to YHWH, with their grain offering and their drink offerings, an offering made by fire for a sweet aroma to YHWH. [19] Then you shall sacrifice one kid of the goats as a sin offering, and two male lambs of the first year as a sacrifice of a peace offering. [20] The priest shall wave them with the bread of the firstfruits as a wave offering before YHWH, with the two lambs. They shall be set apart to YHWH for the priest. [21] And you shall proclaim on the same day that it is a set apart rehearsal to you. You shall do no customary work on it. It shall be a statute throughout the ages (olam) in all your dwellings throughout your generations. [22] When you reap the harvest of your land, you shall not wholly reap the corners of your field when you reap, nor shall you gather any gleaning from your harvest. You shall leave them for the poor and for the stranger: I am YHWH your Elohim. [23] Then YHWH spoke to Mosheh, saying, [24] Speak to the children of Yisrael, saying: In the seventh month, on the first day of the month, you shall have a Sabbath, a memorial of blowing, a set apart rehearsal. [25] You shall do no customary work on it; and you shall offer an offering made by fire to YHWH [26] And YHWH spoke to Mosheh, saying: [27] Also the tenth day of this seventh month shall be the Day of Atonement. It shall be a set

apart rehearsal for you; you shall afflict your souls, and offer an offering made by fire to YHWH. ²⁸ And you shall do no work on that same day, for it is the Day of Atonement, to make atonement for you before YHWH your Elohim. ²⁹ For any person who is not afflicted in soul on that same day shall be cut off from his people. ³⁰ And any person who does any work on that same day, that person I will destroy from among his people. ³¹ You shall do no manner of work; it shall be a statute throughout the ages (olam) throughout your generations in all your dwellings. ³² It shall be to you a Sabbath of solemn rest, and you shall afflict ×ד your souls; on the ninth day of the month at evening, from evening to evening, you shall observe your Sabbath. ³³ Then YHWH spoke to Mosheh, saying, ³⁴ Speak to the children of Yisrael, saying: The fifteenth day of this seventh month shall be the Feast of Succot for seven days to YHWH. ³⁵ On the first day there shall be a set apart rehearsal. You shall do no customary work on it. ³⁶ For seven days you shall offer an offering made by fire to YHWH . On the eighth day you shall have a set apart rehearsal, and you shall offer an offering made by fire to YHWH. It is a atzeret, and you shall do no customary work on it. ³⁷ These are the Appointed Times (Moadi) of YHWH which you shall proclaim to be set apart rehearsals, to offer an offering made by fire to YHWH, a burnt offering and a grain offering, a sacrifice and drink offerings, everything on His day ³⁸ besides the Sabbaths of YHWH, besides your gifts, besides all your vows, and besides all your freewill offerings which you give to YHWH. ³⁹ Also on the fifteenth day of the seventh month, when you have gathered in the fruit of the Land, you shall "keep the feast of YHWH" (hagag ×ד-hag-YHWH) for seven days; on the first day there shall be a Sabbath,

and on the eighth day a Sabbath. 40 And you shall take for yourselves on the first day the fruit of beautiful trees, branches of palm trees, the boughs of leafy trees, and willows of the brook; and you shall rejoice before YHWH your Elohim for seven days. 41 You shall keep (hagag) it as a feast (hag) to YHWH for seven days in the year. It shall be a statute throughout the ages (olam) in your generations. You shall celebrate it in the seventh month. 42 You shall dwell in booths for seven days. All who are native Yisraelites shall dwell in booths, 43 that your generations may know that I made the children of Yisrael dwell in booths when I brought them out of the land of Egypt: I am YHWH your Elohim. 44 So Mosheh declared to the children of Yisrael the Feasts of YHWH." Vayiqra 23:4-44.

Notice in this passage how much more detail is provided concerning dates. There is even mention of other appointments, beyond the three Pilgrimage Feasts. As Yisrael continued on their Covenant journey more information is provided concerning the Appointed Times. It is not that things were added or changed, simply more was being revealed. Throughout the rest of this text we will be examining all of these Times in light of additional information provided in the Scriptures. We will look at their meanings and relationships with one another.

YHWH commanded the children of Yisrael to "proclaim" these times. The Hebrew word is "tiqra" (𐤕𐤒𐤓𐤀) and it means: "to call out, proclaim, pronounce." So we are to keep these times, which includes guarding protecting and preserving, but we are also to proclaim them. They are rehearsals for a Covenant people to guide them in their path, and lead them in the ways of YHWH. As we continue our discussion we will see how these Times have had past fulfillment, but also these rehearsals are preparing the Covenant people of YHWH for a very exciting future.

We will begin our examination of the individual Appointed Times at the point YHWH told Mosheh and Aharon would be the beginning of months – the First month which points to the Passover and the Feast of Unleavened Bread.

8

Passover and Unleavened Bread

Having been given a detailed schedule of the Appointed Times in Vayiqra 23, we are now equipped to examine each one in order. It was already established that the first month is calculated according to the Rule of the Equinox. The Scriptural Year begins in the spring, and that is the month of the abib. In other words we should expect to see abib barley in that month.

The Rule of the Equinox determines when the first month of the year begins using the sun and the moon – not the barley. A crop of grain can never control the celestial bodies that mark the month and the years. Rather, the abib barley in the Land is a confirmation and reminder that there is an important barley offering made during the first month. That offering marks the beginning of a count that starts in the middle of the month and leads to another Appointed Time.

Unlike all of the other Appointed Times, those that occur in the first month were revealed to Yisrael while they were in Egypt. This, of course is no coincidence, because the Passover and Unleavened Bread are about deliverance and freedom. The word for "Egypt" in Hebrew is "Mitsrayim," and actually has become likened with "bondage." So the Feasts of the first month are particularly relevant to those enslaved needing deliverance.

The observance really begins on the First Day because you have to see the new moon and know when the first day of the month begins in order to start counting. Here is the

command given to Yisrael while they were in Egypt.

"*1 Now YHWH spoke to Mosheh and Aharon in the land of Egypt, saying, 2 This month shall be your beginning of months; it shall be the first month of the year to you. 3 Speak to all the congregation of Yisrael, saying: On the tenth of this month every man shall take for himself a lamb, according to the house of his father, a lamb for a household. 4 And if the household is too small for the lamb, let him and his neighbor next to his house take it according to the number of the persons; according to each man's need you shall make your count for the lamb. 5 Your lamb shall be without blemish, a male of the "first" (⌐□) year. You may take it from the sheep or from the goats. 6 Now you shall keep (✕⌂ᴟᴡᴟ) it until (∪⊙) the fourteenth day of the same month. Then the whole assembly (⌐ᴝᛃ) of the congregation (✕∪⊙) of Yisrael shall kill it in the evening (ᴟ⌐□⌂⊙ᴝ ⌐⌐□). 7 And they shall take some of the blood and put it on the two doorposts and on the lintel of the houses where they eat it. 8 Then they shall eat the flesh on that night; roasted in fire, with unleavened bread and with bitter herbs they shall eat it. 9 Do not eat it raw, nor boiled at all with water, but roasted in fire - its head with its legs and its entrails. 10 You shall let none of it remain until morning, and what remains of it until morning you shall burn with fire. 11 And thus you shall eat it: with a belt on your waist, your sandals on your feet, and your staff in your hand. So you shall eat it in haste. It is YHWH's Passover. 12 For I will pass through the land of Egypt on that night, and will strike all the firstborn in the land of Egypt, both man and beast; and against all the gods of Egypt I will execute judgment: I am YHWH. 13 Now the blood shall be a sign for you on the houses where you are. And when I see the blood, I will pass over you;*

and the plague shall not be on you to destroy you when I strike the land of Egypt. ¹⁴ So this day shall be to you a memorial; and you shall keep it as a Feast to YHWH throughout your generations. You shall keep it as a Feast by an ordinance through the ages (olam). ¹⁵ Seven days you shall eat unleavened bread. On the first day you shall remove leaven from your houses. For whoever eats leavened bread from the first day until the seventh day, that person shall be cut off from Yisrael. ¹⁶ On the first day there shall be a set apart rehearsal, and on the seventh day there shall be a set apart rehearsal for you. No manner of work shall be done on them; but that which everyone must eat - that only may be prepared by you. ¹⁷ So you shall observe the Feast of Unleavened Bread, for on this same day I will have brought your armies out of the land of Egypt. Therefore you shall observe this day throughout your generations as an ordinance through the ages (olam). ¹⁸ In the first month, on the fourteenth day of the month at evening, you shall eat unleavened bread, until the twenty-first day of the month at evening. ¹⁹ For seven days no leaven shall be found in your houses, since whoever eats what is leavened, that same person shall be cut off from the congregation of Yisrael, whether he is a stranger or a native of the land. ²⁰ You shall eat nothing leavened; in all your dwellings you shall eat unleavened bread. ²¹ Then Mosheh called for all the elders of Yisrael and said to them, Pick out and take lambs for yourselves according to your families, and kill the Passover lamb. ²² And you shall take a bunch of hyssop, dip it in the blood that is in the basin, and strike the lintel and the two doorposts with the blood that is in the basin. And none of you shall go out of the door of his house until morning. ²³ For YHWH will pass through to strike the

Egyptians; and when He sees the blood on the lintel and on the two doorposts, YHWH will pass over the door and not allow the destroyer to come into your houses to strike you. 24 And you shall observe this thing as an ordinance for you and your sons through the ages (olam). 25 It will come to pass when you come to the Land which YHWH will give you, just as He promised, that you shall keep this service. 26 And it shall be, when your children say to you, 'What do you mean by this service?' 27 that you shall say, 'It is the Passover sacrifice of YHWH, who passed over the houses of the children of Yisrael in Egypt when He struck the Egyptians and delivered our households.'" So the people bowed their heads and worshiped. 28 Then the children of Yisrael went away and did so; just as YHWH had commanded Mosheh and Aharon, so they did."* Shemot 12:1-28.

The Passover was a critical part of the deliverance of the Hebrews, and it was all about the Covenant made with Abraham. Remember that Abram had once been in Egypt, and his wife was held captive by the Pharaoh. Pharaoh was plagued and ultimately released Abram and his bride, Sarai. He was given riches and came out of Egypt with Hagar - The Stranger - who would later become his wife and bear him a child. (Beresheet 16:3). This was a pattern that a future Pharaoh would have done well to remember.

Later Abraham was given a promised son through Sarah. The son was born on Passover, and there was a direct link hinted in the text between this son and the Appointed Time of Passover. Therefore, the time of bondage and the release from captivity was a fulfillment of the patterns and Covenant promises established through Abraham.

Clearly the message behind Passover is the protective covering of the blood of the lamb, and the Passover is closely related to the Covenant. In fact, in Shemot 12:13, YHWH specifically states that the blood was a "sign" which demonstrates that it is a Covenant event. It was this shedding of blood that would "mark" the next phase in this Covenant journey involving the seed of Abraham.

From Abraham we saw that YHWH would provide His Lamb and it would be His "only Son." Prior to the Passover, the people were to select a lamb and bring it into their home on the tenth day of the first month. Interestingly, we read that the lamb is to be of the "first" year. In the Hebrew we read ben (ﬨﬦ), which means "son."

This lamb was to be a son. It would reside in their home for four (4) days, and become part of their family before it is slain. As with the number forty (40), the number four (4) is also linked to the Messiah.[108] On the fourteenth day the lamb was slaughtered, and the blood was placed on the doorposts of the house.

The doorway was the way in and out of the house. It represented the authority, ownership and control of the house. Many people place their names and street numbers on or near the entrance to their home to identify their ownership.

A doorway without a door would be meaningless. The door provides protection for the occupants of the house. It provides a separation and keeps those unwanted outside. Only members of the house and invited guests are supposed to pass through the door. As a result, the blood on the doorposts symbolizes that YHWH lays claim to the inhabitants. Those inside are part of His family, and the blood of His Lamb protects those in the Covenant house.

Remember that the Hebrew pictograph "dalet" (ᴜ) means "door." This is the dalet (ᴜ) that we originally saw in the midst of the am (ᵐᵼ) in the name Adam (ᵐᴜᵼ). Yaakob was renamed "am Yisrael," pointing to the fact that a Covenant people would flow through him. The text describing the Passover is actually shouting out for us to recognize what is being demonstrated through this event.

If we examine the Ancient Hebrew we can see messages hidden beneath the grammatical rules and translations developed by the modern Hebrew language. An examination of Shemot 12:6 provides incredible insight. Immediately after referring to the lamb as "the son," we then read that we are to guard over the Lamb like watchmen "until" (ᵁ⌐) the fourteenth day. Ayin Dalet (ᵁ⌐) literally means "see the door" in the ancient script. Remember that ᵁ⌐ is also at the heart of the word moadim (ᴹᵞᵁ⌐ᛁᴹ).

The whole "assembly of the congregation of Yisrael" was to kill the lamb that they once guarded and protected. A closer look at the Hebrew reveals more depth because we now see the ayin dalet (ᵁ⌐) literally attached to Yisrael. Commonly translated as "the congregation of Yisrael" we see the following in the Hebrew: ᛁᵞ⟡ᵂᵞ-ᵡᵁ⌐. Read from right to left we literally read: "see the door to the covenant-Yisrael."

In this case the ayin dalet (ᵁ⌐) points the way for the Covenant people Yisrael, and again, the way is established through the Appointed Times. So the Lamb of Elohim is the door for the people of Elohim. The blood on the door represented that the occupants of the house were the am (ᴹᵞ) – the people of Elohim. This was the message provided from the very beginning. Through this rehearsal, the Hebrews were getting a vivid picture of how the restoration of mankind would be accomplished through the Covenant.

This lamb, which was a son, was killed and eaten by families in their homes. It is important to remember that there were no priests officiating at a Temple. This was a service done at the entrance of the homes of the people. Only later would it be done at the entrance of the House of YHWH. Further, at this point in time, the firstborn were the ones responsible for the priestly duties. So this was essentially an event where the firstborn of Yisrael were shedding the blood and officiating for their families.

Once the blood was shed and placed on the doorposts

of each house, the lambs were hung on a stake. Their hooves were bound and their flesh was stripped away. They hung stripped down to the flesh before they were then placed in the fire and cooked. The flesh of this former family member then becomes food which is ingested while the blood provides protection from death for those who dwell in the home, specifically the first born who did the killing.

The Passover was a meal eaten in haste. You were to wear your outer garments with your sandals on your feet and your walking stick or rod in your hand. All were to keep vigil that night. (Shemot 12:42). A picture that we might envision in this age is that they were fully clothed with their shoes on their feet, their bags packed, the keys were in the ignition, the gas tank was full and the car was running. They were ready to leave.

This particular Feast is all about leaving slavery and going to freedom, which is life with YHWH. The freedom comes not just from leaving slavery though. It primarily involves going somewhere special – to the Land of promise – the Covenant Land.

Notice the progression to this day of deliverance. You must first recognize the beginning of the month – the first day. You then need to count ten days until Day 10 when you select a lamb. You must inspect and purchase a lamb which you essentially adopt into your family. You must watch over it and protect it for 4 days to insure that nothing happens to it before the meal. If you have children in the house, this lamb likely becomes their pet. To them this is a family member until Day 14, when the lamb becomes the Pesach.

The Pesach is the first and very profound Appointed Time, because it is all about a sacrifice and a meal, which is the ritual of a Covenant. So the yearly cycle of Appointed Times starts off with a Covenant meal, which signifies that the entire process is about the Covenant. It begins with bloodshed and death experienced by each and every family.

This was not some remote ritual conducted within the

dark chambers of a temple complex. Rather, it was an event seen, heard, smelled, felt and even tasted by all of the Covenant participants. It was a Covenant experience that all families were required to undergo. In fact, this was only to be experienced by those in Covenant. The commandment is clear that no foreigner was to partake in the meal. All the males had to be circumcised, which was a mark of the Covenant.[109]

So while Pesach is a Feast, there is no commandment to rejoice as there is with the other Pilgrimage Feasts. It is really quite bitter sweet - particularly the first Pesach. In fact, in Egypt it was full of the unknown, and likely a terrifying time. The people had just witnessed a series of 9 plagues on the Egyptians. The Messenger of death was killing the firstborn in homes throughout the land. There was likely panic and terror all around, except for the homes that were protected by the blood of their slaughtered lambs.

This is often called "The night of YHWH" and it is important to note that the entire Passover observance occurs at night. (Shemot 12:42; Vayiqra 23:5; Bemidbar 9:3, 9:5). The commandment is to kill the lamb *in the evening.* Shemot 12:6. The Hebrew text reads "bein ha'arbayim" (ﬦיﬨﬠﬠﬠ ﬩﬩ﬠ), which literally translates as "between the evenings." Between the evenings is not such a good translation in English, because there is actually a day between two evenings, and we know that this meal took place in the dark. In fact, there is a specific commandment that none could go out of their homes until morning. (Shemot 12:22).

Other translations which provide more focus are "twilight" and "dusk." We know that this is the general time when one day is ending and another day is beginning – the evening. Therefore, the two demarcation points between which the lamb was slaughtered were – 1) the setting of the sun and 2) total darkness. These two demarcation points both occur at the very beginning of a new day. The moment of sunset divides one day from another, and darkness comes shortly after sunset at the beginning of the day. Therefore, the commandment involved killing the lamb "between the evenings" of sunset and total darkness.

Presently there is much debate as to when exactly this occurred relative to the day count. This is not difficult from a clear reading of the Torah. Since a day begins at sunset, the killing of the lamb occurred after sunset on Day 14, the meal was eaten at night on Day 14, and the remains were disposed of by the morning of Day 14.

There really is no doubt on this point from the Torah, even though adherents of Rabbinic Judaism, Karaite Judaism as well as the majority of Messianic sects do not presently understand or obey this command. The proof text is Bemidbar 9:3. "*On the fourteenth day of this month, at twilight, you shall keep it at its appointed time. According to all its statutes and ordinances you shall keep it.*" As all the statutes and ordinances of the Passover must take place on Day 14 of Month 1, and as the lamb must be slain "bein ha'arbayim," then the first "evening" or demarcation point must be sunset.

The reason for much of the confusion is because of a tradition developed by Judaism that merged the Passover with the First day of the Feast of Unleavened Bread beginning on day 15. This fact is readily admitted in Judaism. The Jewish Encyclopedia says, "Vayiqra 23, however, seems to distinguish between Passover, which is set for the fourteenth day of the month, and the Festival of Unleavened Bread, appointed for the fifteenth day." While the Encyclopedia Judaica says, "The feast of Passover consists of two parts: The Passover ceremony and the feast of Unleavened Bread. Originally, both parts existed separately."

The Torah also explains in Debarim 16:6 that the Passover should be sacrificed, "*in the evening at the going down of the sun*" (בערב כבוא השמש). In case there was any confusion about when to begin the sacrifice, YHWH makes it clear that it is in the evening when the sun goes down.

This is important to understand because some falsely

teach that the sun starts to go down after mid-day. At mid-day, the sun is at its highest point in the sky, and although it begins to decline after it reaches its zenith, it is not true that the sun is going down below the horizon at this point, nor is it true that it is evening at this time. It is very likely the rabbis, who did not receive Yahushua as their Messiah, who have peddled this explanation in the Talmud that "the going down of the sun" mid-day and that "evening" is when the sun is in its highest point in the sky. (see Pesachim 58A). This would result on the offering occurring during the day before the Passover began at sunset. This is contrary to the Torah.

You see certain chief priests and scribes in Yahushua's day believed that they were losing their power and that the whole world was going after Yahushua according to Yahanan 12:19. That is why they conspired to kill Him. However, after Yahushua was crucified on the Passover and resurrected on the Third day of Unleavened Bread, they had an even bigger problem to contend with. The disciples (talmidim) of Yahushua were now taking the Passover and turning it into a remembrance of Him – exactly as commanded in Luke 22:19.

Paul (Shaul) of Tarsus was apparently teaching people throughout his "missionary" travels to keep the Passover in remembrance of Yahushua. (1 Corinthians 11:24-26). And so it was likely sometime after the resurrection of Yahushua, when Rabbinic Judaism was in its infancy, that Passover was moved to the First Day of Unleavened Bread.

Now this notion goes against popular understanding which asserts that the move was made shortly after the Babylonian exile, however this cannot be true.[110] Those taken into captivity were likened to "good figs" by YHWH. The captivity was for their own good, and their return was meticulously orchestrated by YHWH. (Yirmeyahu 24:5). They returned after their seventy year exile zealous to obey the Torah. This can be read through the accounts of Ezra, Nehemiah and the many prophets involved in the return and

rebuilding of the Temple and Jerusalem.

Hundreds of years after the House of Yahudah's return from exile, the Levitical priesthood continued to faithfully conduct the Temple service during the Second Temple Period. While the High Priest had become a politicized and corrupted institution, the service itself was closely guarded by the Pharisees who were trusted by the people of Yisrael in these matters. If things were not done properly, the people were often quick to voice their displeasure, prompted by the Pharisees.

The father of Yahanan the Immerser, often referred to as John the Baptist, was Zechariah, a Levitical priest who served in the Second Temple. Zechariah was on duty in the Second Temple when he encountered Gabriel, a messenger of YHWH, according to an account in Luke 1:5-22. In this account, the Scriptures clearly say that Zechariah and his wife Elizabeth walked in all of the commandments and ordinances of YHWH blamelessly. "*5 There was in the days of Herod, the king of Judea, a certain priest named Zechariah, of the division of Abiyah. His wife was of the daughters of Aharon, and her name was Elizabeth. 6 And they were both righteous before Elohim, walking in all the commandments and ordinances of YHWH blameless.*" Luke 1:5-6.

As Zechariah was a priest from the order of Abiyah, he must have kept all of the Appointed Times on the Creator's Calendar. Likewise, the priestly order within which he served must also have kept all of the Appointed Times at the correct time on the Creator's Calendar. And so, from the testimony of Luke 1:6, it is provable that the shift to observe Passover on Day 15 – one day late – did not occur as late as 4 BCE.

It is the testimony of Josephus, himself a Levitical priest from the course of Yehoiarib, that proves the change of Passover from Day 14 to Day 15 did not occur until after the Second Temple period. For Josephus says that the Passover was kept on Day 14 of Month 1.

"(311) Elohim, having revealed that by yet one more plague He would constrain the Egyptians to release the Hebrews, now commanded Moses to instruct the people to have ready a sacrifice, making preparations on the tenth day of the month Xanthicus over against the fourteenth day (this is the month called by the Egyptians Pharmuthi, by the Hebrews Nisan, and by the Macedonians termed Xanthicus) and then to lead the Hebrews away with all of their possessions. (312) He accordingly had the Hebrews ready ahead of time for their departure, and ranging them in fraternities kept them assembled together; then when the fourteenth day was come the whole body, in readiness to start, sacrificed, purified the houses with the blood, using bunches of hyssop to sprinkle it, and after the repast burnt the remnants of the meat as persons on the eve of the departure. (313) Hence it is that to this day we keep this sacrifice in the same customary manner, calling the feast Pascha, which signifies "passing over," because on that day Elohim passed over our people when he smote the Egyptians with plague. For on that selfsame night destruction visited the first-born of Egypt, insomuch that multitudes of those whose dwellings surrounded the palace trooped to Pharaoh to urge him to let the Hebrews go. (314) And he, summoning Moses, ordered him to depart, supposing that, once his people were gone out of the country, Egypt's sufferings would cease. They even honored the Hebrews with gifts, some to speed their departure, others from neighborly feelings towards old acquaintances." Josephus, Antiquities, 2 / 311-314.

Josephus also said the feast of Unleavened Bread lasted for 8 days. "Hence it is that, in memory of that time of scarcity, we keep for eight days a feast called the feast of Unleavened Bread. Now the entire multitude of those that went out, including the women and children, was not easy to be numbered; but those that were of an age fit for war, were six hundred thousand." Josephus, Antiquities, 2 / 317.

Josephus also clearly says that the Feast of Unleavened Bread succeeded the Passover. "(248) In the month of Xanthicus, which is by us called Nisan, and is the beginning of our year, on the fourteenth day of the lunar month, when the sun is in Aries (for in this month it was that we were delivered from bondage under the Egyptians, the law ordained that we should every year slay that sacrifice which I before told you we slew when we came out of Egypt, and  which was called the Passover; and so we do celebrate this Passover in companies, leaving nothing of what we sacrifice till the day following. (249) The feast of Unleavened Bread succeeds that of the Passover, and falls on the fifteenth day of the month, and continues seven days, wherein they feed on unleavened bread; on every one of which days two bulls are killed, and one ram, and seven lambs. Now these lambs are entirely burnt, besides the kid of the goats which is added to all the rest, for sins; for it is intended as a feast for the priest on every one of those days." Josephus, Antiquities, 3 /248-249.

The testimony of Josephus is very compelling because he was born around 37 CE and lived until around 100 CE. He fought in the First Jewish Roman war between 66-73 CE, and personally witnessed the destruction of the Second Temple in 70 CE when he acted as a negotiator during the siege of Jerusalem. Josephus says the "High Priests" slew their

Passover sacrifices from the ninth hour until the eleventh hour.

"(423) So these high priests, upon the coming of their feast which is called the Passover, when they slay their sacrifices, from the ninth hour till the eleventh, but so that a company not less than ten belong to every sacrifice (for it is not lawful for them to feast singly by themselves), and many of us are twenty in a company, (424) found the number of sacrifices was two-hundred and fifty-six thousand five hundred; (425) which, upon the allowance of no more than ten that feast together, amounts to two million seven hundred thousand and two hundred persons that were pure and set apart." Josephus, Wars, 6 / 423-435.

Josephus is obviously reckoning in Roman hours here, meaning that the High Priests slew their sacrifices approximately between 9:00 – 10:00 pm. The people presumably began slaughtering their sacrifices immediately after sunset beginning Day 14 of Month 1, while the High Priests slew their sacrifices later on in the evening when their service was complete.

As Josephus wrote all of his works under Roman patronage, it is understandable that he reckoned hours in Roman style. This is an important distinction to understand when examining New Testament manuscripts. While Mattityahu, Mark and Luke reckon in Hebrew hours, Yahanan, like Josephus, reckoned in Roman hours.

It is most probable then, that the Passover was changed subsequent to the destruction of Jerusalem in 70 CE. After the Romans destroyed Jerusalem, Rabbi Yahanan ben Zakkai founded an academy at Yavneh, also called Jamnia. Jamnia became the headquarters of Rabbinic Judaism, and it was at Jamnia that a council was formed which issued a curse against the Judeans who believed in Yahushua the Messiah.

The curse of the "Minim," as the followers of Yahushua were called, was a distinctive point of separation between Judeans who believed that Yahushua was the

Messiah, and those who did not.[III] It was this decree that drove the wedge so deep between the Judeans that they eventually developed into two distinct world religions – Rabbinic Judaism and Christianity.

It is therefore highly possible that this was the time in history, or some time thereafter, that this group of Pharisees at Jamnia took it upon themselves to alter the Torah of Mosheh, and change the observance of Passover from Day 14 of Month 1 to Day 15 of Month 1, in direct violation of Debarim 5:32.

Very interestingly, the argument that the change occurred around this later point in history is supported by a controversy that occurred in the fledgling Christian religion after the destruction of Jerusalem. Remember that Jerusalem had also been the center of the sect of followers of Yahushua. With the destruction of the City, the "headquarters" of this sect ultimately migrated to the west – to Rome. Rome was the very capital of the destroyers of Jerusalem. The irony is quite profound when you recognize how Rome also created and profaned the religion of Christianity.

When we examine history, around 159 CE, we see that there were true followers of Yahushua, arguing in support of the Day 14 Passover. This came to be known as the Quartodeciman Controversy – The Day 14 Controversy. The controversy took place within the context of the debate involving Easter.

Just as Rabbinic Judaism was separating from the "Minim," there was a corresponding trend in Christianity to move away from anything deemed "Jewish." The Christians were moving rapidly from a faith centered around a renewed Covenant with Yisrael, to a new and different covenant with the Church. A part of the shift away from Yisrael was to replace the Feasts with new and different pagan centered holy days. Thus, the Christians were rejecting Passover and focusing on Easter, a pagan fertility celebration originating in Babylon.

History records that Polycarp, a disciple (talmid) of Yahanan, was taught to keep the Passover on Day 14 of Month 1. He travelled to Rome and met with Anicetus expressing his resistance against Rome's attempts to move the observance to a Sunday, Easter celebration. The issue continued for centuries as Eastern assemblies continued observing Day 14, while Western assemblies changed to Easter Sunday observance. The matter was  ultimately resolved by the Council of Nicea, when the sun worshippers prevailed by essentially establishing the new religion of Christianity, with its own separate holy days rooted in paganism. (See Encyclopedia Brittanica 1911, Easter).

The bottom line is that the controversy rested on the fact that the proper celebration of Passover was known to be Day 14 of Month 1. The Christians desired to separate from things considered "Jewish," and they moved the Easter celebration because the "Jewish" Passover was on Day 14 of Month 1. There was so much division after the destruction of Jerusalem that it is sometimes difficult to see this very important and dramatic separation. What began as two different sects of Yisrael divided into two separate and distinct religions.

All of this division, strife and confusion is a good reason why every person must shamar (guard, watch and protect) the commandments. If you blindly follow a tradition or calendar which is not founded in truth, you will be misled.

There are those who expound the notion that for the sake of unity everyone should simply follow the Jewish calendar. I trust it is obvious to the reader that to willingly follow an erroneous tradition is ludicrous. This is particularly true when examining the likely motives for developing the calendar. Indeed, it could have perilous implications in the future if you are rehearsing something at the wrong time.

The Jewish Holidays on the Rabbinic calendar unsuccessfully execute the Appointed Times. The Appointed Times belong to YHWH and are determined by the Torah. The Jewish Holidays belong to the adherents of Rabbinic Judaism, and are based upon the invented calendar of Hillel II from 359 CE, and the postponement of Passover that was likely instituted sometime after the Council in Jamnia was formed.

When the Yisraelites were preparing to leave Egypt there was no such religion as Rabbinic Judaism. There were 12 tribes of Yisrael, which included the Tribe of Judah, better known as Yahudah.[112] Mosheh and Aharon were chosen by YHWH to lead Yisrael, and they transmitted the Commandments to the Elders and the people directly from YHWH. They did not make things up as they went along. If they did, there would have been serious consequences as we saw with Aharon and the golden calf incident.

Accordingly, there was no confusion, speculation or false tradition on the first Pesach. Mosheh gave the directions and Yisrael followed them precisely. Failure to do so meant the death of the firstborn in the household. It did not matter if you were circumcised at that point. Their circumcision alone would not save them. They had to be circumcised to partake of this Covenant event, but they would only be saved if they were protected by the blood of the Lamb.

I hope that this point is clearly understood. The act of circumcision alone did not provide protection from death, it only permitted the people into the Covenant meal and to reap the benefits of the Covenant promise of protection afforded by the blood of the Lamb. The protection did not come from the blood shed by those who were circumcised.

So the bottom line is that the Passover meal is to take place at the

beginning of Day 14. It was after sunset, when there was some light, before total darkness. Interestingly, this is still how the Samaritans rehearse the Passover on Mt. Gerizim each year, albeit on their own corrupted calendar. They are a small community, and they do not have a problem slaughtering their lambs "between the evenings" as each family attends to their own lamb at the same time.

When each Yisraelite family slaughtered their own lamb in Egypt, it was not a logistical problem to slaughter and roast the lamb within this short period, especially if you had an entire household working on it. In fact, the Scriptures even record that the lamb was to be cooked with its entrails.[113] This entire process of slaughtering the lambs between the evenings was accomplished quickly on the Passover preceding the Exodus. Only later in Yisrael's history, when worship was centralized around the Temple in Jerusalem, did the logistics of slaughtering lambs extend later into the night.[114]

According to the Torah, the Passover occurs at the beginning of Day 14, which begins in the evening. It happens in the dark of the night because it is a watch (shamar) night. This is the root meaning of the word shamar (𐤔𐤌𐤓): "to keep, to watch, to guard, to protect." You stay awake, in your homes. This observance is at night and precedes the next Appointed Time known as The Feast of Unleavened Bread.

Those who kept the Pesach were spared from judgment and death. They were then ready to be delivered from slavery. It is a two step process that is distinguished by two different Appointments.

The Feast of Unleavened Bread known as Hag HaMatzah, The Feast of Matzah[115] is a seven day Feast when no leaven was to be eaten. This Feast begins on Day 15, a full day after the Passover began. The Feast of Unleavened Bread begins and ends with a Sabbath.

This is important to understand. We know from the first week of Creation that time was divided into days and

weeks. The seventh day of Creation week was a Sabbath Day, and this righteous cycle of seven days has been repeating in an unbroken cycle ever since. The seven day cycle (seven rotations of the earth on its axis) is completely independent from the monthly cycle (one rotation of the moon around the earth).

The month and the year count is dependent upon the sun and the moon, and in that count there are also Sabbath Days which occur on very specific days of the lunar month. We know that in every Month 1, there will be Sabbath Days occurring every seven days on the weekly cycle which is not dependent upon the sighting of the New Moon. There will also be Sabbath Days which land on very specific days of the lunar month which are dependent on sighting the New Moon. The dates are specifically provided for all of the annual Sabbath days in Month 1. Specifically, days 15 and 21 are declared to be set apart rehearsals when no work is done.

"⁶ And on the fifteenth day of the same month is the Feast of Unleavened Bread unto YHWH: seven days you must eat unleavened bread. ⁷ In the first day you shall have a set apart rehearsal: you shall do no servile work therein. ⁸ But you shall offer an offering made by fire unto YHWH seven days: in the seventh day is a set apart rehearsal, you shall do no servile work therein." Vayiqra 23:6-8. The allusion to the Sabbath cannot be ignored, and indeed on other Appointed Times with the same description, those days are specifically called Sabbaths.

Since they are not specifically labeled Sabbaths, some dispute their being called Sabbaths. The tradition is clear that they were treated as "Shabbatons," which are deemed High Sabbaths. There is even evidence in the New Testament texts which support that position. (see Yahanan 19:31).

So then it is important to recognize that there will be a Sabbath Day on Day 15 and a Sabbath Day on Day 21. These are not weekly Sabbaths, they are "High Sabbaths" related to the monthly cycle that are associated with the annual Appointed Times. This is a mystery, and if you do not grasp this dual reckoning of time established at the beginning of Creation you will not be able to understand how the Creator's Calendar works. So when we speak about the Appointed Times determined by the sun and the moon, and we read about a "High Sabbath" we must understand that it is not referring to a weekly Sabbath.

Now during the first Feast of Unleavened Bread the children of Yisrael, including the "mixed multitude," were in the process of leaving Egypt. They "borrowed" jewels, gold, silver and clothing from the Egyptians on Day 14 following the nightly observance of the Passover. They then assembled together, and began their departure on Day 15, which began at sunset. The Scriptures confirm that they left at night. (Debarim 16:1).

At this point they had Pharaoh's permission to take their journey into the wilderness (bemidbar) and sacrifice to YHWH. Pharaoh actually asked Mosheh to bless him, although he did not give them permission to leave Egypt indefinitely.

They did not take the most direct route to the Promised Land. This would have taken them to the north and the east – "the way of the Philistines." Rather, they journeyed from Ramses to Succot - a very significant place and time. Succot is actually an Appointed Time that we will discuss in more detail.

They were on the move throughout this entire process as they traversed what is now known as the Sinai Peninsula. They travelled through the wilderness, and through wadis until they came upon what is presently known as Nuweiba in Egypt. It was there that YHWH parted the waters and they crossed the Red Sea on an underwater land bridge into the land of Midian where Mosheh had once lived. This is where they found the Mountain where Mosheh saw the burning bush. Mount Sinai is located in the land of Midian, currently called Saudi Arabia.[116]

The entire process of Passover and Unleavened Bread has very much to do with the firstborn. This was made very

clear from the beginning. When Mosheh originally confronted the Pharaoh of Egypt he proclaimed: "*²² Thus saith YHWH, Yisrael is My son, even My firstborn. ²³ And I say unto you Let My son go, that he may serve Me, and if you refuse to let him go, behold, I will slay your son, even your firstborn.*" Shemot 4:22-23.

The Pharaoh refused this initial demand, and he ended up suffering the consequences. The firstborn of Egypt had been slain, and the firstborn of the Covenant had been spared by the Passover Lamb, the Lamb of Elohim. The firstborn of Yisrael were now to be set apart. Here is what YHWH told Mosheh.

"*² Sanctify unto Me all the firstborn, whatsoever opens the womb among the children of Yisrael, both of man and of beast: it is Mine. ³ And Mosheh said unto the people, Remember this day, in which you came out from Egypt, out of the house of bondage; for by strength of hand YHWH brought you out from this place: there shall no leavened bread be eaten. ⁴ This day came you out in the month of the abib. ⁵ And it shall be when YHWH shall bring you into the land of the Canaanites, and the Hittites, and the Amorites, and the Hivites, and the Jebusites, which He swore unto thy fathers to give you, a land flowing with milk and honey, that thou shall keep (abad) ×Ɏ-this service in this month. ⁶ Seven days thou shall eat unleavened bread, and in the seventh day shall be a Feast to YHWH. ⁷ Unleavened bread shall be eaten seven days; and there shall no leavened bread be seen with thee, neither shall there be leaven seen with thee in all thy quarters. ⁸ And thou shall show thy son in that day, saying, This is done because of that which YHWH did unto me when I came forth out of Egypt. ⁹ And it shall be for a sign unto thee upon thine hand, and for a memorial between thine eyes, that YHWH's Torah may be in thy mouth: for with a strong hand hath YHWH brought thee out of Egypt. ¹⁰ You shall therefore keep (shamar) this ×℧-ordinance in His Appointed Time (moad) from year to year. ¹¹ And it shall be when YHWH shall bring you into the land of the Canaanites, as He swore to you and your fathers, and shall give it to you, ¹² That you shall set apart unto YHWH all that opens the matrix, and every firstling that comes of a beast which thou hast; the males shall be YHWH's. ¹³ And every firstling of an ass you shall redeem with a lamb; and if thou wilt not redeem it, then thou shalt break his neck: and all the firstborn of man among thy children shalt thou redeem. ¹⁴ And it shall be when thy son asketh thee in time to come, saying, What is this? that thou shalt say unto him, By strength of hand YHWH brought us out from Egypt, from the house of bondage: ¹⁵ And it came to pass, when Pharaoh would hardly let us go, that YHWH slew all the firstborn in the land of Egypt, both the firstborn of man, and the firstborn of beast: therefore I sacrifice to YHWH all that opens the matrix, being males; but all the firstborn of my children I redeem. ¹⁶ And it shall be for a sign upon thine hand, and for frontlets between thine eyes: for by strength of hand YHWH brought us forth out of Egypt.*" Shemot 13:1-16.

So while the Passover was about saving the firstborn in the Covenant houses from physical death, the emphasis of Unleavened Bread is how YHWH delivered Yisrael with a strong hand from the house of bondage. The act of eating unleavened bread is actually a sign. Interestingly, it is to be a sign upon your hand and frontlets between your eyes. This is the same command given in the Shema. (Debarim 6:4-8).

Notice that we are to "keep this service" (Shemot 13:5) and "keep this ordinance." (Shemot 13:10). In each instance there is the Aleph Taw (✗𝒱) attached to the "service" and "ordinance." This should make us aware that the Messiah is directly associated with this command. Indeed, the word translated as "keep" in Shemot 13:5 is abad (∪꛷◌). In the ancient Hebrew it literally means: "see house door." Once again, we are supposed to see this as the door back to the house. The word translated as "keep" in Shemot 13:10 is shamar (𝟫ᵐꟸ), and we already discussed the aspects of "watching, guarding and protecting" attributed to this word.

Amazingly, these two words - abad and shamar - were the two specific instructions given to Adam in the Garden. Adam was placed in the Garden and instructed to "abad and shamar." (see Beresheet 2:15). Adam was to "keep" and "watch" the Garden, which was the House. These are the same instructions that we are given concerning the Torah and the Appointed Times.

So we see that how we treat the Torah is how we treat the House - the Garden. The Messiah, as the Torah in the flesh, is the door. Once we are included into the Covenant through the Messiah, we join Yisrael and become firstborn sons. We are given the task that was originally given to Adam to abad and shamar. Essentially, the Torah and the Garden are one - echad.

So when people question whether we should "keep the Feasts" the answer is unequivocally – yes! We are specifically told to remember the Feast and tell our children about it. In fact, when we recount the history we are supposed to make it personal. It is our story. We are to tell our children: "*This is done because of that which YHWH did unto me when I came forth out of Egypt.*" (Shemot 13:8).

Now there is something very unique about this seven day Feast which is preceded by a one day event - the Passover. As previously stated, there were actually two Sabbaths associated with Unleavened Bread. The first day of the Feast which always occurs on day 15 of month 1, and the last day of the Feast which always occurs on day 21 of month 1. So this seven day feast began and ended with a Sabbath. You begin to see the significance of this fact when you recognize the interrelationship between this Feast and the harvest Feast called Shabuot, as well as the parallels with the Feasts of the seventh month. Before we delve any deeper into those connections, we must first examine the remaining commandments concerning the Passover and Unleavened Bread.

Here is the Commandment concerning the Feasts of the first month as found in the text of Vayiqra. "*⁴ These are the Appointed Times (Moadi) of YHWH, set apart rehearsals which you shall proclaim at their Appointed Times (Moadim). ⁵ On the fourteenth day of the first month at twilight is YHWH's Passover. ⁶ And on the fifteenth day of the same month is the Feast of Unleavened Bread to YHWH; seven days you must eat unleavened bread.⁷ On the first day you shall have a set apart gathering; you shall do no customary work on it.⁸ But you shall offer an offering made by fire to YHWH for seven days. The seventh day shall be a set apart gathering, you shall do no customary work on it.*" Vayiqra 23:4-8.

These Times are also described in Bemidbar as follows: "*¹⁶ On the fourteenth day of the first month YHWH's Passover is to be held. ¹⁷ On the fifteenth day of this month there is to be a festival; for seven days eat bread made without yeast. ¹⁸ On the first day hold a set apart rehearsal and do no regular work. ¹⁹ Present to YHWH an offering made by fire, a burnt offering of two young bulls, one ram and seven male lambs a year old, all without defect. ²⁰ With each bull prepare a grain offering of three-tenths of an ephah of fine flour mixed with oil; with the ram, two-tenths; ²¹ and with each of the seven lambs, one-tenth. ²² Include one male goat as a sin offering to make atonement for you. ²³ Prepare these in addition to the regular morning burnt offering. ²⁴ In this way prepare the food for the offering made by fire every day for seven days as an aroma pleasing to YHWH; it is to be prepared in addition to the regular burnt offering and its drink offering. ²⁵ On*

the seventh day hold a set apart rehearsal and do no regular work."
Bemidbar 28:16-25.

We can see that the first and the seventh days of the
Feast of Unleavened Bread are repeatedly referred to as set
apart rehearsals where no work is done – Sabbath days. These
are not weekly Sabbaths, but rather Sabbaths that occur at
specific times in the annual Moadim cycle. As we see the
progression of the Torah, in Vayiqra there is mention of
burnt offerings, and in Bemidbar there are very specific
offerings for the Appointed Times.

The first sacrifice of the annual Moadim cycle that we
read about is the Passover Lamb. The blood of the Lamb was
needed to protect the firstborn. Those were the only ones
who were killed, everyone else was exempted. The firstborn
were generally the ones who inherited and took the place of
the father. The firstborn also acted as the priests of their
families and tribes. They were the ones who offered sacrifices
to YHWH. So with the firstborn we see the representatives
of the tribes and the houses.

After the Passover in Egypt we understand that the
firstborn are represented by the Levites. The Levites
functioned along with the Cohenim, The Priests, as servants
in the House of YHWH. It was now the Levites who would
assume the priestly duties of the firstborn, the bakar (𐤒𐤔𐤓),
by serving before YHWH. So this Feast centered on the
firstborn was ultimately about the House.

After the Passover Lamb, the most predominant
theme of the Feast of Unleavened Bread is leaven, also
referred to as yeast. The object was to get rid of the leaven
during this Feast. Now there is nothing particularly bad or
good about yeast. Yeast is simply a leavening agent. When it
is combined with something it grows. It is actually alive and
mixes in with its host. It is very useful in cooking, and makes
a very good spiritual analogy for sin.

The Feast of Unleavened Bread was not only kept by
Native Yisraelites, but also the alien who resided with

Yisrael. "*¹⁷ Celebrate the Feast of Unleavened Bread, because it was on this very day that I brought your divisions out of Egypt. Celebrate this day as a lasting ordinance for the generations to come. ¹⁸ In the first month you are to eat bread made without yeast, from the evening of the fourteenth day until the evening of the twenty-first day. ¹⁹ For seven days no yeast is to be found in your houses. And whoever eats anything with yeast in it must be cut off from the community of Yisrael, whether he is an alien or native-born. ²⁰ Eat nothing made with yeast. Wherever you live, you must eat unleavened bread.*" Shemot 12:17-20.

Notice that there were no exceptions to this requirement not to consume leaven. No one living in the Land was exempt from this requirement. This is because the leaven was intended to symbolize sin and the removal of the leaven was to teach everyone to examine and remove the sin from their lives. All of Yisrael was to be free from sin for the seven day Feast with the number 7 symbolizing spiritual perfection in YHWH. Everyone was to remove the leaven from their homes, and the Land was to be free from all leaven.

Sadly, there are some in Judaism who remove the leaven from their homes each year and ask their non-Jewish neighbors to keep their leaven filled food items until the Feast is over. They then bring the items back into their home. What a tragedy. The symbolism of what they are doing is profound.

First of all, the point is to get rid of the leaven for good. Remove it and destroy it – don't give it to someone else. Imagine asking someone to hold onto your sins for seven days, and then ask them to give it back to you after seven days so that you can bring the same old sins back into your home and into your lives. This practice provides a terrible witness to their "Gentile" neighbors. Those who practice such a religion are involved in nothing more than a legalistic process of do's and don'ts, which are twisted and maneuvered around to the point that the intended lesson is missed altogether.

Currently, there are vast quantities of leaven in modern society, which appears to correlate with the existence of sin. Anyone who has attempted to remove the leaven from their homes can testify to the inclusion of leaven in numerous food products that we consume – not simply bread. As a result, some

stores in modern Israel actually close down for the Festival of Unleavened Bread as it would prove too costly to remove the leaven, or too difficult to cover their shelves. Some grocery stores in Israel actually do go through the work of taping off, with white sheets of plastic, the shelves that contain products with leaven, in an attempt to comply with the commandment that: *"No leaven shall be seen among you in all your territory for seven days."* Debarim 16:4. Whether YHWH actually thinks this complies with the commandment is an interesting question.

Ultimately however, YHWH does not want us to simply *cover* our sin, He wants our lives to be *free* from the effects of sin altogether by *removing* sin from our lives. While He commands Yisrael not to consume leaven for seven days and to remove the leaven from our *houses*, ultimately the *entire Covenant Land* will be purged of all leaven (sin) in the Millennial Kingdom.

This is the goal of the seventy sevens prophecy in Daniel 9:24. For YHWH has already determined that in the 70th seven He will finish the transgression, make an end of sin, make reconciliation for iniquity, bring in the righteous age, seal up vision and prophecy and anoint the Most Set Apart. Gabriel informed Daniel that YHWH would make an end of sin when He brings in the righteous age, which is the Age of Life or the Millennial Kingdom.

This was also taught by Yahushua the Messiah in the Parable of the Leaven, albeit in a slightly different way. In

Matthew 13:33 we read this very peculiar parable. "*The kingdom of heaven is like leaven, which a woman took and hid in three measures of meal till it was all leavened.*" Another text provides the following: "*²⁰ To what shall I liken the kingdom of Elohim? ²¹ It is like leaven, which a woman took and hid in three measures of meal till it was all leavened.*" Luke 13:20-21.

Yahushua was saying the same thing that He sent Gabriel to tell Daniel. The three measures of meal in the Parable of the Leaven symbolized 3 ages of 2,000 years. This is the same 6,000 years allotted to man, however Yahushua was revealing this truth as 3 measures of 40 Jubilee Cycles in each measure or "age."

At the end of the 6,000 years, during Jubilee Year 120, YHWH will bring in the righteous age - the Age of Life. At that time the entire Covenant Land will finally be free from sin. The meal that Yahushua referred to was grain, which constitutes the yield of the harvest. So we can see how the Plan of YHWH, and time itself, is centered on the harvest – the Harvest of the Kingdom.

It is no coincidence that "3 measures" is the quantity of fine flour that Abraham used to prepare a meal for YHWH when He appeared at the plains of Mamre. That meal took place around Passover, when the promise of a son was provided at the Appointed Time. (see Beresheet 18). Yahushua was clearly referencing the fact that the 3 measures of time provided were for the fullness of the Covenant, and the Kingdom will consist of those within the Covenant.

From the Passover we saw that the innocent blood of another, the Lamb of Elohim, must be applied to the houses of those who are in Covenant with YHWH. Only the blood of the Lamb can save those in the Covenant. Of course, just as with Noah, the inhabitants of the Covenant house must diligently obey the Commandments in order to be in the position to receive that salvation. What you think or what you have been taught is irrelevant if it is not in accordance with the Way prescribed by YHWH.

Those who have been passed over may then proceed to the Feast of Unleavened Bread. The removal of the leaven ahead of time, and the abstinence from leaven represents purification from sin. Leaven is essentially alive and it can cause serious health problems if left unchecked. Amazingly, there may have been health benefits associated with this yearly purging.[117]

From a purely spiritual perspective, the leaven makes a good analogy of sin in our lives. As the Covenant people prepared to unite with YHWH and dwell with Him, they were given a powerful reminder of the purity required to dwell with a set apart Elohim.

This Feast begins with a Sabbath rest day and ends with a Sabbath rest day. The doorway into this time of rest and redemption was splashed with blood. Passing through that door symbolizes the protection and benefits of the Covenant. Those males passing through must have spilled the blood of the Covenant themselves and bear the sign of the Covenant. They can then pass through and partake in the Covenant meal. They will be nourished and sustained by the same being (the Lamb) which shed the blood that protected them.

When you view this event in the context of the Covenant, the patterns established through the life of Abraham start to take shape. We read about the promised son (lamb) taken to be slaughtered. The firstborn son of the Covenant represented the Lamb of Elohim. This Lamb of Elohim was also connected with the fire and the smoke passing through the Covenant pieces while Abram was in a symbolic state of death.

During the seven day Feast of Unleavened Bread, another very important event occurs, sometimes referred to as the Counting of the Omer. It is the counting of seven sevens that has often been seen as a great mystery to many. The count begins at an important barley offering. This event is often called the Feast of First fruits, but it is more

accurately called the First or Resheet Offering. It is not an Appointed Time or a Feast, it is a special offering made by the Priest which begins the count to a Feast.

Interestingly, the general grain offerings could come in different forms - 1) fine flour; 2) baked in an oven; and 3) cooked on a griddle. Every grain offering was to be presented without yeast. (Vayiqra 2:11). Every grain offering was to be presented with salt. It was to be presented with oil and incense upon it. People were permitted to bring their new grain as a first fruits offering, but they would not be offered on the altar. New grain (abib) brought as first fruits (bikkurim) would be crushed and roasted in fire. It would be presented with oil and incense as a grain offering, even though it was not yet ripe.

Typically when you think about first fruits you envision each individual bringing baskets of the best of their harvest. That is not how the grain offering was presented before YHWH as a first fruits offering, and it is not what the first (resheet) barley offering was all about.

The first (resheet) barley offering made during the Feast of Unleavened Bread was exactly what it sounds like – the very first. Just like the first word in the Scriptures was beresheet or b'resheet – in the beginning. This was not a first fruits (bikkurim) that the people brought from their dwellings. That would not have been possible since the harvest could not begin until the Priest presented the first (resheet) offering.

We read about it in the following passage. "⁹ And YHWH spoke to Mosheh, saying, ¹⁰ Speak to the children of Yisrael, and say to them: When you come into the Land which I give to you, and reap its ✕ℽ harvest, then you shall bring ✕ℽ a omer of the firsts (resheet) of your harvest to the priest. ¹¹ He shall wave ✕ℽ the omer before YHWH, to be accepted on your behalf; on the day after the Sabbath the Priest shall wave it. ¹² And you shall offer on that day, when you wave ✕ℽ the omer, a male lamb of the first year, without blemish, as a burnt offering to YHWH. ¹³ Its grain offering shall be two-tenths of an ephah of fine flour mixed *with oil, an offering made by fire to YHWH, for a sweet aroma; and its drink offering shall be of wine, one-fourth of a hin.* [14] *You shall eat neither bread nor parched grain nor fresh grain until the same day that you have brought an offering to your Elohim; it shall be a statute throughout the ages (olam) throughout your generations in all your dwellings."* Vayiqra 23:9-14.

So it was the Priest who would present this resheet offering. Many translations speak of a wave sheaf offering, but the Hebrew text clearly indicated an omer. An omer is literally "a heap," and it is typically a dry measure of grain. It is also used to describe a sheaf which would be expected to amount to an omer after it was processed.

I like to consistently use the specific word omer, because it is a direct link to the manna, the bread provided by YHWH. Aharon was instructed to take an omer of manna and put it in a jar for future generations, so that they could see the manna provided by YHWH. Therefore, this omer offering was a link to the manna, both of which have very strong Messianic implications.

There was a set of offerings that were made on this day including a lamb of the first year without blemish, the same description that we read concerning the pesach. There is also flour mixed with oil, essentially matzah and a drink offering. This is symbolic of a meal. Notice that no new grain could be eaten until this offering was made. This reinforces the fact that nothing was harvested at this point – only the first omer by the Priest.

That first or beginning offering would then essentially mark the beginning of the barley harvest. It was presented on behalf of Yisrael by the Priest so that the people could then begin a new grain harvest season after purging all the leaven out of their systems. It is important to understand that this "first" offering is a priestly mandate, made on behalf of the people. When viewed in the context of a Messianic pattern, the reasons become highly apparent and significant.

The people had come to Jerusalem to celebrate the Passover, and would depart for the harvest season. According to the commandment, they did not come empty handed – they came either with money to purchase a lamb or they brought their lambs. They might also be bringing a tithe or a free-will offering. They would not be bringing their firstfruits (bikkurim), because all of this is taking place in the month of the abib. The barley could be in this unripe state for some or all of the month. The point of this Feast taking place in the month of the abib was so that it could occur before the harvest season. The grain was green and not ready to harvest.

We know from historical records of an elaborate ceremony that would be conducted by the priests on this day, "the day after the Sabbath."[118] Now we often can observe traditions developed by men which contradict the express commands found within the Torah, such as the merging of the Appointed Time on Day 14 of Month 1 with the Appointed Time on Day 15 of Month 1. On the other hand, not all traditions carried out in the past are wrong. Regarding the barley cutting and presentation of the omer on the 16th day, that is correct.

For the past two millennia there has been a debate concerning when this event should occur because of confusion concerning the phrase "the day after the Sabbath" also rendered "the morrow after the Sabbath." Some believe that this passage refers to the day after the "weekly" Sabbath, but we already established that the weekly Sabbath is separate and distinct from the Appointed Times determined by the sun and the moon. The annual Appointed Times occur on specific days in specific months, as do their Sabbath days. When you attempt to mix these two systems of reckoning it leads to confusion and error.

So when it refers to the day after the Sabbath it must be referring to day 15 of month 1, the first Sabbath in the Feast of Unleavened Bread. It would not be referring to the Final Sabbath, Day 21 of month 1, because that would place the first barley offering outside the parameters of the Feast that it is contained within. Again, the point of all of this is for the offering to be made as soon as possible, before the barley was ripe, so that the people could return home to begin the harvest season.

According to the ancient Gezer Calendar discovered at the beginning of the 20th century, and dating to the 10th century BCE, the barley harvest lasted for one month followed by a month of harvesting wheat and measuring grain. So it would make sense that the Priest would make the offering as early as possible so that the people could then return to the grain harvest.

Gezer Calendar
10th Century B.C.E.

This can clearly be seen in another passage concerning the events that took place in the month of the abib. *"¹ Observe the month of the abib and celebrate the Passover of YHWH your Elohim, because in the month of the abib He brought you out of Egypt by night. ² Sacrifice as the Passover to YHWH your Elohim an animal from your flock or herd at the place YHWH will choose as a dwelling for His Name. ³ Do not eat it with bread made with yeast, but for seven days eat unleavened bread, the bread of affliction, because you left Egypt in haste - so that all the days of your life you may remember the time of your departure from Egypt. ⁴ Let no yeast be seen in all your land for seven days. Do not let any of the meat you sacrifice on the evening of the first day remain until morning. ⁵ You must not sacrifice the Passover in any town YHWH your Elohim gives you ⁶ except in the place He will choose as a dwelling for his Name. There you must sacrifice the Passover in the evening, when the sun goes down, on the anniversary of your departure from Egypt. ⁷ Roast it and eat it at the place YHWH your Elohim will choose. Then in the morning return to your tents. ⁸ For six days eat unleavened bread and on the seventh day hold a atzeret to YHWH your Elohim and do no work. ⁹ Count off seven weeks from the time you begin to put the sickle to the standing grain."* Debarim 16:1-9.

It is important to recognize that this particular passage was given to the Yisraelites after the wilderness wanderings on Day 1 of Month 11. (Debarim 1:3). This was immediately preceding the entrance into the Land. They had not been circumcised, so they could not have been observing the Passover. They had not been harvesting crops so they needed a refresher, and this is what Mosheh was providing. It appears that their first year in the Land was also unique since they were invading the Land during the harvest season. (See Joshua 5).

Notice something interesting concerning the last day of the Feast. It is not only a Sabbath, but it is also described as an "atzeret" (×ᛘ+☉). Often referred to as "a solemn assembly" the word "atzeret" is better understood from its' root "atzar" (ᛘ+☉) which means: "to hold back, to retain, to restrain, to detain, to stay."

It is at the end of the Feast as a barrier, or restraining device. In other words, do not leave early. Stay to the very end. This is clearly seen in the Ancient characters which mean: "see, hook, head, covenant." The letter tsade (+) represents a hook, and is related to the word "tsadiq" (ᛈᛥᚢ+) which means: "righteous."

So the righteous ones are gathered and restrained by the hook of YHWH to see the head of the Covenant. This is the first atzeret that we read about relative to the Appointed Times, but it is not the last. After the seventh day, the atzeret, the people are then released to do the work of the harvest as they continue the counting of weeks and days.

The Yisraelites were to count off seven weeks from the time that they began "to put the sickle to the standing grain." That event occurred when the Priest cut the first sheaf and presented it on day 16 of month 1. This had to be the way that it occurred since during the harvest season, not all of the Yisraelites would begin harvesting their grain at the same time. The ripeness of the barley crops varies throughout the Land. They needed one definite and fixed starting point for the count which was provided by the actions of the Priest.

The count was not initiated on a multiple of

different days when everybody and anybody began harvesting their personal crops. This was an offering made for all of Yisrael, and it began a count for all of Yisrael. It was performed by the Priest on behalf of Yisrael. Therefore, once the first barley offering was made by the Priest, during Unleavened Bread, the count would commence, and the Yisraelites would return to their homes and start harvesting their crops in preparation for the Feast of Firstfruits, known as Weeks.

9

Weeks

The count is an exercise and a commandment which actually connects two Appointed Times. Essentially this count is occurring throughout the grain harvest season leading up to the Appointed Time previously mentioned as the Feast of the Cutting (Shemot 23:16) and the Feast of Weeks. (Shemot 34:22). In each of those passages it is designated as one of the three Pilgrimage Feasts where the males would congregate at the place that YHWH chose.

Remember that in the initial references to this Appointed Time, there was no specific time given for the observance, except for the theme of weeks. Each of those references mentioned the firstfruits (bikkurim) of their labors. In Shemot 23:16 we read "*And the Feast of cutting, the firstfruits (bikkurim) of your labors which you have sown in the field.*" In Shemot 34:22 we read "*And you shall observe the Feast of Weeks, of the firstfruits (bikkurim) of the wheat harvest . . .*"

So we can see the firstfruits (bikkurim) of the wheat harvest are the focus of this Feast – a Feast that occurs after the counting of weeks. The word "weeks" in Hebrew is "shabuot" (✗⊙▢ѡ). Therefore, the Feast is commonly referred to as Shabuot (Shavuot), although it is also referred to as Bikkurim or Firstfruits. There are four different occasions in the Scriptures where it is referred to as the Feast of Weeks. (Shemot 34:22; Debarim 16:10 and 16:16; 2 Chronicles 8:13). This repeated emphasis on weeks is important to remember as it helps to resolve a translation issue which is problematic for some. There can be no doubt

that weeks is the predominant theme.

In Vayiqra 23:15-21 we read much more specific information concerning the counting of the weeks. *"¹⁵ From the day after the Sabbath, the day you brought the sheaf of the wave offering, count off seven complete "weeks." ¹⁶ Count off fifty days up to the day after the seventh "week," and then present an offering of new grain to YHWH. ¹⁷ From wherever you live, bring two loaves made of two-tenths of an ephah of fine flour, baked with yeast, as a wave offering of firstfruits to YHWH. ¹⁸ Present with this bread seven male lambs, each a year old and without defect, one young bull and two rams. They will be a burnt offering to YHWH, together with their grain offerings and drink offerings - an offering made by fire, an aroma pleasing to YHWH. ¹⁹ Then sacrifice one male goat for a sin offering and two lambs, each a year old, for a fellowship offering. ²⁰ The Priest is to wave the two lambs before YHWH as a wave offering, together with the bread of the firstfruits. They are a set apart offering to YHWH for the Priest. ²¹ On that same day you are to proclaim a set apart assembly and do no regular work. This is to be a lasting ordinance for the generations to come, wherever you live."*

So we have this process of counting seven "weeks" and 50 days, commonly called the counting of the omer. This is an exercise which involves counting seven weeks and 50 days. These are two separate but united counts at the same time. The count begins with the resheet barley offering of one omer, and ends with the bikkurim wheat offering of two omers. At first glance, the commandment concerning the omer count seems fairly simple. We shall soon see the counting of the omer is one of the most mysterious and elusive commandments involving the Appointed Times. It even sounds unusual to those unfamiliar with the Hebrew language. In order to count something you first need to know what it is.

The first time that the Scriptures mention the omer is when they reference the manna, the bread from heaven, provided by YHWH to His people. The omer is actually a measurement, and it was mentioned along with the manna.

"This is the word which YHWH has commanded, Let every man gather of it according to each one's need, an omer for every being, according to the number of your beings. Let every man take for those who are in his tent." Shemot 16:16.

We already saw a previous quantitative provision of food in the Scriptures - the Passover Lamb. A suitable size lamb was to be selected for a family. If there was more, it could be shared with neighbors. This was a yearly event. Now we have an omer for every being – a daily event only while the Yisraelites were in the wilderness. (Shemot 16:35). After they entered into the Land, they would eat the grain from the Land.

The omer is represented as 𐤏𐤌𐤓 in Ancient Hebrew. The literal meaning of the characters is "eye" "water" "head". It has great spiritual significance because the amount was sufficient for everyone. No matter the age or size of the person the omer was enough. It was a uniform measure that satisfied each being. The omer could be considered to be "our daily bread." (see Mattityahu 6:11; Luke 11:3).

Since the omer was intimately connected with the manna, we should be thinking of the bread from heaven, the bread that gives life in the wilderness. We should remember the manna. In fact, YHWH commanded Mosheh to keep an omer of manna before the Ark of the Covenant, known as "the witness."

"*32 And Mosheh said, This is the word which YHWH has commanded, Fill an omer with it to be kept for your generations; that they may see ×𐤏 the bread with which I fed you in the wilderness, when I brought you forth from the land of Egypt. 33 And Mosheh said unto Aharon, take a pot, and put an omer full of manna therein, and lay it up before YHWH, to be kept for your generations. 34 As YHWH commanded Mosheh, so Aharon laid it up before the Witness, to be kept." Shemot 16:32-34.*

Interestingly, an omer was to be kept for future generations to see ×𐤏 the bread. The Aleph Taw (×𐤏) is intimately connected with the omer of manna, the bread from heaven. Once again, we should be looking to the

Messiah as the Bread that gives life - the Manna that comes down from Heaven to nourish Yisrael.

The omer of manna was laid up before YHWH, so Aharon laid it up before the Witness. The word for witness is "adut" (ᚷᚢᚩ). This word is literally: "eye, door, covenant" or "see the door which leads to the Covenant." So the witness was essentially testifying to the manna.

Later on in the Scriptures we are given more information concerning the omer as a unit of measurement. *"Now an omer is the tenth part of an ephah."* Shemot 16:32-36. The fact that the omer was a one-tenth portion connects it with the tithe.[119] How interesting that this dry measure has the symbol for water at its center. Again, when thinking about the manna in the desert we cannot help but remember the water that came from the rock. These were both the miraculous provisions of life provided directly from YHWH.

After reading about the omer and the manna, the next time we read about an omer is during the commandment concerning the count. *""[15] And you shall number to yourselves from the day after the Sabbath, from the day on which you shall offer ᚷᚩ the omer of the heave offering, seven complete "weeks." [16] until the morrow after the last "week" you shall number fifty days, and shall bring a new grain offering to YHWH."* Vayiqra 23:15-16.

Notice the connection between this offering – the omer – and the bread. This is supposed to make us think about the manna, and likewise, the Messiah. In fact, we see a direct reference to the Messiah next to the omer in the Hebrew text which now draws our attention to Vayiqra 23:15-16, because there are issues concerning the count that rely upon the underlying language.

If you note the parenthesis around the words "weeks" and "week" in Vayiqra 23:15, that is where much of the mystery and confusion lie. This citation including the word "weeks" derives from the Septuagint.[120] Here is the same passage in a translation derived from the Masoretic text.[121] "[15]

From the day after the Sabbath, the day you brought ✕∀ *the omer wave offering, count off seven full "Sabbaths."* [16] *Count off fifty days up to the day after the seventh "Sabbath," and then present an offering of new grain to YHWH." Vayiqra 23:15-16.* This was the source text for the translation previously provided in Chapter 6. I am providing both of these translations so that the reader can clearly see the problem. Are we counting Sabbaths, weeks or both?

We read that the count begins on the day after the Sabbath, and both texts are clear in that regard. As we already mentioned, exactly which Sabbath is another point of contention. The fact that the weekly Sabbaths are on a separate and independent count would reasonably lead a person to understand this to be the first Sabbath of the Feast of Unleavened Bread, Day 15 of month 1. So we see that the count begins on the day of the resheet omer wave offering. This has been determined to be Day 16 of month 1. We can see that there is a difference in translations which has resulted in confusion concerning the subsequent count.

The Septuagint supports a Day 16 resheet barley offering, and a subsequent count of 7 complete weeks followed by day 50. The Masoretic text speaks of counting seven Sabbaths, and determining day 50 after the seventh Sabbath. This is definitely inconsistent with the notion that the annual Appointed Times deal with their own Sabbaths, separate and independent from the weekly Sabbath cycle. It also contradicts the historical observance of the count.

The fact is, there are usually 8 Sabbaths in the first 49 days of the count, one High Sabbath on Day 21 of Month 1 and seven weekly Sabbaths. So logically, it would be impossible to count seven Sabbaths in the first 49 days as there are usually eight. The only time there are seven is when Day 21 of Month 1 falls on a weekly Sabbath. Elohim is not the source of confusion. He would never ask Yisrael to count 7 Sabbaths in seven weeks, when most of the time there are 8 Sabbaths in seven weeks.

The confusion associated with Vayiqra 23:16 causes many to follow the method involving a mandatory Sunday First Barley Offering (the morrow after the weekly Sabbath), which inevitably leads to counting seven consecutive weeks of weekly Sabbaths leading to the 50th day, always occurring on a Sunday.

While at first glance this seems logical and consistent with the text, it was not the method used by the Priests in the Jerusalem Temple. This is confirmed by historical and Scriptural information.[122] There were differences of opinion that developed over time, which we will examine.

Obviously, at one point there was unity as we saw in the days of Mosheh and Joshua (Yahushua).[123] As time progressed Yisrael was divided into two Kingdoms, namely the Northern Kingdom known as the House of Yisrael, and the Southern Kingdom known as the House of Yahudah. These two different kingdoms came to represent two sons – Joseph and Yahudah.

These two "sons" both sinned and were dealt with differently by YHWH. In the pattern of Joseph, the House of Yisrael was exiled from the Land, and essentially grafted into the world power system then represented by Egypt. Joseph has yet to be revealed as his period of punishment was exceptionally longer than Yahudah's. Yahudah was initially exiled for a period of seventy years, and ultimately some of those exiles returned.

While a remnant of Yahudah returned from Babylon, and retained their connection and identity with YHWH, Yoseph remained hidden and lost – the lost sheep of the House of Yisrael. After the return of the House of Yahudah, unity was problematic and continually diminished. These returning exiles from the House of Yahudah came to represent Yisrael. These Yahudim, later referred to as "Jews" remained fractured and divided into various sects with differing beliefs and traditions. They ultimately developed their own unique religion called Judaism, dominated by the

traditions of the Pharisaic sect.[124]

We know that Yahushua the Messiah came around what we refer to as the First Century of the Common Era. At this point in time, the House of Yisrael remained scattered throughout the world, like lost sheep without a shepherd. Some from the House of Yahudah had returned from their Babylonian exile, but they were subject to the Romans. These Yahudim were divided into different sects, and at that time there were three main opinions concerning the count.

The majority position, held by the Pharisees and Sadducees, followed the Septuagint rendering of waving the first barley omer offering on Day 16 of Month 1, and then counting seven complete weeks to the fiftieth day, which would always fall on day 5, day 6 or day 7 of month 3. There were other minority views. Two of particular note were the Boethusians and the Essenes, believed incorrectly by some to be the sect responsible for the Dead Sea Scrolls.

"The 'Boethusians' were most likely a branch of the Sadducees, gaining their name from Simeon b. Boethus who was appointed high priest by Herod the Great in 24 BCE . . . the Boethusians held that the waving of the sheaf should occur, not the day following the Sabbath of the festival (i.e., on the 16th) but on the first day of the week following the weekly Sabbath. This variation in the starting point for counting the omer meant that their celebration of Shavuot was also at variance with the Pharisees, and presumably the majority of Sadducees. Since they waved the sheaf on the first day of the week, Shavuot also fell on a Sunday. We also know that the Qumran sect differed in their calculations for counting the omer and thus the day they celebrated Shavuot. They understood the word "Sabbath" of Leviticus 23:15 to be the weekly Sabbath following the last day of Unleavened Bread (which is also a Sabbath). Thus, like the Boethusians, they began counting the omer on the first day of the week, and celebrated Shavuot on the first day of the week, but in

both cases a week later than the Boethusians. These three different perspectives (Pharisees, Boethusians, sect of the Dead Sea Scrolls), then, are those known to exist in the 1st Century CE."[125]

The Boethusians believed that the omer should be offered on the first day of the week, and therefore Shabuot should fall on the first day of the week. Although the Boethusians held these beliefs, they did not control the way the Levitical priesthood operated, as it was the opinion of the Pharisees that were followed by the Sadducees, and a majority of the populace.[126]

When Messiah walked upon the earth in the flesh, the majority view of the Pharisees and Sadducees was predominant. We know that Yahushua provided correction to the Pharisees and Sadducees in many areas of the Torah. One of the greatest debates occurring at the time was on a point that these two majority sects could not agree - the subject of the resurrection. Yahushua answered that question decisively through His own resurrection. Accordingly, His actions supported the Pharisaic position.

Interestingly, other than the dates of His birth and death, we have no record of Yahushua giving any direct or specific instruction concerning the calendar. We read about Him travelling to Jerusalem during the three Pilgrimage Feasts. He was even in Jerusalem on the Feast of Dedication, known as Hannukah.[127]

One could reasonably assume that Yahushua would have provided correction on such an important subject if it were needed. Instead, we see Yahushua presumably walking in synchronicity with the calendar of that day, appearing in Jerusalem along with all of the Yahudim.

After the establishment of the Christian religion, hundreds of years following the death of Yahushua, the Catholic Church weighed in on this matter. The Catholic

Church, which felt empowered to change the Sabbath day to Sunday, decided to fix Sunday as the day of the resheet offering to coincide with their tradition of a Sunday resurrection.[128] Since Catholicism incorporated many aspects of sun worship, we can see the tendency for them to move from the Sabbath to Sunday. This resulted in a Sunday Feast of Weeks, called Pentecost. This essentially took the emphasis away from counting seven weeks after the High Sabbath on Day 16 of Month 1, and focused on having the count always end on a Sunday, their sabbath day - the day traditionally reserved to worship the sun.[129]

Many people who have a Christian background prefer this rendering, because they are trying to parallel an Easter Sunday resurrection with the resheet offering, which they call "firstfruits" and actually erroneously treat as a separate feast. The essential problem is the fact that the Messiah was not resurrected on a Sunday, and they may be misunderstanding the purpose of the event.

It is quite clear that Yahushua was actually placed in the ground before sundown on Day 14, following the night of Passover, which was a Wednesday.[130] We know that He was in sheol[131] for three days, and three nights according to the sign of Jonah.[132] Therefore, He was subsequently resurrected on the weekly Sabbath, during the Feast of Unleavened Bread.[133]

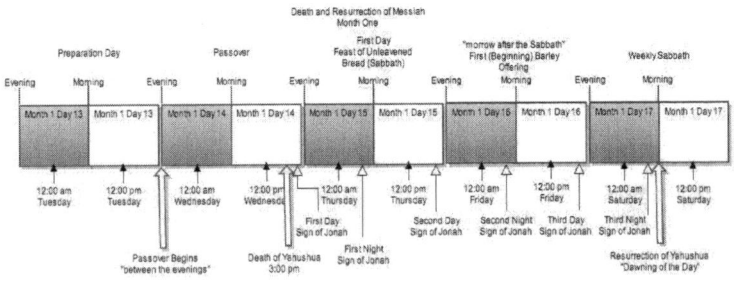

There is no valid Sunday connection that can be made with the resheet offering or the resurrection. Yahushua was

the Lamb of Elohim that was slain on Passover Day – Day 14 of Month 1, which was a Wednesday. The First Day of the Feast of Unleavened Bread occurred on Day 15 of Month 1, which was a Thursday. The resheet offering occurred on the day after the Festival Sabbath, day 16 of month 1, which was a Friday. Since Yahushua was in sheol three days and three nights, He was resurrected on the weekly Sabbath.[134]

How appropriate for the Master of the Sabbath.[135] There is no doubt a deep mystery associated with this day, this offering and this count – all leading to another Appointed Time focused on weeks – shabuot.

The similarities between the word shabuot (X⊙□w) and shabat (X□w) cannot be ignored. The only difference between the two is the existence of the ayin (⊙) between bet (□ - the house) and taw (X - the mark or the covenant). In essence, it is shouting out "do you see the sabbath in the weeks?"

Interestingly, there will be seven weekly Sabbaths within the seven weeks, but the emphasis is on the shabuot – the weeks. This reckoning is actually confirmed by Mosheh and by the New Testament Scriptures.[136] We can therefore accept that the historical counting was accurate. Again, just because the Pharisees were doing something does not automatically mean it was wrong. Yahushua corrected the Pharisees on many matters where they were in error, but not everything they did was wrong.

In fact, Josephus makes it clear that right up until the end of the Second Temple Period, the resheet offering of barley was offered on Day 16 of Month 1. "(250) But on the second day of unleavened bread, which is the sixteenth day of the month, they first partake of the fruits of the earth, for before that day they do not touch them. And while they suppose it proper to honor Elohim, from who they obtain this plentiful provision, in the first place, they offer the first fruits of their barley, and that in the manner following: (251) They take a handful of the ears, and dry them, then beat them small, and purge the barley from the bran; they then bring one tenth deal to the altar, to Elohim; and, casting one handful of it upon the fire, they leave the rest for the use of the priest; and after this it is that they may publicly or privately reap their harvest. They also at this participation of the firstfruits of the earth, sacrifice a lamb, as a burnt offering to Elohim." Josephus, Antiquities, 3 / 250-251.

The Talmud - speaking of the Creator's Calendar that Yisrael was on before the Rabbinic calendar was invented - states that Shabuot could be observed on Day 5, Day 6 or Day 7 of Month 3. (see Rosh Hashanah 6B). This means that throughout all of Yisrael's history until 359 CE, the first visible crescent was being used to reckon months, and that every month could independently contain either 29 or 30 days. It also means that the omer was being counted from Day 16 of Month 1.

This is confirmed by examining the existing possibilities. When the first 2 months each contain 30 days, Shabuot will fall on Day 5 of Month 3 counting from Day 16 of Month 1. When month 1 contains 30 days and month 2 contains 29 days (or visa versa), Shabuot will fall on Day 6 of month 3 counting from Day 16 of Month 1. And when the first 2 months each contain 29 days, Shabuot will fall on Day 7 of Month 3 counting from Day 16 of Month 1.

This Talmud reference in Rosh Hashanah 6B speaks volumes about how to reckon months and how to count the days and weeks to Shabuot. It proves that the ancient Yisraelites reckoned the month from the first visible crescent, and that they counted the omer from the day after the High Sabbath on Day 15 of Month 1.

Again, history provides all of the evidence necessary for Yisrael to recalibrate itself to the Appointed Times of YHWH and His calendar. And if the Levitical priests in the Second Temple were counting in this manner, then Yahushua the Messiah would have counted in this way. According to the New Testament Scriptures Yahushua never

sinned. (Hebrews 4:15, 9:28 and 1 Peter 2:22). He kept the Appointed Times in Jerusalem throughout His life, and if the Levitical priests were not counting properly, Yahushua either would not have participated on their calendar or He would have corrected them. Since He did neither, we can safely assume that the count was being performed properly.

While there are several systems of counting available, all other methods lack the support found in the weekly count beginning on Day 16 of Month 1. Most importantly, that method is supported by the Scriptures and overwhelming historical evidence.[137]

Only when the resheet offering was presented by the Priest could they begin the count, and the subsequent harvest. At the end of the harvest, the people would then bring the firstfruits of their harvest, known as the bikkurim, from their homes. This is made clear through various passages.

Here is the passage from Vayiqra. "You shall bring _out of your habitations_ two wave loaves of two tenth parts: they shall be of fine flour; they shall be baked with leaven; they are the firstfruits (bikkurim) unto YHWH." Vayiqra 23:17. We can now see that at Shabuot the people would bring their firstfruits (bikkurim) from their homes. This time they bring two loaves of two omers – baked with leaven. So while the resheet barley offering was at the beginning of the harvest and consisted of a single omer presented by the Priest without any leaven, the bikkurim was much different.

The Shabuot bikkurim offering was brought by the people from their dwellings. It was the firstfruits from their own crops brought at the end of the harvest. It consisted of two loaves, which were set apart, baked with leaven and waved before YHWH. If leaven is representative of sin then we see the single resheet offering without sin and the two bikkurim loaves, the two omers with leaven, brought from throughout the Land and waved as one before YHWH.

This may seem strange, but it must be viewed within the larger context of the Appointed Times, and the Covenant plan. We already discussed the problems that stemmed from the Garden, and progressed through Yisrael. Yisrael consists of the Covenant people, and is the firstfruits of YHWH. (Yirmeyahu 2:2). Yisrael was married to YHWH, but later divided into two houses because of their sin. The Prophets foretold of a time when Yisrael would be regathered, reunited and restored.

The two loaves coming together at Shabuot represent the House of Yisrael and the House of Yahudah coming together over Shabuot. Even though both houses contain leaven, they are set apart to YHWH. The House of Yisrael has not been taught the instructions in the Torah – which were given at Shabuot on Day 7 of Month 3 in 1437 BCE.* The House of Yahudah has not received the Spirit of Messiah – which was also given at Shabuot on Day 7 of Month 3 in 34 CE.* It is highly significant that both of these fulfillments occurred when Shabuot landed on Day 7 of Month 3.

At a future date, the House of Yisrael and the House of Yahudah, along with a large mixed multitude, will be regathered and restored under Yahushua the Messiah. Then, the Commonwealth of Yisrael will be keeping the commandments of Elohim (The Torah) and having the testimony of Yahushua the Messiah (The Spirit). This, in fact, is prophesied to occur before the Messiah returns. (Revelation 12:17 and 14:12).

Only after the resheet (first) omer offering (representing the Messiah) was presented could the House of Yisrael and the House of Yahudah be reaped, gathered together and presented before YHWH as firstfruits (bikkurim). This would occur through a process of seven sevens, concluding with 50. One cannot ignore the allusion to the restoration of Yisrael occurring in the last year of a 50 year Jubilee count. That 50 day count to Shabuot began when the resheet offering was cut and waved by the Priest. This point, as well as the counting of seven weeks, is made clear

by a subsequent text.

"*⁹ You shall count seven weeks (×⊙☐w) for yourself; you shall begin to count seven weeks (×⊙☐w) from the time you begin to put the sickle to the standing grain. ¹⁰ Then you shall celebrate the Feast of Weeks (×ꟷ⊙☐w) to YHWH your Elohim with a tribute of a freewill offering of your hand, which you shall give just as YHWH your Elohim blesses you.*" Debarim 16:9-10. Again, notice the emphasis on seven and weeks.

So we can now see that the Feast of Weeks, Shabuot, does not have a fixed calendar date in the Scriptures, but rather falls on the day after the completion of seven weeks, or 49 days. It occurs on the 50th day so we must count the passage of seven weeks and 50 days. There is a parallel counting of weeks and days occurring simultaneously. Without question, the count is related to the Jubilee. In fact, there is a text that hints at the purpose:

"*¹⁶ And if a man shall sanctify unto YHWH some part of a field of his possession, then thy estimation shall be according to the seed thereof: an homer of barley seed shall be valued at fifty shekels of silver. ¹⁷ If he sanctify his field from the year of Jubilee, according to thy estimation it shall stand. ¹⁸ But if he sanctify his field after the Jubilee, then the Priest shall reckon unto him the money according to the years that remain, even unto the year of the Jubilee, and it shall be abated from thy estimation. ¹⁹ And if he that sanctified the field will in any wise redeem it, then he shall add the fifth part of the money of thy estimation unto it, and it shall be assured to him. ²⁰ And if he will not redeem the field, or if he have sold the field to another man, it shall not be redeemed any more. ²¹ But the field, when it goeth out in the Jubilee, shall be set apart unto YHWH, as a field devoted; the possession thereof shall be the priest's. ²² And if a man sanctify unto YHWH a field which he hath bought, which is not of the fields of his possession; ²³ Then the Priest shall reckon unto him the worth of thy estimation, even unto the year of the Jubilee: and he shall give thine estimation in that day, as a set apart thing unto YHWH. ²⁴ In the year of the Jubilee the field shall return unto him of whom it was bought, even to him to whom the possession of the land did belong.*" Vayiqra 27:16-24.

For those unfamiliar with the Jubilee, here is the primary commandment. *"[1] YHWH said to Mosheh on Mount Sinai, [2] Speak to the Yisraelites and say to them: When you enter the Land I am going to give you, the Land itself must observe a Sabbath to YHWH. [3] For six years sow your fields, and for six years prune your vineyards and gather their crops. [4] But in the seventh year the land is to have a Sabbath of rest, a Sabbath to YHWH. Do not sow your fields or prune your vineyards. [5] Do not reap what grows of itself or harvest the grapes of your untended vines. The Land is to have a year of rest. [6] Whatever the land yields during the Sabbath year will be food for you - for yourself, your manservant and maidservant, and the hired worker and temporary resident who live among you, [7] as well as for your livestock and the wild animals in your land. Whatever the land produces may be eaten. [8] Count off seven Sabbaths of years - seven times seven years - so that the seven Sabbaths of years amount to a period of forty-nine years. [9] Then have the shofar sounded everywhere on the tenth day of the seventh month; on the Day of Atonements sound the shofar throughout your Land. [10] Consecrate the fiftieth year and proclaim liberty throughout the Land to all its inhabitants. It shall be a Jubilee for you; each one of you is to return to his family property and each to his own clan. [11] The fiftieth year shall be a Jubilee for you; do not sow and do not reap what grows of itself or harvest the untended vines. [12] For it is a Jubilee and is to be set apart for you; eat only what is taken directly from the fields. [13] In this Year of Jubilee everyone is to return to his own property."* Vayiqra 25:1-13.

The Hebrew word for "jubilee" is "yobel" (יוֹבֵל). It derives from yabal, which means "to conduct, to bring or to carry – as in a procession." The picture is a procession carrying possessions to the house. This was a day to blow the shofar, a ram's horn, throughout the Land. On this day, every 50 years, Yisrael was to proclaim liberty. The primary themes of the Jubilee year are release, return, redemption and restoration to the way it was in the Garden of Eden in the beginning.

Pay particular attention to the count. Notice the

reference to Sabbaths. That is why so many desire to count the omer based upon seven weekly Sabbaths, but that is really no basis at all, because these Sabbaths are not the seventh day Sabbaths. They are seven year Sabbaths, which reveals that the word Sabbath does not exclusively apply to the weekly Sabbath.

The Jubilee actually counts special years called "Shemitah" years. A Shemitah year occurs every seven years, and it is called a "Sabbath" just like the Appointed Times contain their own annual Sabbaths. The Shemitah year is a year of rest, and after seven Shemitah cycles the yobel begins – not on Day 1 of Month 1, but rather Day 10 of Month 7.

In many ways, the Feast of Weeks is essentially a yearly reminder of the Jubilee, which links Passover, Unleavened Bread and Shabuot together. Shabuot occurs at the end of the grain harvest while the 50 year Jubilee cycle culminates in the end of the Fall harvest.

Shabuot is a time of rejoicing for all people. On one occasion there is a commandment to rejoice. "*And you shall rejoice before YHWH your Elohim, you, and your son, and your daughter, and your manservant, and your maidservant, and the Levite that is within your gates, and the stranger, and the fatherless, and the widow, that are among you, in the place which YHWH your Elohim has chosen to place His Name there.*" Debarim 16:11. The Jubilee is the ultimate time of rejoicing, although it is tempered by the fact that it begins on the Day of Atonement on Day 10 of Month 7, a day of affliction.

The overriding question we should ask is: "What is so important about the number 50 that there would be such mystery and emphasis associated with the 50th day and the 50th year?" YHWH could have made this all perfectly clear. Instead, He allowed some mystery to be built into this elusive count, which should tell us that there is something special to be learned. We gain understanding through our participation in the Appointed Times.

Once we recognize how to count the weeks, we are

brought to the culmination of the Feast of Weeks, the fiftieth day. Let us look at what happened on the 50th day as offerings and sacrifices were presented at a threshing floor where YHWH ultimately established a Temple (Hekal) in Jerusalem. For those unfamiliar with the construction of the Temple, known as the Hekal, a little background might be in order.

While Shlomo, the son of David, actually oversaw the building of the Hekal in Jerusalem, it was David who was integral in making the necessary plans and preparations. One of the most significant details was the location – the threshing floor of Araunah. It was the location where the plague of YHWH stopped. (see 2 Shemuel 24). The threshing process was intimately connected with the various grains harvested in the Land, so there is a link that cannot be ignored between the grain Feasts and what happens at the Hekal.

Here is the command concerning the offerings made on the fiftieth day, at the conclusion of weeks. *"¹⁷ You shall bring out of your habitations two wave loaves of two tenth deals: they shall be of fine flour; they shall be baked with leaven; they are the firstfruits (bikkurim) unto YHWH. ¹⁸ And you shall offer with the bread seven lambs without blemish of the first year, and one young bullock, and two rams: they shall be for a burnt offering unto YHWH, with their grain offering, and their drink offerings, even an offering made by fire, of sweet savour unto YHWH. ¹⁹ Then you shall sacrifice one kid of the goats for a sin offering, and two lambs of the first year for a sacrifice of peace offerings. ²⁰ And the Priest shall wave them with the bread of the firstfruits for a wave offering before YHWH, with the two lambs: they shall be set apart to YHWH for the Priest. ²¹ And you shall proclaim on the selfsame day, that it may be a set apart gathering unto you: you shall do no servile work therein: it shall be a statute throughout the ages (olam) in all your dwellings throughout your generations. ²² And when you reap the harvest of your land, thou shalt not make clean riddance of the corners of thy field when thou reapest, neither shalt thou gather any gleaning of thy harvest: thou shalt leave them*

unto the poor, and to the stranger: I am YHWH your Elohim."
Vayiqra 23:17-22.

We can see this as a culmination of the Passover. Instead of the first (resheet) of the barley harvest brought by the Priest, these are the firstfruits brought by the people *from their habitations*. Instead of one omer of unleavened barley we have two loaves, two omers, of leavened wheat. Instead of one lamb of the first year we see seven lambs of the first year along with a young bull and two rams offered as burnt offerings which were a sweet smell unto YHWH.

It is incredible to recognize that there was a physical act in the Temple Service that provided physical pleasure to YHWH involving one of the senses. The lesson is that we too can please YHWH through our thoughts, our speech and our behavior – this is the lesson blessing associated with keeping the Appointed Times.

These burnt offerings were made with wine offerings (ᛗᚤᚤᛃᛃᛉ) and grain offerings (ᛗᚷᚼᛃᛗ). This was a Feast after all, and the provision essentially reveals who is at this Feast. The existence of ten animals at this Feast should not be lost upon the reader. Another offering that should not be lost is the "kid of the goats" made for a sin offering and two lambs made for a peace offering. These were waved with the bread of the firstfruits which contains the yeast.

Another passage that details the offerings made on Shabuot is found in Bemidbar. *"²⁶ On the day of firstfruits (bikkurim), when you present to YHWH an offering of new grain during the Feast of Weeks, hold a set apart rehearsal and do no regular work. ²⁷ Present a burnt offering of two young bulls, one ram and seven male lambs a year old as an aroma pleasing to YHWH. ²⁸ With each bull there is to be a grain offering of three-tenths of an ephah of fine flour mixed with oil; with the ram, two-tenths; ²⁹ and with each of the seven lambs, one-tenth. ³⁰ Include one male goat to make atonement for you. ³¹ Prepare these together with their drink offerings, in addition to the regular burnt offering and its grain offering. Be sure the animals are without defect."* Bemidbar 28:26-31.

Notice what appears to be a problem between Bemidbar 28:27, which describes two bulls and one ram, and Vayiqra 23:18 which describes one bull and two rams. The difference is not a contradiction, but merely a description of different offerings altogether. The offerings in Vayiqra describe the offerings made with the wave loaves, and those in Bemidbar are for the Appointed Time. Thus all of them are offered on the 50th day.

Bemidbar also describes a grain offering along with each sacrifice - 3 omers with each bull, 2 omers with each ram and 1 omer with each lamb. Both passages provide a male goat as an atonement. So on the 50th day there would be 2 lambs offered followed by 3 young bulls, 3 rams, 14 lambs and 2 kids.[138]

Finally, in Debarim 16:10 we read: "*And you shall keep the Feast of Weeks unto YHWH your Elohim with a tribute of a freewill offering of your hand, which thou shalt give unto YHWH your Elohim, according as YHWH your Elohim has blessed you.*" Notice the emphasis on the relationship - "YHWH your Elohim." This is stressed throughout Debarim 16 and is found 3 times relative to Shabuot, which is the date associated with the giving of the Torah at Sinai. That was a Marriage Covenant event and relationship with YHWH is central to this Appointed Time. It is also about giving back to YHWH according to the blessings you have received.

The Feast of Shabuot is the last Appointed Time before a period of time that leads to other Appointed Times in the seventh month. Before we proceed to discuss those Appointed Times there is an interesting passage in the Scriptures that is found between the Feasts, which at first glance seems out of place. A further review provides a powerful teaching.

"*When you reap the harvest of your land, you shall not wholly reap the corners of your field when you reap, nor shall you gather any gleaning from your harvest. You shall leave them for the poor and for the stranger (* 𐤂𐤓 *). I am YHWH your Elohim.*"

Vayiqra 23:22. This speaks to a time during the harvest, and there is specific provision for the poor and the stranger – the ger (𐤂𐤓). How interesting that this commandment falls between the text describing the Appointed Times in spring and the text describing the Appointed Times in the fall. In the midst of these Feasts there is provision for the stranger - those outside of the Covenant.

The Scriptures provide a vivid example of this commandment in the Book of Ruth. Ruth, a Moabitess, was a stranger who asserted her rights to glean the fields of Boaz during the grain harvest. She ultimately became his wife and through that union came King David and eventually Yahushua the Messiah. We also see a powerful example of the kinsman redeemer through the story of Ruth, and these are all working within the framework of the Appointed Times.[139]

As Yisrael walks the Covenant path, through the Appointed Times, there will be provision for those outside the Covenant. This is ultimately an important purpose of Yisrael, to help draw the Nations to YHWH. We saw that on Passover YHWH redeemed the firstborn of Yisrael and that Yisrael was saved by the blood of the Lamb on Day 14 of Month 1. On the first day of Unleavened Bread they left Ramses as a mixed multitude on Day 15 of Month 1, and on the last day of Unleavened Bread this multitude crossed over the Red Sea and left Egypt on Day 21 of Month 1. They received instructions at Mount Sinai at Shabuot on Day 7 of Month 3, but they had not entered the Promised Land yet. We will now continue our study of Yisrael's Covenant journey as we examine the Appointed Times of the seventh month.

10

The Seventh Month

The remaining focus of the Appointed Times is directed to the seventh month - the Sabbath month. Again, all of these cycles of seven are meant to attract our attention to the perfection and completion of the Covenant plan. We trace the Covenant journey through the Appointed Times from the first month, beginning with the shed blood of the Passover Lamb. It continues through the grain harvest by the counting of seven weeks, and then culminates through a series of Appointed Times found within the seventh month. We already read about one of those Appointed Times as a Pilgrimage Feast, referred to as the Feast of Ingathering.

Just as the Passover was to occur around the tequfah – the vernal equinox, the Feast of Ingathering was to occur around the tequfah - the autumnal equinox. (Shemot 23:16). The Feast of Ingathering, in month 7, will occur around the turn of the year. It was at the end of the harvest season which began in the month of the abib - Month 1. This turn is sometimes referred to as "the end of the year" or "the end of days." Only when we recognize the significance of the tequfah do these reckonings make sense. It also is another confirmation that The Rule of the Equinox is an accurate calculation for keeping the Appointed Times in their proper places.

So we see the Appointed Times of the seventh month occurring around the turn of the year, the end of days, which will involve a different harvest from the previous Appointed Times. Instead of grains, we will see the fruit harvests. This

is an important distinction to understand when we view certain Scriptures, including prophecies.

Let us begin our examination of the Appointed Times of the seventh month by quoting the remaining text of Vayiqra 23: "*[23] Then YHWH spoke to Mosheh, saying, [24] Speak to the children of Yisrael, saying: In the seventh month (chodesh), in the first (echad) of the month (chodesh), you shall have a Sabbath rest (shabbaton) a memorial of blowing, a set apart rehearsal (miqra-qadosh). [25] You shall do no customary work and you shall offer an offering made by fire to YHWH. [26] And YHWH spoke to Mosheh, saying: [27] Also the tenth of this seventh month let it be the Day of Atonement. It shall be a set apart rehearsal (miqra-qadosh) for you; you shall afflict your souls, and offer an offering made by fire to YHWH. [28] And you shall do no work on that same day, for it is the Day of Atonement, to make atonement for you before YHWH your Elohim. [29] For any person who is not afflicted in soul on that same day shall be cut off from his people. [30] And any person who does any work on that same day, that person I will destroy from among his people. [31] You shall do no manner of work; it shall be a statute throughout the ages (olam) throughout your generations in all your dwellings. [32] It shall be to you a Shabbat Shabbaton, and you shall afflict your souls; on the ninth day of the month at evening, from evening to evening, you shall celebrate your Sabbath. [33] Then YHWH spoke to Mosheh saying, [34] Speak to the children of Yisrael, saying: The fifteenth day of this seventh month shall be the Feast of Succot for seven days to YHWH. [35] On the first day there shall be a set apart rehearsal (miqra-qadosh) You shall do no customary work on it. [36] For seven days you shall offer an offering made by fire to YHWH. On the eighth day you shall have a set apart rehearsal (miqra-qadosh), and you shall offer an offering made by fire to YHWH. It is a atzeret, and you shall do no customary work on it. [37] These are the Appointed Times of YHWH which you shall proclaim to be set apart rehearsals, to offer an offering made by fire to YHWH, a burnt offering and a grain offering, a sacrifice and drink offerings, everything on its day - [38] besides the Sabbaths of YHWH, besides your gifts, besides all your vows, and besides all your freewill offerings which you give to YHWH.* [39] *Also on the fifteenth day of the seventh month, when you have gathered in the fruit of the Land, you shall keep a Feast unto YHWH for seven days; on the first day there shall be a Shabbaton, and on the eighth day a Shabbaton.* [40] *And you shall take for yourselves on the first day the fruit of beautiful trees, branches of palm trees, the boughs of leafy trees, and willows of the brook; and you shall rejoice before YHWH your Elohim for seven days.* [41] *You shall keep it as a Feast to YHWH for seven days in the year. It shall be a statute throughout the ages in your generations. You shall celebrate it in the seventh month.* [42] *You shall dwell in succot for seven days. All who are native (ezrach) Yisraelites shall dwell in succoth,* [43] *that your generations may know that I made the children of Yisrael dwell in succot when I brought them out of the land of Egypt: I am YHWH your Elohim.* [44] *So Mosheh declared to the children of Yisrael the Feasts of YHWH."* Vayiqra 23:23-44.

From this passage we can see many interrelated events occurring in the seventh month, beginning with the first day, commonly referred to as the Feast of Trumpets. This is not accurate because the first day is not referred to as a Feast (hag). While it is an Appointed Time, it is not a Pilgrimage Feast when Yisraelite males were commanded to go to the House of YHWH.

For many reasons, it is probably the most underrated and misunderstood Appointed Time. Its meaning is often lost within the Jewish celebration of Rosh Hashanah. Rosh Hashanah means "head of the year" and many treat it as simply a New Year celebration.[140]

Remember the "paradigm shift" that occurred when Mosheh and Aharon helped deliver the Yisraelites out of Egypt. That event occurred in 1437 BCE* and prior to that point, it is believed that mankind reckoned a year from Month 7 to Month 7.

To celebrate Day 1 of Month 7 as a New Year celebration is essentially a recognition of creation Day 1. This fact is not specifically mentioned in the Scriptures, although it is called "ha-yom ha-rat olam" or "The Birthday of the

World" in Hebraic thought. As it commemorates the creation of the physical universe, we can discern that it is a very significant Appointed Time relative to the restoration of all things. That being the case we should focus on the spiritual significance and meaning of this day instead of simply treating it as a New Year celebration.

The actual name of the Appointed Time is Yom Teruah, which means: "day of blowing" or "day of blasting." The blowing of trumpets and shofars (ram's horns) on Day 1 of Month 7 has been associated with the day that YHWH will raise the righteous from the dead. So this time is about resurrection.

The first reference to Yom Teruah is found in Vayiqra 23:24: *"In the seventh month, on the first day of the month, shall be a solemn rest (Shabbaton) unto you, a memorial blowing (teruah), a set apart gathering (miqra-qadosh)."* Notice the word "Shabbaton" translated as solemn rest. Some translations provide for a "Sabbath-rest." The connection with sabbath cannot be ignored, because it is a Sabbath. In this instance it is not necessarily a weekly sabbath, but rather a Sabbath based upon the lunar cycle.

The word shabbaton has also been used while referring to the weekly sabbath.[41] The word "shabbaton" is used relative to all of the Appointed Times which are designated as Sabbaths in the seventh month - the Day of Atonement (Vayiqra 16:3) and the first day of Succot (Vayiqra 23:39) and the eighth day called Shemini Atzeret (Vayiqra 23:39). It is also used to refer to the Shemitah Year - the seventh year.

All of these Shabbat Shabbaton events are related by sevens. So while the first day of the seventh month is a Shabbat, it is usually not a weekly Shabbat. Likewise, Day 10, Day 15 and Day 22 are also described as Shabbat Shabbatons, and just as Day 1 of Month 7, they are determined by the lunar cycle rather than the seven day weekly cycle.

The Hebrew word *teruah*, often translated as trumpet,

literally means "blast or blowing." It is not the instrument of blasting that is mentioned, but the sound. Indeed the sound is referenced as a "memorial blast."

There is another reference to this Appointed Time found in Bemidbar 29:1. *"On the first day of the seventh month you shall have a set apart gathering. You shall do no laborious work. It is a day of blowing."* The Hebrew phrase "yom teruah" literally means: "a day of blowing." Now this is interesting because blowing trumpets or shofars is not a unique event. In fact, there are numerous instances when shofars and trumpets are used in the Scriptures. Probably the most common usage for Yisrael was to assemble or gather the people.

One thing that makes this day unique is the fact that it is the only Appointed Time that occurs on Rosh Chodesh – the head of the month. It is a unique day as it combines a High Sabbath with a New Moon Day. This is a time when shofars would traditionally be blown to announce the "resheet" or the beginning of the month. It is also a time when people would be looking up – eagerly searching out the sky to sight the first light of the new moon which would mark the beginning of the month. It is not just any Rosh Chodesh - it marks the beginning of the seventh month.

The blast of this day is a memorial - zikrone (ﬡﬡﬡ). As we already mentioned, it can be a remembrance of Creation. Again, the emphasis of this day is sound and we know that Elohim created with His voice - sound. The voice of YHWH is a mighty sound (Tehillim 29). It could actually be seen. When the Children of Yisrael heard and saw the sound they thought that they would die if YHWH continued to speak His words. (Shemot 20:19). As a result, the Children of Yisrael only heard the Ten words spoken by the voice of YHWH. The rest of the Torah was given to them through Mosheh.[142]

So when we think of this day we think of a mighty blast that gets the attention of all of the people. It is the voice of the Trumpet that was heard at Sinai, and this fact actually takes us back to Sinai on Shabuot when that voice was heard. (Shemot 19). We remember Sinai, but we also remember that the Covenant was thereafter broken.

Mosheh had to specifically intercede, and he prayed that the Children of Yisrael not be blotted out from His book, or rather scroll. "*32 Yet now, if You will forgive their sin, and if not, blot me, I pray thee, out of Your Scroll which You have written. 33 And YHWH said unto Mosheh, Whosoever hath sinned against Me, him will I blot out of My scroll.*" Shemot 32:32-33. The inference is that the appearance of your name in this Scroll is a good thing, while being blotted out is bad.

So when we think about this Scroll, could it be that this also relates with the notion of remembrance. It is possible that this might also be a day that YHWH remembers, and thus the reason that we make the blasting sounds. Could it be that we are trying to get His attention on this day so that He will remember us? When thinking about a text in the Hebrew Scriptures it is important to think about a scroll rather than a codex. The scroll, known as a "sefer" (𐤎𐤐𐤓) in Hebrew, is rolled up and sometimes sealed, while a codex is bound by a spine. The scroll is what is referenced in the text and fits perfectly with the cyclical nature of Hebrew thought and language.

The Scriptures provide further information regarding the Scroll that YHWH has written. That Scroll is connected with judgment and the Covenant people. Let us review what the prophet Malachi has to say about this very important issue:

"*1 Behold, I will send My messenger, and he shall prepare the way before Me: and the Master, whom you seek, shall suddenly come to His Hekal, even the Messenger of the Covenant, whom you delight in. Behold, He shall come, says YHWH of hosts. 2 But who may abide the day of His coming? And who shall stand when He appeareth? For He is like a refiner's fire, and like fullers' soap: 3 And He shall sit as a refiner and purifier of silver: and He shall purify the sons of Levi, and purge them as gold and silver, that they*" may offer unto YHWH an offering in righteousness. ⁴ Then shall the offering of Yahudah and Jerusalem be pleasant unto YHWH, as in the days of old, and as in former years. ⁵ And I will come near to you to judgment; and I will be a swift witness against the sorcerers, and against the adulterers, and against false swearers, and against those that oppress the hireling in his wages, the widow, and the fatherless, and that turn aside the stranger from his right, and fear not Me, saith YHWH of hosts. ⁶ For I am YHWH, I change not; therefore you sons of Yaakob are not consumed. ⁷ Even from the days of your fathers you are gone away from My ordinances, and have not kept them. Return unto Me, and I will return unto you, saith YHWH of hosts. But you said, Wherein shall we return? ⁸ Will a man rob Elohim? Yet you have robbed Me. But you say, Wherein have we robbed you? In tithes and offerings. ⁹ You are cursed with a curse: for you have robbed Me, even this whole nation. ¹⁰ Bring you all the tithes into the storehouse, that there may be meat in mine house, and prove Me now herewith, saith YHWH of hosts, if I will not open you the windows of heaven, and pour you out a blessing, that there shall not be room enough to receive it. ¹¹ And I will rebuke the devourer for your sakes, and he shall not destroy the fruits of your ground; neither shall your vine cast her fruit before the time in the field, saith YHWH of hosts. ¹² And all nations shall call you blessed: for you shall be a delightsome land, saith YHWH of hosts. ¹³ Your words have been stout against Me, saith YHWH. Yet you say, What have we spoken so much against thee? ¹⁴ You have said, It is vain to serve Elohim: and what profit is it that we have kept His ordinance, and that we have walked mournfully before YHWH of hosts? ¹⁵ And now we call the proud happy; yea, they that work wickedness are set up; yea, they that tempt Elohim are even delivered. ¹⁶ Then they that feared YHWH spake often one to another: and YHWH hearkened, and heard it, and a Scroll of remembrance (Sefer Zikrone) was written before Him for them that feared YHWH, and that thought upon His Name. ¹⁷ And they shall be Mine, saith YHWH of hosts, in that day when I make up My jewels; and I will spare them, as a man spareth his own son that serveth him. ¹⁸ Then shall you return, and discern between the

righteous and the wicked, between him that serveth Elohim and him that serveth Him not." Malachi 3:1-18.

This text speaks of a time of restoration when the people of YHWH return to Him. It describes a time when YHWH opens His Scroll of Remembrance (Sefer Zikrone), and remembers His People. This Scroll contains the Names of those in the Covenant - those who feared YHWH, and thought upon His Name. Those who fear YHWH obey Him. They bear the sign, and are covered by the blood of the Lamb of Elohim.

Again, we cannot ignore the fact that both of these events, the blowing and the opening of the scroll, deal with zikrone - remembrance. So when we approach the special new moon day, the seventh new moon of the year, we must place it in context. It was presented after the 3 Pilgrimage Feasts were originally revealed. In fact, it was revealed after the sin at Sinai, and there is a powerful connection with Sinai. The blasting and the remembrance should make us recall Sinai when YHWH gathered His people.

We need to remember what His people did after hearing and seeing the sound from the Mountain. As we remember, our prayer should be that we be remembered by Him. Indeed, on this day of remembrance we prepare for another Appointed Time not originally mentioned with the 3 Pilgrimage Feasts.

The Day of Blowing begins what is commonly referred to as the 10 Days of Awe. These 10 days are traditionally a period of reflection, prayer and repentance leading up to the Day of Atonement - Yom Kippur.

II

Yom Kippur

Yom Kippur is another Appointed Time that was not initially mentioned along with the three Pilgrimage Feasts. It is not a Feast, and the first mention of this Appointed Time in the Scriptures is after the death of Aharon's two sons Nadab and Abihu. Even though the text does not specifically state that they are linked, the connection is nonetheless notable.

First let us examine the incident, then we will examine the Commandment describing Yom Kippur. "¹ *And Nadab and Abihu, the sons of Aharon, took either of them his censer, and put fire therein, and put incense thereon, and offered strange fire before YHWH, which He commanded them not.* ² *And there went out fire from YHWH, and devoured them, and they died before YHWH.*" Vayiqra 10:1-2.

Now remember that these were the two sons who went up on Mt Sinai with Mosheh, Aharon and the seventy elders. They "saw the Elohim of Yisrael" and "they ate and drank." (Shemot 24:10,11). They were anointed to serve in the Tabernacle of YHWH, and were in the midst of serving YHWH when they were consumed.

This event has baffled many because it is not always clear what happened. Many speculate that they added a ritual or were drunk. We do not know for certain, but the focus is on the fire. They offered "strange fire."

This event is memorialized on two other occasions in the Scriptures, namely Bemidbar 3:4 and Bemidbar 26:61. In each case the reason for their demise is that they "*offered strange fire before YHWH.*" In Vayiqra 10:1 it specifically indicated that they did something which was not commanded, or they did something that they were commanded not to do.

So the question is: What were they doing? The event is prefaced by the description of the Tabernacle being set up on Day 1 of Month 1, and the beginning of the Priestly service of Aharon and his sons. The text then moves to "the eighth day" when the esteem of YHWH appeared to the people. Some might interpret this to be day 8 of month 1, but that was not the case. You see there is a deep mystery hidden here. Fire came from the presence of YHWH, and consumed the offerings on the Altar. (Vayiqra 9:23). There was an eight day period to prepare the Tabernacle, this will become more significant when we discuss the eighth day as an Appointed Time.

This event occurred in the year 1436 BCE* and "the eighth day" was actually the eighth day following the seven days of preparation which occurred between Day 3 and Day 9 of Month 1. Thus the eighth day was actually Day 10 of Month 1, Yom Rishon – the first day of the week following Shabbat. This is highly significant as we continue to consider the parallels between the first and the seventh months.

There is an interesting parallel that exists between this event on Day 10 of Month 1 involving Nadab and Abihu, and the incident involving Qayin and Hebel on Day 10 of Month 7. One occurred 10 days into the Spiritual Year, and the other occurred 10 days into the Civil Year. Each involved a service before YHWH by two brothers and in each case, something went terribly wrong. These events are not recorded for our reading pleasure. They are there so that we can learn from the mistakes of the past, and hopefully not repeat them.

The event involving Nadab and Abihu likely revolved around the lighting of incense, which required fire. There were two instances when incense would have been brought into the House of YHWH. The first involved the Golden

Altar of Incense. Here is the command concerning the Altar of Incense.

"[7] *Aharon shall burn on it sweet incense every morning; when he tends the lamps, he shall burn incense on it.* [8] *And when Aharon lights the lamps at twilight (𐤁𐤉𐤍 𐤄𐤏𐤓𐤁𐤉𐤌), he shall burn incense on it, a perpetual incense before YHWH throughout your generations.* [9] *You shall not offer strange incense on it, or a burnt offering, or a grain offering; nor shall you pour a drink offering on it.* [10] *And Aharon shall make atonement upon its horns once a year with the blood of the sin offering of atonement; once a year he shall make atonement upon it throughout your generations. It is most set apart to YHWH."* Shemot 30:7-10.

First, we see that this is a duty prescribed for Aharon or one of his descendants. The incense is burned in the morning and the evening, when Aharon lights the lamps. Aharon lit the Menorah at "bein ha'arbayim" (𐤁𐤉𐤍 𐤄𐤏𐤓𐤁𐤉𐤌), which is the same time that the Passover sacrifice is slaughtered. The lamps were obviously lit before dark, so the incense would be burned around the tequfah or turn of each day - morning and evening at sunrise and sunset.

YHWH is specific that nothing strange is to be put on it. The Hebrew word translated as strange is "zarah" (𐤆𐤓𐤄) which derives from the root "zar" (𐤆𐤓). It means: "foreign, strange, profane, illegitimate" also "adultery." In other words, it is out of place, out of order. In this case, "unholy" and contrary to the Commandments. Nothing was to be placed on the Altar except for the prescribed incense at the prescribed times by the prescribed person.

Notice also the mention of atonement. Once a year blood would be placed upon the horns of this Altar - blood from the sin offering of atonement. This also happened to be the other time when the Priest would bring incense into the House of YHWH. We will read more about this further on, but in each case the incense was to be lit with fire from the brazen Altar in front of the Tabernacle which was supposed to burn perpetually.

"¹² And the fire upon the Altar shall be burning in it; it shall not be put out: and the Priest shall burn wood on it every morning, and lay the burnt offering in order upon it; and he shall burn thereon the fat of the peace offerings. ¹³ The fire shall ever be burning upon the Altar; it shall never go out." Vayiqra 6:12-13.

Where did the sons of Aharon get the unauthorized fire? It must not have been from the Altar, because is was described as "zarah" (ᚨ). It is very possible that their offering was profane because it was out of order. It is quite possible that Aharon himself was supposed to be offering the incense.

Let us examine the context of the event to gain even more insight. These were sons of Aharon so they were priests - Cohenim. Essentially, Aharon was from the Tribe of Levi, and his clan was chosen to head the Levites. The Tribe of Levi was chosen to serve in the House of YHWH. They were literally substitutes for the firstborn of Yisrael. (Bemidbar 3:12; 8:15-19). The clan of Aharon, designated Cohenim, were thus the head or "the first" of the firstborn.

The Levites were actually offered to YHWH as a firstborn offering. The message is loud and clear that the firstborn are those who get into the House of YHWH. They are the ones who belong to Him. This, of course, was a pattern for a greater future fulfillment.

While the Levites were chosen to serve in the House, only Aharon and his descendants were selected for offering the incense. Therefore, their censers alone would hold the fire from the Altar. The Cohenim had separate and distinct duties from the Levites. The Cohenim essentially worked in the House, in the inner chambers, close to YHWH. The Levites worked in the Courts of the House, and served closer to the people. Together they acted as a bridge between the people and YHWH. This was the order established by YHWH.

There is a very powerful story in the Scriptures concerning the hierarchy of the Aharonites when the Korahites rebelled and questioned the position and authority of Aharon. They felt that Aharon should not be elevated above them. As a result, all were told to bring their censers before YHWH, and light them the next day. Mosheh asked YHWH not to respect their offering.

The next day, 250 men along with Korah lit their censors and they paid the price. YHWH did not respect their offering. The earth opened up and consumed Korah and his family. A fire came out of YHWH and consumed the 250 men who offered incense, just as fire had devoured the sons of Aharon. The censers of the 250 "sinners" (ᙏᔓᘓᐤᕼ) were then beaten into plates for covering the altar. This was meant to be a memorial - a zikrone. (Bemidbar 16).

"To be a memorial unto the children of Yisrael, that no stranger, which is not of the seed of Aharon, come near to offer incense before YHWH; that he be not as Korah, and as his company: as YHWH said to him by the hand of Mosheh." Bemidbar 16:40. The lesson should have been clear. YHWH has His established order, and we must respect it whether we like it or not. Do it His way, especially when dealing with His fire, or suffer His judgment.

Immediately after that incident, the people ignored the lesson of Korah, and they rebelled against Mosheh and Aharon. This brought a plague upon the people. *"[43] And Mosheh and Aharon came before the Tabernacle of the congregation. [44] And YHWH spoke unto Mosheh, saying, [45] Get you up from among this congregation, that I may consume them as in a moment. And they fell upon their faces. [46] And Mosheh said unto Aharon, Take a censer, and put fire therein from off the Altar, and put on incense, and go quickly unto the congregation, and make an atonement for them: for there is wrath gone out from YHWH; the plague is begun. [47] And Aharon took as Mosheh commanded, and ran into the midst of the congregation; and, behold, the plague*

was begun among the people: and he put on incense, and made an atonement for the people. ⁴⁸ And he stood between the dead and the living; and the plague was stayed. ⁴⁹ Now they that died in the plague were fourteen thousand and seven hundred, beside them that died about the matter of Korah. ⁵⁰ And Aharon returned unto Mosheh unto the door of the Tabernacle of the congregation: and the plague was stayed." Bemidbar 16:43-50.

So here we see the fire from the Altar along with the incense, brought by Aharon himself, which stopped the wrath of YHWH. This was another endorsement that the offering of Aharon, pursuant to the instruction of Mosheh, was respected by YHWH. It literally saved the people. So the point should be clear, only a Priest chosen by YHWH may make the prescribed offerings which will be respected by YHWH.

This aspect of respecting offerings brings us back to Qayin and Hebel, the two sons of Adam. This is essentially a parallel account of the sons of Aharon and in this case the sons of Adam were acting as priests in the order of the High Priest Adam, arguably the first - resheet, in the Order of Melchizedek.¹⁴³ "⁴ And Hebel, he also brought of the firstlings of his flock and of the fat thereof. And YHWH had respect unto Hebel and to his offering: ⁵ But unto Qayin and to his offering he had not respect. And Qayin was very wroth, and his countenance fell." Beresheet 4:4-5.

This event occurred at an altar. Could it have been at the door of Eden from whence mankind previously was expelled? Could it have been at the door to the House of YHWH? We can only speculate on that, but the similarities are quite profound. The Hebrew word for "respect" in the instance involving Qayin is "sha'ah" (𐤔𐤏𐤅). Essentially, YHWH would not acknowledge it or look at it, and Qayin was wroth (𐤒𐤑𐤐). In the case of Korah and his followers, Mosheh was wroth (𐤒𐤑𐤐) and asked YHWH not to

"respect" or "face" (᠆ ᠐Ϟ) Korah's offering. In the case of Korah and the Levites, Mosheh was asking YHWH to turn away from them.

Both of these instances are related as they deal with how we worship YHWH. Much of this has to do with our heart. Are we serving Him in humility and are we giving Him our best? Are we following His prescribed order, or are we presenting foreign and profane offerings before Him? If YHWH does not respect our offerings, we are subject to His judgment. This is a repeating pattern and this is the teaching of Yom Kippur.

It is within this context that we now read the actual Commandment concerning the 10th day of the seventh month.

> *" And YHWH spoke unto Mosheh after the death of the two sons of Aharon, when they offered before YHWH, and died; ² And YHWH said unto Mosheh, Speak unto Aharon thy brother, that he come not at all times into the set apart place within the veil before the mercy seat, which is upon the Ark; that he die not: for I will appear in the cloud upon the mercy seat. ³ Thus shall Aharon come into the set apart place: with a young bullock for a sin offering, and a ram for a burnt offering. ⁴ He shall put on the set apart linen coat, and he shall have the linen breeches upon his flesh, and shall be girded with a linen girdle, and with the linen mitre shall he be attired: these are set apart garments; therefore shall he wash his flesh in water, and so put them on. ⁵ And he shall take of the congregation of the children of Yisrael two kids of the goats for a sin offering, and one ram for a burnt offering. ⁶ And Aaron shall offer his bullock of the sin offering, which is for himself, and make an atonement for*

himself, and for his house. ⁷ And he shall take ✕Ⅎ the two goats, and present them before YHWH at the door of the tabernacle of the congregation. ⁸ And Aharon shall cast lots upon the two goats; one (echad) lot for YHWH, and one (echad) lot for azazel. ⁹ And Aaron shall bring ✕Ⅎ the goat upon which YHWH's lot fell, and offer him for a sin offering. ¹⁰ But the goat, on which the lot fell to be the scapegoat, shall be presented alive before YHWH, to make an atonement with him, ✕Ⅎ and to let him go for azazel into the wilderness. ¹¹ And Aharon shall bring ✕Ⅎ the bullock of the sin offering, which is for himself, and shall make an atonement for himself, and for his house, and shall kill ✕Ⅎ the bullock of the sin offering which is for himself: ¹² And he shall take a censer full of burning coals of fire from off the Altar before YHWH, and his hands full of sweet incense beaten small, and bring it within the veil: ¹³ And he shall put the incense upon the fire before YHWH, that the cloud of the incense may cover the mercy seat that is upon the testimony, that he die not: ¹⁴ And he shall take of the blood of the bullock, and sprinkle it with his finger upon the mercy seat eastward; and before the mercy seat shall he sprinkle of the blood with his finger seven times. ¹⁵ Then shall he kill ✕Ⅎ the goat of the sin offering, that is for the people, and bring ✕Ⅎ his blood within the veil, and do with that ✕Ⅎ blood as he did with the blood of the bullock, and sprinkle it ✕Ⅎ upon the mercy seat, and before the mercy seat: ¹⁶ And he shall make an atonement for the set apart place, because of the uncleanness of the children of Yisrael, and because of their transgressions in all their sins: and so shall he do for the Tabernacle of the congregation, that remaineth among them in the midst of their uncleanness. ¹⁷ And there shall be no man in the Tabernacle of the

congregation when he goeth in to make an atonement in the set apart place, until he come out, and have made an atonement for himself, and for his household, and for all the congregation of Yisrael. [18] And he shall go out unto the Altar that is before YHWH, and make an atonement for it; and shall take of the blood of the bullock, and of the blood of the goat, and put it upon the horns of the Altar round about. [19] And he shall sprinkle of the blood upon it with his finger seven times, and cleanse it, and hallow it from the uncleanness of the children of Yisrael. [20] And when he hath made an end of reconciling the set apart place, and the Tabernacle of the congregation, and the Altar, he shall bring the live goat: [21] And Aharon shall lay both his hands upon the head of the live goat, and confess over him all the iniquities of the children of Yisrael, and all their transgressions in all their sins, putting them upon the head of the goat, and shall send him away by the hand of a fit man into the wilderness: [22] And the goat shall bear upon him all their iniquities unto a land not inhabited: and he shall let go the goat in the wilderness. [23] And Aaron shall come into the tabernacle of the congregation, and shall put off the linen garments, which he put on when he went into the set apart place, and shall leave them there: [24] And he shall wash his flesh with water in the set apart place, and put on his garments, and come forth, and offer his burnt offering, and the burnt offering of the people, and make an atonement for himself, and for the people. [25] And the fat of the sin offering shall he burn upon the Altar. [26] And he that let go the goat for the scapegoat shall wash his clothes, and bathe his flesh in water, and afterward come into the camp. [27] And the bullock for the sin offering, and the goat for the sin offering, whose blood was brought in to make atonement in the set *apart place, shall one carry forth without the camp; and they shall burn in the fire their skins, and their flesh, and their dung.* [28] *And he that burneth them shall wash his clothes, and bathe his flesh in water, and afterward he shall come into the camp.* [29] <u>And this shall be a statute throughout the age (olam) unto you: that in the seventh month, on the tenth day of the month, you shall afflict your souls, and do no work at all, whether it be one of your own country, or a stranger that sojourneth among you:</u> [30] <u>For on that day shall the Priest make an atonement for you, to cleanse you, that you may be clean from all your sins before YHWH.</u> [31] <u>It shall be a Shabbat Shabbaton unto you, and you shall afflict your souls, by a statute throughout the ages (olam).</u> [32] <u>And the Priest, whom he shall anoint (moshiach) את and whom he shall consecrate את to minister in the Priest's office in his father's stead, shall make the atonement, and shall put on את the linen clothes, even the set apart garments:</u> [33] *And he shall make an atonement for* את *the set apart sanctuary, and he shall make an atonement for* את *the Tabernacle of the congregation, and for* את *the Altar, and he shall make an atonement for the Priests, and for all the people of the congregation.* [34] *And this shall be a statute throughout the age (olam) unto you, to make an atonement for the children of Yisrael for all their sins once a year. And he did as YHWH commanded Mosheh."* Vayiqra 16:1-34.

Understanding the context of this day certainly helps gain a greater understanding. There are limits to our service and boundaries that must be respected when dealing with a set apart Elohim. As we can see from the text, even the Priest could not go before the mercy seat on just any day or in any manner. Only the High Priest was permitted to enter in and only on one day.

He first needed to make atonement for himself and his house. We then see a detailed procedure for providing atonement for the congregation of Yisrael which involved two goats. The instruction reveals how atonement is made for the Covenant people, and the two goats bring us right back to the beginning - the two brothers Qayin and Hebel.

In fact, Hebrew tradition indicates that Qayin and Hebel made their offerings when they were 40 years old, on Day 10 of Month 7. This was Yom Kippur beginning the first Jubilee Year! As previously mentioned, the phrase "*the end of days*" which is "m'qetz yomim" in Hebrew (ᛗᛘᛋᛗᛘᛋ ᛏᛈᛗ), is another term for the Jubilee.

Prior to that event there had already been the blood of animals shed due to the transgression of Adam and Hawah. Indeed, Hebel had shed the blood of an animal in a fashion acceptable to YHWH. Qayin was the first to shed the blood of a man - his brother Hebel. The blood of Hebel cried out, and Qayin was forced to wander, separated from YHWH, like the goat for Azazel. Hebel was killed, like the goat of YHWH.

Both goats from the congregation of Yisrael were for atonement. They were both acceptable sacrifices, and both were presented before YHWH at the door of the Tabernacle. The High Priest cast lots, and that was what sealed their fate. One was chosen for YHWH, and the other for azazel. The goat for YHWH was killed, while the goat for azazel was permitted to live. This all occurred on the 10th day of month seven.

At this point, the connection with the Passover cannot be ignored. Remember that the Passover could be a lamb or a goat (Shemot 12:5). The Passover was selected on the 10th day of the first month. It was later slaughtered on the 14th day, and the blood was sprinkled with hyssop on the doorposts of the houses of those in Covenant with YHWH. It was a sign to be seen by all who passed by, and the Messenger of death particularly, which would pass over

those with the mark of the blood.

Here, on the 10th day of the seventh month, we see the High Priest laying both hands upon the goat of YHWH while he confessed the sins of the people. The goat was then killed, and the blood of the goat for YHWH was sprinkled before the mercy seat, and on the mercy seat in the Most Set Apart Place. The mercy seat was the cover of the Ark where the blood was sprinkled, and it was actually called the Atonement Cover.[144]

The blood of the goat is to atone for the Covenant people - Yisrael. The blood is sprinkled by the finger of the High Priest seven times, because this is in the Sabbath month, and this day is a Shabbat Shabbaton – the Sabbath of Sabbaths. The High Priest (Cohen Gadol) put fire from the Altar in his censor, and heaped it full of fine incense. This would make for a faster, fuller burn. The point was to create a lot of smoke to cover the mercy seat so that he would live and not die.

Clearly, even this earthly High Priest needed covering. He was limited in his relationship with YHWH, and his ability to draw near. While there is presently no House, or Hekal, to conduct this elaborate procedure, that was always the duty of the High Priest alone, and the entire event cried out for a greater High Priest. The Cohen Gadol was revealing the pattern, but his service was not completely fulfilling the meaning behind his actions.

The fulfillment is actually alluded to in the text. In verses 32 and 33 of Vayiqra 16 we read about how the anointed son, the Moshiach, will act in his father's stead, and make atonement for all. On the surface, this text simply allows for the hereditary succession of the Priesthood. As we look at the Hebrew we see numerous instances of the Aleph Taw (✕𝄐), and there is the allusion to the Messiah as that greater Priest Who will make a final atonement. There are also allusions throughout the text that the Aleph Taw (✕𝄐) is the atonement.

The events of Yom Kippur reveal many things, and contain numerous levels of revelation. They can be studied, and also experienced as we participate in this very important Appointed Time. The Commandments were not strictly limited to the High Priest. There were other commandments requiring conduct by the people. Everyone is required to keep this Appointed Time by "afflicting their souls."

"27 *Also the tenth day of this seventh month shall be the Day of Atonements. It shall be a set apart rehearsal for you. You shall afflict* ×ʊ *your souls, and offer an offering made by fire to YHWH.* 28 *And you shall do no work on that same day, for it is the Day of Atonements, to make atonement for you before YHWH your Elohim.* 29 *For any person who is not afflicted in soul on that same day shall be cut off from his people.* 30 *And any person who does any work on that same day, that person I will destroy from among his people.* 31 *You shall do no manner of work; it shall be a statute through the ages (olam) throughout your generations in all your dwellings.* 32 *It shall be to you a Shabbat Shabbaton, and you shall afflict your souls; on the ninth day of the month at evening, from evening to evening, you shall celebrate your Sabbath.*" Vayiqra 23:26-32.

It is here that the Appointed Time is actually given a name - the Day of Atonements. It is Yom Kippurim because there are various atonements being made - not just one. The word "kippurim" (ᴹᵞ♅ᚱᵂ) is particularly interesting to see in the ancient Hebrew text. Our sins are primarily committed through our hands (ᵂ) and our mouths (ᚱ). Our heads (♅) control our mouths (ᚱ) and our arms (᪣) control our hands (ᵂ). This is the process through which sin gets expressed through each one of us.

This is why we are instructed to bind the commandments on our hands as signs, and as frontlets between our eyes. (See Debarim 6:8) It is for our own good, so that we do not sin. Thankfully, when we do sin, there is atonement. Atonement is often described as "covering," and that is an aspect of atonement. The blood of the sacrifice

covers our sins so that our sins are not in YHWH's Face. There is a deeper meaning attributed to this Day of Atonements as we see the word ending with mem (^{m}) which means: "water." So then we see that the ultimate atonement will not only involve the blood covering our sins, but also washing, and cleansing us from our sins.

Therefore, all atonements are made on this day, because all have transgressed in their beings, by their actions. As a result, everyone is required to "afflict their souls." The Hebrew word for "afflict" derives from the root "anah" (𐤏‎‎) which means: "to speak, to respond, to give account." All souls will give an account this day. This is a day connected with judgment and punishment.

In fact, the command to "afflict your souls" is directly linked with the command to "offer an offering made by fire to YHWH." This offering was a whole burnt offering - everything went to YHWH. Interestingly, the text could read that everyone must afflict their souls and offer a whole burnt offering this day. The word "soul" is "nefesh" (𐤅𐤔‎), and it is a person's soul that is figuratively placed upon the Altar when a sacrifice is presented.

Indeed this embodied the whole notion of atonement and substitution. The sacrificial system was meant to reveal that innocent blood was required to atone for our sins. It showed that the blood which contains the life, or soul of a being, was what was placed upon the Altar. Therefore, it was on this Day of Atonements that everyone was supposed to afflict their souls, recognizing that their souls should be up on that Altar. They should be whole burnt offerings, completely incinerated to ashes for their sins.

It is with this understanding that we see a wonderful revelation in the Hebrew text. When we read where everyone must afflict their souls, instead of simply reading "afflict" ($^mX\lrcorner\curvearrowright\odot$) and "souls" ($^m\text{\WW}\lrcorner X\text{w}\text{?}\curvearrowright$) we read $^m\text{\WW}\lrcorner X\text{w}\text{?}\curvearrowright\text{-}X\text{\textbf{Y}}\ ^mX\lrcorner\curvearrowright\odot$. So it is the Aleph Taw ($X\text{\textbf{Y}}$) at the center of this afflicting our souls. This points to the

Aleph Taw (✕𝒱) as the true atonement for our souls on this Day of Atonements. Of course, this works perfectly with the need for the Messiah to act as our High Priest. He is the only One Who can enter in to the Most Set Apart Place, and stand before the Mercy Seat - the Throne of Elohim.

Interestingly, this verse also defines a day and a Sabbath "from evening to evening." This is a full 24 hour period, not just the time from sunrise to sunset as some try to define a day. Remember how critical timing was concerning the Passover. If the Passover was not kept at the correct time, it meant death to the firstborn. The same holds true for everyone on this day. There was death prescribed for all who did not obey at the right time.

On Passover, the firstborn would be eating a meal while receiving the protection of the blood. On the Day of Atonements, everyone would be fasting in order to receive the atonement provided by the blood of the goat, and the service of the High Priest. The Day of Atonements was when the sins of all Yisrael would be atoned. This is in contrast to the redemption of the firstborn provided by the Passover. The similarities and contrasts are profound, and have deep significance. In each case, obedience is required from those in the Covenant - those receiving the benefit of the shed blood.

There is another interesting aspect to the commandment concerning this day, which can only be gleaned from the Hebrew text. In an English translation of Vayiqra 23:32 we typically read the concluding phrase "*you shall celebrate your Sabbath.*" This does not make much sense as this day of affliction is quite somber, and not really a time to celebrate. Some translations tone it down a bit by providing "you shall observe your Sabbath."

The reason for the difficulty is found in the Hebrew text which provides "ti<u>shabatu shabat</u>kem" (ᴍ山✕□山 ꟾ✕□山✕). Essentially, we are to "shabbat shabbat" which is not so easy to translate. The Hebrew text is emphatically telling us to treat this particular Shabbat very seriously. This adds to the solemnity of the day.

The various sacrifices for this day are detailed further in Bemidbar as follows: "⁷ *And you shall have on the tenth day of this seventh month a set apart rehearsal; and you shall afflict עו your souls: you shall not do any work therein:* ⁸ *But you shall offer a burnt offering unto YHWH for a sweet savour; one young bullock, one ram, and seven lambs of the first year; they shall be unto you without blemish:* ⁹ *And their grain offering shall be of flour mingled with oil, three tenth deals to a bullock, and two tenth deals to one ram,* ¹⁰ *A several tenth deal for one lamb, throughout the seven lambs:* ¹¹ *One kid of the goats for a sin offering; beside the sin offering of atonement, and the continual burnt offering, and the grain offering of it, and their drink offerings.*" Bemidbar 29:7-11.

Yom Kippur is the culmination of the Ten Days of Awe which began at Yom Teruah, and ended on the tenth day of the seventh month. On this day there were 10 additional sacrifices, besides the 2 goats. Therefore, we see an emphasis on 10 and 12. The number 10 is typically associated with ordinal perfection (10 Commandments) and the number 12 is typically associated with governmental perfection (12 Tribes). (see E.W. Bullinger, *Number in Scripture*, Kregel Publications 1967).

Traditionally, this span of 10 days is treated as a period of repentance and humility, which is clearly a healthy spiritual exercise. As we saw that Day 1 was a Day of Remembrance when the Scroll is opened, many believe that there is a 10 day period until final judgment. Yom Kippur is when judgment for the new Civil Year is finally rendered, so it is an extremely somber day. When Yom Kippur of Jubilee Year 120 arrives, the theme of final judgment will take on an eternal dimension.

As a result of the severity and consequences associated with this day, Yom Kippur is probably the most significant moadee observed in Judaism today. Even in the modern State of Israel, where the majority of people are not particularly religious, everything shuts down on Yom Kipper, albeit on the false Rabbinic calendar. On that day, nothing moves, mostly out of fear and reverence toward YHWH, but sometimes out of fear of getting a stone thrown at your car if you do decide to venture out. It is taken very seriously.

This begs the question: What does it mean to afflict our souls? Most people fast on this day in obedience to the command to afflict yourself. Afflicting our souls is often simplified as mere fasting. That is one aspect, but it runs far deeper than food and water. Should we play games, throw a party or go shopping on Yom Kippur? Obviously not. We could go on to create a list of thousands of things prohibited on this day of affliction, but that would miss the point entirely.

Therefore, we see that this affliction is as much, or more, about the spiritual and internal things, as it is about depriving our flesh. It is about dying to oneself and ones own desires, so that YHWH can then fill you up and replace your desires with His desires. It is not just about "putting your time in," and then going about your business as soon as the sun sets. It is a matter of the heart, and often times when dealing with the heart, you get out of the experience what you put into it.

This is really the case with all of the Appointed Times. They are about seeking and developing a relationship with YHWH, not just going through the motions or putting in our time. Part of this process involves understanding why we are participating in the Appointed Times. We can discern the purpose from the patterns provided. The Prophet Yeshayahu provides more insight on why we afflict our souls.

"57:14 *And he will say, Cast ye up, cast ye up, prepare the way, take up the stumbling-block out of the way of My people.* 15 *For thus saith the high and lofty One that inhabiteth eternity, Whose Name is Set Apart: I dwell in the high and set apart place, with him also that is of a contrite and humble spirit, to revive the spirit of the humble, and to revive the heart of the contrite.* 16 *For I will not contend throughout the ages (olam), neither will I be always wroth;*

for the spirit would faint before Me, and the souls that I have made. [17] For the iniquity of his covetousness was I wroth, and smote him; I hid My face and was wroth; and he went on backsliding in the way of his heart. [18] I have seen his ways, and will heal him: I will lead him also, and restore comforts unto him and to his mourners. [19] I create the fruit of the lips: Peace, peace, to him that is far off and to him that is near, saith YHWH; and I will heal him. [20] But the wicked are like the troubled sea; for it cannot rest, and its waters cast up mire and dirt. [21] There is no peace, saith my Elohim, to the wicked. [58:1] Cry aloud, spare not, lift up thy voice like a shofar, and declare unto My people their transgression, and to the House of Yaacob their sins. [2] Yet they seek Me daily, and delight to know My ways: as a nation that did righteousness, and forsook not the ordinance of their Elohim, they ask of Me righteous judgments; they delight to draw near unto Elohim. [3] Wherefore have we fasted, say they, and Thou seest not? Wherefore have we afflicted our soul, and Thou takest no knowledge? Behold, in the day of your fast you find your own pleasure, and exact all your labors. [4] Behold, you fast for strife and contention, and to smite with the fist of wickedness: you fast not this day so as to make your voice to be heard on high. [5] Is such the fast that I have chosen? The day for a man to afflict his soul? Is it to bow down his head as a rush, and to spread sackcloth and ashes under him? wilt thou call this a fast, and an acceptable day to YHWH? [6] Is not this the fast that I have chosen: to loose the bonds of wickedness, to undo the bands of the yoke, and to let the oppressed go free, and that you break every yoke? [7] Is it not to deal thy bread to the hungry, and that thou bring the poor that are cast out to thy house? When thou seest the naked, that thou cover him; and that thou hide not thyself from thine own flesh? [8] Then shall thy light break forth as the morning, and thy healing shall spring forth speedily; and thy righteousness shall go before thee; the glory of YHWH shall by thy rearward. [9] Then shalt thou call, and YHWH will answer; thou shalt cry, and He will say, Here I am. If thou take away from the midst of thee the yoke, the putting forth of the finger, and speaking wickedly; [10] and if thou draw out thy soul to the hungry, and satisfy the afflicted soul: then shall thy light rise in darkness, and thine obscurity be as the noonday; [11] and YHWH *will guide thee continually, and satisfy thy soul in dry places, and make strong thy bones; and thou shalt be like a watered garden, and like a spring of water, whose waters fail not. ¹² And they that shall be of thee shall build the old waste places; thou shalt raise up the foundations of many generations; and thou shalt be called The repairer of the breach, The restorer of paths to dwell in. ¹³ If thou turn away thy foot from the Sabbath, from doing thy pleasure on My set apart day; and call the Sabbath a delight, and the Set Apart of YHWH honorable; and shalt honor it, not doing thine own ways, nor finding thine own pleasure, nor speaking thine own words: ¹⁴ then shalt thou delight thyself in YHWH; and I will make thee to ride upon the high places of the earth; and I will feed thee with the heritage of Yaacob thy father: for the mouth of YHWH hath spoken it."* Yeshayahu 57:14-58:14.

So we can see that this day of affliction is really to get us in a place where YHWH can hear us. It is about forgiveness and deliverance. *"¹⁸ Who is a Elohim like unto Thee, that pardoneth iniquity, and passeth over the transgression of the remnant of his heritage? He retaineth not His anger throughout the ages (olam), because He delighteth in lovingkindness. ¹⁹ He will again have compassion upon us; He will tread our iniquities under foot; and thou wilt cast all their sins into the depths of the sea. ²⁰ Thou wilt perform the truth to Yaacob, and the lovingkindness to Abraham, which thou hast sworn unto our fathers from the days of old."* Micah (Mikayahu)¹⁴⁵ 7:18-20.

YHWH has shown that He will turn away His anger, and actually forget our sins. He will remember the Covenant promises of old. As we follow that Covenant path and afflict our souls, we learn to walk in the ways of the Covenant, and we will reap the blessings associated therewith. As we choose to do His will, rather than our own, we are set free.

Amazingly, this day of Affliction is also linked with an incredible time of release - the Jubilee. After counting seven Sabbath years, also known as Shemitah years, we recognize the 50th year on the Day of Atonements as the Jubilee. This was already discussed previously, but it warrants another mention since the beginning of the Jubilee falls not at the beginning of the month, but on Day 10. On this day, the shofars were sounded throughout the Land. (Vayiqra 25:9). This is how we know that Yeshayahu was speaking specifically about the Day of Atonements. (see Yeshayahu 58:1).

Tradition prescribes that when Mosheh came down from the Mountain with the second set of tablets that it was on Yom Kippurim - The Day of Atonements which marked a Jubilee Year.[146] As tradition indeed appears to be true, it provides a wonderful message about forgiveness from sin and the mercy of Elohim. For it appears that it was on Yom Kippur beginning Jubilee Year 51, on the very Hebrew day of the fall equinox, that Yisrael was given a second chance with YHWH.

It was 50 Jubilee cycles previously that Qayin was given a second chance. He was marked and forced to wander in the wilderness, but he was allowed to live. Here Yisrael was given a second chance. They were not blotted out of the Scroll. They were permitted to renew the Covenant that had been broken. Eventually, they too would end up wandering in the wilderness for their further transgressions. Repeatedly, YHWH provides us with a second chance, and allows us an opportunity to repent before His judgment falls upon us.

So this Day of Judgment is also connected with atonement for sin, and release from debts. The picture should be clear by now. The debt of sin, which we all carry from the Garden, is a debt which we cannot repay. We cannot satisfy this debt that we all inherited without an anointed High Priest, authorized by YHWH, to come before His throne. Only a High Priest from the Order of Melchizedek, can take fire from the Altar, enter into the Most Holy Place and offer up the requisite blood in the Temple in heaven. Yahushua the Messiah will surely accomplish this task on Yom Kippur beginning Jubilee Year 120, when Yisrael is given their third and final chance with YHWH.

Having received atonements, the stage is set for the

rehearsal that is full of joy. The Covenant people are now ready to proceed to a Feast that finds its ultimate fulfillment in a Jubilee Year - the Feast of Succot.

12

Succot

Without a doubt, the most joyous Appointed Time within the yearly cycle is Succot (𐤎𐤊𐤅𐤕). It is even referred to as "the season of our joy." Sometimes referred to as The Feast of Tabernacles, this is the last of the 3 Pilgrimage Feasts, which began with Unleavened Bread. Interestingly, there was no commandment to rejoice during Unleavened Bread, and the second Pilgrimage Feast, Shabuot, contains only one commandment to rejoice. The Feast of Succot is the crescendo of the Feasts, when the people are specifically and repeatedly commanded to rejoice.

"13 *Celebrate the Feast of Succot for seven days after you have gathered in the produce of your threshing floor and of your winepress:* 14 *And thou shall rejoice in your Feast, you and your son, and your daughter, and your manservant, and your maidservant, and the Levite, the stranger, and the fatherless, and the widow, that are within your gates.*" Debarim 16:13-14. Also in Vayiqra 23:40 we read *"you shall rejoice before YHWH your Elohim for seven days."*

The Hebrew word for "rejoice" is "simchat" (𐤔𐤌𐤇𐤕). It derives from "samach" which means: "brighten, joy, glee, cheer, gladness." So it is interesting how the joy was to increase throughout the harvest season until it culminated at Succot. Succot was always to occur at "the end of days" - the end of the harvest season around the tequfah. (Shemot 23:16; 34:22).

The grain had previously been cut, gathered, winnowed, threshed and the bikkurim presented at Shabuot.

Now the fruits had been harvested, and those bikkurim would be brought before YHWH. There was new wine, and that was especially helpful relative to the command to rejoice. It was time to go to the House of YHWH and celebrate.

Here is the command setting the specific time for Succot. "*34 Speak unto the children of Yisrael, saying, The fifteenth day of this seventh month shall be the Feast of Succot for seven days unto YHWH. 35 On the first day shall be a set apart gathering: you shall do no servile work therein.*" Vayiqra 23:34-35.

This was like a homecoming event, and it was unique in that it is named after a place. Two times in the Scriptures a geographical location is mentioned bearing the name Succot. It is first mentioned after Yaakob, renamed "am Yisrael," was leaving his servitude with Laban and returning to the Promised Land. The second mention occurs immediately after the Children of Yisrael were departing their captivity in Egypt on their way to the Promised Land.

In each case, there was an important event that occurred before Yisrael arrived at a location bearing the name Succot. In the case of Yaacob, he was on his way back to the Promised Land after having essentially become a tribe. He wrestled with a "man" and was renamed "am Yisrael." He crossed through the waters into the Land. He divided his tribe into two tribes, and then reunited them before journeying to Succot, where he built a house (×﬩ℸ). The Covenant Land is all about the House, and this is an important theme of Succot. (Beresheet 33). This entire event was prophetic, and it is noteworthy that his youngest son Benjamin was not present, because he was not yet born.

There is another mention of a place called Succot. It is not the same place, but once again it involved "am Yisrael." After the Passover in Egypt, the Children of Yisrael, along with a mixed multitude, left victoriously on their journey out of Egypt. They left Ramses on Day 15 of Month 1 according to Bemidbar 33:3, and arrived at Succot on the day when the Resheet would later be offered, on Day 16 of Month 1.

(Shemot 12:37, Bemidbar 33:5).

During this return to the Promised Land, "am Yisrael" was expanded beyond the physical descendants of Yaacob. Once again, this was prophetic that the nations would be gathered and "grafted in" to Yisrael at Succot. What makes this event so profound is that it essentially links the Feast of Succot with Unleavened Bread in time and space - the two Feasts that begin on Day 15 and end on Day 21.

So there is a common theme of going to the Promised Land. There is a place, as well as a time, associated with Succot and it is all a part of the Covenant process between YHWH and His people - am Yisrael. Essentially, this Feast is typified by its very name. A succah, the singular for succot, is a tent or temporary dwelling place - sometimes referred to as a tabernacle. It is something that the Covenant people construct and reside in each year to commemorate living with YHWH. Our succah is a temporary house as we look forward to dwelling in the permanent House of YHWH that He builds.

There are other significant events and traditions linked with this Feast. For instance, it would appear that Noah's ark came to rest during Succot. "[3] *The water receded steadily from the earth. At the end of the hundred and fifty days the water had gone down, [4] and on the seventeenth day of the seventh month the ark came to rest on the mountains of Ararat."* Beresheet 8:2-4.

Here is another interesting example of significant events falling at opposite ends of the calendar. Noah's ark came to rest on the mountains of Ararat on Day 17 of Month 7, exactly 17 days into the Civil Year. And as we shall soon see, a very significant event occurred in the life of the Messiah on Day 17 of Month 1, exactly 17 days into the Spiritual Year.

Joshua (Yahushua) led the Covenant people, Yisrael, across the Jordan on Day 10 of Month 1. This hearkened back to when Yisrael crossed through the Red Sea 40 years earlier.

Both of these events were corporate mikvah's, or washings, of Yisrael that were to cleanse Yisrael before they entered the Promised Land. This is why Peter instructed people to repent and be immersed. In other words, get cleaned up if you want to follow the Covenant path and receive the Covenant Promises. (Acts 2:38).

We need to follow the same path that YHWH led Yisrael, like a Shepherd. As a result, the day that Yisrael crossed over the Jordan on Day 10 of Month 1 has great prophetic significance for Yisrael. It was the day that Nadab and Abihu died, and also the day the lamb for the Passover was chosen.

There is another interesting tradition in Judaism that is carried out at Succot. In the synagogue, they circle the Bema once each day during the first six days of Succot. Then on the seventh day of Succot, on Day 21 of Month 7, they circle the Bema seven times shouting "save now" and "send salvation now," following the pattern of Jericho.[147] The Battle of Jericho is filled with symbolism, as it was Yisrael's first victory upon entering the Promised Land where the battle was entirely fought by YHWH.[148] This event is apparently prophetic of a future deliverance that YHWH will perform for the Covenant people of Yisrael.

Now looking back in the text, we read the first direct mention of Succot was the commandment regarding the Feast of Ingathering at Sinai, prior to the golden calf event. *"[16] Celebrate the Feast of Harvest with the firstfruits of the crops you sow in your field. Celebrate the Feast of Ingathering at the end of the year, when you gather in your crops from the field. [17] "three times a year all the men are to appear before the Sovereign YHWH."* Shemot 23:16-17.

After the calf event, there is a very detailed discussion of the Passover, the Feast of Unleavened Bread and the Firstborn followed by a description of the two remaining Pilgrimage Feasts. *"And you shall observe the Feast of weeks, of the bikkuri of wheat harvest, and the Feast of ingathering at the*

year's tequfot." Shemot 34:22.

There is a much more detailed description of this time found in Vayiqra. "*[33]* *And YHWH spoke unto Mosheh, saying,* *[34]* *Speak unto the children of Yisrael, saying, The fifteenth day of this seventh month shall be the Feast of Succot for seven days unto YHWH.* *[35]* *On the first day shall be a set apart rehearsal: you shall do no servile work therein.* *[36]* *Seven days you shall offer an offering made by fire unto YHWH: on the eighth day shall be a set apart rehearsal unto you; and you shall offer an offering made by fire unto YHWH: it is a atzeret; and you shall do no servile work therein.* *[37]* *These are the Appointed Times of YHWH, which you shall proclaim to be set apart rehearsals, to offer an offering made by fire unto YHWH, a burnt offering, and a grain offering, a sacrifice, and drink offerings, every thing upon His day:* *[38]* *Beside the Sabbaths of YHWH, and beside your gifts, and beside all your vows, and beside all your freewill offerings, which you give unto YHWH.* *[39]* *Also in the fifteenth day of the seventh month, when you have gathered in the fruit of the Land, you shall keep a "Feast unto YHWH"* (hagag ×ʮ-hag-YHWH) *seven days: on the first day shall be a Sabbath, and on the eighth day shall be a Sabbath.* *[40]* *And you shall take you on the first day the boughs of goodly trees, branches of palm trees, and the boughs of thick trees, and willows of the brook; and you shall rejoice before YHWH your Elohim seven days.* *[41]* *And you shall keep it a "Feast unto YHWH"* (hagtem ʾ×ʮ hag YHWH) *seven days in the year. It shall be a statute throughout the ages (olam) in your generations: you shall celebrate (tahagu) it in the seventh month.* *[42]* *You shall dwell in booths seven days; all that are Yisraelites born shall dwell in booths:* *[43]* *That your generations may know that I made the children of Yisrael to dwell in booths, when I brought them out of the land of Egypt: I am YHWH your Elohim.*" Vayiqra 23:33-43.

So we see that Sukkot is a hag (∧ㅐ), which is a Feast. It lasts for seven days, the first of which is a rest day. Take special note of the "also" in verse 39, as well as the text that follows. The previous verses had essentially described Succot along with the other Appointed Times, and then seemed to conclude with the phrase "these are the Appointed Times of

YHWH." The description appeared to be concluded, but then the text went on to describe Succot again.

This is not a mistake or mere redundancy. The second enhanced description is meant to reveal something special about this time. For one thing, we are not simply instructed to "keep" or "celebrate" this Feast as some translations provide. Instead, the command is to "hagag the hag." The word hagag (∧∧日) is clearly related to the word hag (∧日), which is commonly translated as "feast." The word hagag (∧∧日) means: "to move in a circle, to march in a sacred procession." This reminds us specifically of the event at Jericho. The word hagag (∧∧日) also means: "to reel to and fro, to dance, to be giddy." This tends to amplify the notion of rejoicing during this time, and the emphasis can be seen from another mystery hidden within the text.

Of particular note is the existence of the Aleph Taw (×𐤏) essentially connecting this Feast with YHWH. In the very text we can see the Messiah acting as a conduit, or a bridge, between the Covenant people and YHWH. This is particularly significant since this is the Feast which commemorates dwelling with YHWH, and it is here in the second mention, that we are provided with a list of building supplies. The repeated use of the word hagag emphasizes the cyclical nature of this Time as it relates to the Covenant. Year after year, as we rehearse this special time, the Covenant people are being swept in and prepared to dwell with YHWH.

There is another description of Succot in Debarim. *[13] You shall observe the Feast of Succot seven days, after that thou hast gathered in thy corn and thy wine: [14] And thou shalt rejoice in thy Feast, thou, and thy son, and thy daughter, and thy manservant, and thy maidservant, and the Levite, the stranger, and the fatherless, and the widow, that are within thy gates. [15] Seven days shalt thou keep a solemn Feast unto YHWH your Elohim in the place which YHWH shall choose: because YHWH your Elohim shall bless thee in all thine increase, and in all the works of thine hands, therefore thou shalt surely rejoice. [16] Three times in a year* shall all thy males appear before YHWH your Elohim in the place which He shall choose; in the Feast of Unleavened Bread, and in the Feast of Weeks, and in the Feast of Succot: and they shall not appear before YHWH empty: *[17]* Every man shall give as he is able, according to the blessing of YHWH your Elohim which He hath given thee." Debarim 16:13-17

Notice again the emphasis on rejoicing, and it is not limited to just native Yisraelites. Everyone dwelling in the Land, "within thy gates" is invited to this Feast. This is a demonstration of how YHWH desires to fellowship with His Creation, and it includes all of mankind, not just Yisrael. This is made abundantly clear by the sacrifices that are prescribed during the Feast. This is, without a doubt, the most elaborate listing of sacrifices for all of the Appointed Times. Take special note of the number of each animal being presented.

"*[12]* And on the fifteenth day of the seventh month you shall have a set apart rehearsal; you shall do no servile work, and you shall keep a Feast unto YHWH seven days: *[13]* And you shall offer a burnt offering, a sacrifice made by fire, of a sweet savour unto YHWH; thirteen young bullocks, two rams, and fourteen lambs of the first year; they shall be without blemish: *[14]* And their grain offering shall be of flour mingled with oil, three tenth deals unto every bullock of the thirteen bullocks, two tenth deals to each ram of the two rams, *[15]* And a several tenth deal to each lamb of the fourteen lambs: *[16]* And one kid of the goats for a sin offering; beside the continual burnt offering, his grain offering, and his drink offering. *[17]* And on the second day you shall offer twelve young bullocks, two rams, fourteen lambs of the first year without spot: *[18]* And their grain offering and their drink offerings for the bullocks, for the rams, and for the lambs, shall be according to their number, after the manner: *[19]* And one kid of the goats for a sin offering; beside the* continual burnt offering, and the grain offering thereof, and their drink offerings. ²⁰ And on the third day eleven bullocks, two rams, fourteen lambs of the first year without blemish; ²¹ And their grain offering and their drink offerings for the bullocks, for the rams, and for the lambs, shall be according to their number, after the manner: ²² And one goat for a sin offering; beside the continual burnt offering, and his grain offering, and his drink offering. ²³ And on the fourth day ten bullocks, two rams, and fourteen lambs of the first year without blemish: ²⁴ Their grain offering and their drink offerings for the bullocks, for the rams, and for the lambs, shall be according to their number, after the manner: ²⁵ And one kid of the goats for a sin offering; beside the continual burnt offering, his grain offering, and his drink offering. ²⁶ And on the fifth day nine bullocks, two rams, and fourteen lambs of the first year without spot: ²⁷ And their grain offering and their drink offerings for the bullocks, for the rams, and for the lambs, shall be according to their number, after the manner: ²⁸ And one goat for a sin offering; beside the continual burnt offering, and his grain offering, and his drink offering. ²⁹ And on the sixth day eight bullocks, two rams, and fourteen lambs of the first year without blemish: ³⁰ And their grain offering and their drink offerings for the bullocks, for the rams, and for the lambs, shall be according to their number, after the manner: ³¹ And one goat for a sin offering; beside the continual burnt offering, his grain offering, and his drink offering. ³² And on the seventh day seven bullocks, two rams, and fourteen lambs of the first year without blemish: ³³ And their grain offering and their drink offerings for the bullocks, for the rams, and for the lambs, shall be according to their number, after the manner: ³⁴ And one goat for a sin

offering; beside the continual burnt offering, his grain offering, and his drink offering." Bemidbar 29:12-40.

We already saw that this was a Feast for everyone, and the detail should make everyone take note. What is particularly interesting is the bulls. There are 70 bulls offered over the seven days of Succot, but only the bulls sacrificed on the first two days were specified by YHWH to be "young bulls." On day 1 and 2 there are 13 and 12 "young bulls" offered respectively. The Hebrew words translated as "young bulls" is beni-baqar (𐤒𐤓𐤟-𐤍𐤁𐤉).

These two words literally mean "my son" (beni) "breaks forth" (baqar). How profound that during the first two days there is an offering of "sons" and the numbers 12 and 13 are closely linked with the Children of Yisrael and their entry into Egypt. Yaakob became the father of 11 sons in Padan while he worked for his father-in-law Laban. He had a 12th son in Bethlehem, after his name had been changed to Yisrael.

So there were 12 sons of Yisrael. Later, while in Egypt, he adopted the two sons of Joseph - Ephraim and Manasseh to be first in the birth order over Reuben and Simeon. Therefore, the original twelve sons, followed by the elevation of Joseph's two sons in the stead of Joseph, essentially resulted in 13 tribes. Interestingly, the Scriptures never place more than 12 tribes in one group.[149]

There is a mystery revealed, and a powerful message to be discerned, when we examine the Hebrew words with the numerical value of 13. Here are some of the words that we see in the Scriptures that have the Gematria value 13: "echad" (unified, one), abi (my father), ahaba (love), habow (come), b'hag (feast), yahab (give), zedeb (dowry). Obviously, something very special occurred when Yisrael adopted and elevated Joseph's 2 sons, and it involves the Appointed Times.

Indeed, read the prophecy over the Tribe of Joseph

given by Mosheh. *"His glory is like the firstling of his bullock, and his horns are like the horns of ra'am (ᵐ∀ᐌ): with them he shall push the people together to the ends of the earth: and they are the ten thousands of Ephraim, and they are the thousands of Manasseh."* Debarim 33:17. There is dispute over the interpretation of the word ᵐ∀ᐌ which some interpret as "wild ox" while others interpret it as "unicorn."

The message should be loud and clear - Ephraim and Manasseh, who were elevated to Joseph's status of the first born, are likened to the firstlings of the bullocks. The text refers to "My son-breaks forth." This is prophetic of something that is getting ready to occur on the first two days of Succot in Jubilee Year 120.

For those unfamiliar with the history of Yisrael, it may be helpful to provide a brief summary. After the death of King Solomon (Shlomo), Joseph seceded from the Southern Kingdom of Yahudah, and brought along the majority of the Tribes of Yisrael. The Tribe of Joseph ruled over the Northern Kingdom, known as the House of Yisrael, which was later exiled and taken captive by the Assyrians from the north. Their primary sin was the setting up of two altars to, none other than, a golden calf.[150]

Both Kingdoms were exiled. The Kingdom of Yahudah was exiled by the Babylonians, but some of them returned after their 70 year exile. The Northern Kingdom, represented by Joseph, has never returned from the punishment of exile, and the long awaited return is imminent.[151] Essentially, Joseph has been scattered throughout the world and mixed with the nations. For Mosheh truly prophesied of Joseph: *"he shall push the people together to the ends of the earth."* Debarim 33:17.

While the Kingdom of Yahudah never lost their identity during their exile, the House of Yisrael (Joseph) has been completely cut off from YHWH, exactly as prophesied by Hoshea. (see Hoshea 1:9). The House of Yisrael (Joseph) is currently blended in with the nations, essentially hidden from view - unrecognizable. This is a prophetic amplification of what happened to the man Joseph when he was forced into Egypt.

Joseph was originally removed from the Land as a slave, and ultimately elevated to power. He ended up blending in with Egypt. He married an Egyptian woman and essentially looked just like an Egyptian - unrecognizable to his brothers. The same holds true for Joseph - the House of Yisrael. Originally taken from the Land as slaves, the House of Yisrael has blended into the Nations. The House of Yisrael, like Joseph, is virtually unrecognizable to his brothers - Yahudah. Some day soon, YHWH will cast His net and draw back His people from the nations. (Hoshea 1:10-11).

Remember that the Nations are often symbolized by the number 70. As has already been mentioned, there are 70 bullocks slaughtered during this Feast. The first two days they are called "young bulls" (beni-baqar) while the remaining days they are "bullocks" (parim). The slaughtering of the bullocks during this "homecoming Feast" of the seventh month culminates with seven bullocks being slaughtered on the seventh day. The prophetic implications are profound.

Interestingly this is the one Feast that the entire planet will be required to observe during the millennial reign.

"¹ Behold, the Day of YHWH cometh, and thy spoil shall be divided in the midst of thee. ² For I will gather all nations against Jerusalem to battle; and the city shall be taken, and the houses rifled, and the women ravished; and half of the city shall go forth into captivity, and the residue of the people shall not be cut off from the city. ³ Then shall YHWH go forth, and fight against those nations, as when He fought in the day of battle. ⁴ And His feet shall stand in that day upon the mount of Olives, which is before Jerusalem on the east, and the mount of Olives shall cleave in the midst thereof toward the

east and toward the west, and there shall be a very great valley; and half of the mountain shall remove toward the north, and half of it toward the south. ⁵ *And you shall flee to the valley of the mountains; for the valley of the mountains shall reach unto Azal: yea, you shall flee, like as you fled from before the earthquake in the days of Uzziah king of Yahudah: and YHWH Elohi shall come, and all the set apart ones with thee.* ⁶ <u>*And it shall come to pass in that day, that the light shall not be clear, nor dark:*</u> ⁷ <u>*But it shall be one day which shall be known to YHWH, not day, nor night: but it shall come to pass, that at evening time it shall be light.*</u> ⁸ *And it shall be in that day, that living waters shall go out from Jerusalem; half of them toward the former sea, and half of them toward the hinder sea: in summer and in winter shall it be.* ⁹ *And* <u>*YHWH shall be king over all the earth: in that day shall there be one (echad) YHWH, and His Name one (echad).*</u> ¹⁰ *All the land shall be turned as a plain from Geba to Rimmon south of Jerusalem: and it shall be lifted up, and inhabited in her place, from Benjamin's gate unto the place of the first gate, unto the corner gate, and from the tower of Hananeel unto the king's winepresses.* ¹¹ *And men shall dwell in it, and there shall be no more utter destruction; but Jerusalem shall be safely inhabited.* ¹² *And this shall be the plague wherewith YHWH will smite all the people that have fought against Jerusalem; Their flesh shall consume away while they stand upon their feet, and their eyes shall consume away in their holes, and their tongue shall consume away in their mouth.* ¹³ *And it shall come to pass in that day, that a great tumult from YHWH shall be among them; and they shall lay hold every one on the hand of his neighbour, and his hand shall rise up against the hand of his neighbour.* ¹⁴ <u>*And Yahudah also shall*</u>

fight at Jerusalem; and the wealth of all the heathen round about shall be gathered together, gold, and silver, and apparel, in great abundance. ¹⁵ *And so shall be the plague of the horse, of the mule, of the camel, and of the ass, and of all the beasts that shall be in these tents, as this plague.* ¹⁶ *And it shall come to pass, that every one that is left of all the nations which came against Jerusalem shall even go up from year to year to worship the King, YHWH of hosts, and to keep the Feast of Succot.* ¹⁷ *And it shall be, that whoso will not come up of all the families of the earth unto Jerusalem to worship the King, YHWH of hosts, even upon them shall be no rain.* ¹⁸ *And if the family of Egypt go not up, and come not, that have no rain; there shall be the plague, wherewith YHWH will smite the heathen that come not up to keep the Feast of Succot.* ¹⁹ *This shall be the punishment of Egypt, and the punishment of all nations that come not up to keep the Feast of Succot." Zechariah 14:1-19.*

Notice that this Feast is directly associated with the Day of YHWH. The Day of YHWH is a period of time equal to one "shanah" or one Hebrew Year according to Yeshayahu 34:8, 61:2, 63:4. In the 7,000 Year Plan of Elohim, it is year 6,000, and a time when all nations will be gathered against Yisrael. Then YHWH will fight against those Nations "as when He fought in the day of battle." We know that YHWH specifically fought for Yisrael when they left Egypt (Shemot 15:1-10) and when they entered into the Land. (Joshua 10:42), among other times.

Remember at Jericho, when the Yisraelites surrounded the city and marched in a circle in a sacred ceremony - hagag (ᐱᐱᕼ). Joshua (Yahushua) had met beforehand with the Prince of the Host of YHWH. The presence of YHWH was there as Joshua (Yahushua) was instructed to take off his sandals, because he was on "holy ground." This was the same instruction given to Mosheh when he stood before the burning bush. We cannot ignore the fact that this "Prince" was YHWH Himself.

Joshua (Yahushua) was given specific and detailed instructions for taking Jericho. Specifically, seven Priests with seven shofars were to go before the Ark as all the men of battle marched around the city over the course of seven days. The first six days they were to walk around the city once. On the seventh day, they were to walk around the city seven times, followed by the blasting of the shofars and a mighty shout. After that, the walls of Jericho came down.

Jericho was not some random city selected for destruction. There was a reason why it was taken first. Jericho was named after Yerach, the Canaanite moon god. Indeed the Hebrew word for moon was "yerach" (ﬧﬧ). In the future, the Nations will surround Jerusalem, including one group of nations who strongly identify with the crescent moon.

The Fifth Pillar of Islam requires every able-bodied adherent to Islam to make The Hajj, the pilgrimage to Mecca. While at Mecca, the pilgrims participate in the "Tawaf" where they march around the Kaaba seven times. The parallels between what Joshua (Yahushua) did at Jericho, and what Muslims do at Mecca are extraordinary. This is particularly poignant since their god "Allah" is a moon deity, and the basis for the crescent moon as the symbol of Islam. This is why Muslims follow a strictly lunar calendar, with no intercalation, as opposed to the luni-solar calendar prescribed in the Scriptures, which requires intercalation.

When Yisrael, lead by Joshua (Yahushua), conquered Jericho at Succot, it was YHWH Himself Who destroyed the cult center for moon worshippers in the Promised Land. This has prophetic implications for all who worship the moon deity at Succot in the year 6,000.

The tensions between Islam and the Judeo-Christian religions seem to escalate daily, and it is interesting how Jerusalem and the Promised Land remain at the heart of this

conflict. So we can certainly see the Feast of Succot as a rehearsal for a very important future event. In fact, many believe that we are soon approaching the Day of YHWH.

We are surely living in interesting times, and the Feast of Succot has particular significance at this time at the end of the ages. Paul of Tarsus said that the things that happened to Yisrael on the First Exodus under Mosheh, were to provide instruction to those of us living at the end of the ages. *"Now all these things happened to them as examples, and they were written for our admonition, upon whom the ends of the ages have come."* 1 Corinthians 10:1-11.

The account of Yisrael coming into Covenant with YHWH is filled with prophetic clues about exactly how the Covenant journey is going to end. As a result, it is paramount that we understand the Feast of Succot. Indeed, the Feast of Succot was important when the House of Yahudah returned from their Babylonian exile, so we can imagine that it will also be significant when the House of Yisrael - Joseph returns from the long exile that began in 722 BCE.[52]

The Kingdom of Yahudah had witnessed the exile of their Northern brethren to the Assyrians, but did not learn from their mistakes. Yahudah continued in their sins, and was also exiled. The prophet Jeremiah (Yirmeyahu) told them that they would be conquered by the Babylonians and exiled 70 years. The Southern Kingdom of Yahudah was indeed taken captive by the Babylonians who were themselves later conquered by the Medo-Persians. This is the setting in which we find Daniel praying regarding those 70 years, and he receives a message concerning 70 weeks. (Daniel 9).

Exactly 70 years after the last captives were taken from Yahudah, Cyrus decreed they could return to fulfill the prophecy of Yirmeyahu 29:10-14. After the Decree of Cyrus (Ezra 1:1-4), the royal prince Zerubbabel and many others from the House of Yahudah returned to Jerusalem to rebuild the temple on the 1st of Cyrus. Construction began in the 2nd of Cyrus (Ezra 3:8-13), but the people of Yahudah were frustrated in their purposes by their adversaries who were living in the Land and wanted to help them. This was something that the people of Yahudah and Benjamin could not allow (Ezra 4:1-5).

Finally, after much struggle, a second decree was issued in the 2nd of Darius (Haggai 1:1-15, Ezra 6:1-12), and construction of the Second Temple went ahead without delay by royal decree. The Second Temple was completed in the 6th of Darius (Ezra 6:15), which was 70 years after Zerubbabel first returned under the Decree of Cyrus (Ezra 1:1-4). It was at this time that Ezra came from Babylon to Jerusalem with a second wave of immigrants (Ezra 7:1-8:32).

Within a year of his return, Ezra persuaded the House of Yahudah to put away all the foreign wives they had married (Ezra 10:1-44). It was five years after he returned that Ezra, at the conclusion of Sabbath Year 495, read from the Torah on Yom Teruah (Nehemiah 8:1-2).

On the first day of the seventh month, the Day of Blasting, the people heard the Torah. It was translated for them and they wept. They wept for many reasons. One particular reason was because they were hearing about the Appointed Times that they had forgotten while in exile. The people were told not to weep because it was a set apart day of YHWH, an Appointed Time. Instead, the people were told to go eat "the fat" and drink "the sweet," and send portions to those who did not have anything prepared. The congregation was told not to be sorrowful because the joy of YHWH is their strength.[153]

After celebrating the Day of Blasting, the people returned to hear more Scripture reading. Once again the chief fathers of all the people, the Priests, and the Levites returned and taught more from the Torah. They realized that they should keep the Feast of Succot, so they built succas. They made their succas out of olive branches, pine branches, myrtle branches, palm branches, and branches of thick trees

as it is written in the Torah (Vayiqra 23:40).

This was truly a time of rejoicing. Again, this was a homecoming. A return to the Mountain of the House of YHWH after all the years that it took to return and rebuild. Nehemiah wrote that the Feast had not been kept this way since the time of Joshua (Yahushua) the son of Nun.

What we see here is an incredible awakening but also it reveals their hearts to obey. They diligently kept the commandments, including a very important one that occurs during Succot - the reading of the Torah. *"10 And Mosheh commanded them, saying, At the end of every seven years, in the solemnity of the year of release, in the Feast of Succot, 11 When all Yisrael is come to appear before YHWH your Elohim in the place which He shall choose, you shall read this Torah before all Yisrael in their hearing. 12 Gather the people together, men, and women, and children, and thy stranger that is within thy gates, that they may hear, and that they may learn, and fear YHWH your Elohim, and observe to do all the words of this Torah: 13 And that their children, which have not known any thing, may hear, and learn to fear YHWH your Elohim, as long as you live in the Land whither you go over Jordan to possess it."* Debarim 31:10-13.

It is interesting to note that immediately after giving this command, Mosheh was told that it was time for him to die at the age of 120 years. Mosheh would stop short of the Promised Land because of his sin. Yahushua (Joshua) would thereafter lead the Children of Yisrael into the Land. How interesting that 120 Jubilee years leads to the end of the age, the time when Messiah will return to lead the Covenant People Yisrael into their inheritance.

As Mosheh commanded before his death, Ezra read from Debarim for the seven days of Succot at the conclusion of Sabbath Year 495 in Month 7 of 451 BCE. (Nehemiah 8:18). Notice in the command given by Mosheh that even the stranger (ha ger) was to hear the Torah. This reveals that the Torah was for all of Creation, as was the Feast. All of Creation was called to join with YHWH in Covenant and Feast at His table, in His House. As a result, the Feast was a time when all were called to rejoice, and every seven years all would hear the Torah. That would be the year of release. It was a seven year cycle known as the Shemitah cycle that was at the heart of the Jubilee cycle. The Shemitah year was the Sabbath year when even the Land would rest. Just like the count up to Shabuot counted weeks of days, the Shemitah involved weeks of years.

The House of Yahudah continued to endure many struggles and conflicts from the inhabitants of the Land. This was a great source of distress to Nehemiah. In the 20th of Artaxerxes in 443 BCE, Artaxerxes made a decree that Nehemiah could return to Jerusalem to rebuild the walls and the city of Jerusalem. Rebuilding Jerusalem was quite an ordeal. They had to fend off raiding parties as they worked around the city. In fact, the men who worked on the wall had to carry shofars, so they could sound the alarm if they came under attack. It was this Decree of Artaxerxes that initiated the count for the 7 sevens and 62 sevens of Daniel 9:25.

The walls were completed in 52 days on Day 25 of Month 6 in 443 BCE. Not long after this, every man returned to his inheritance in Jubilee Year 71 in 437 BCE. (see Nehemiah 11:20). It was at this time that Nehemiah also fulfilled the commandment to read Debarim during the seven days of Succot at the conclusion of Sabbath Year 497. "*Also day by day, from the first day unto the last day, he read in the Scroll of the Torah of Elohim. And they kept the Feast seven days; and on the eighth day was a atzeret, according unto the manner.*" Nehemiah 8:18.

Notice that they kept the Feast for seven days and on the eighth day was an "atzeret." Succot is a seven day feast followed by an eighth day, a separate day. The discerning individual would see the striking similarity with Passover and Unleavened Bread, only this time somewhat in reverse.

The last day of Succot is the seventh day, Day 21 of Month 7, often called Hoshana Rabbah. Unlike the last day of the Feast of Unleavened Bread, the last day of the Feast of

Succot is not a Shabbat. It is also the final day of harvest or ingathering. Tradition links this day with the last of the days of judgment, or the final judgment.

So the seven day Feast of Succot begins with a Shabbaton, but does not end with a Shabbaton. This reveals that there is work to be done on this day, and the future implication of that fact is quite telling. This final day of harvest leads to another Appointed Time known as the Eighth Day.

13

The Eighth Day

There is a final Appointed Time beyond the seventh day of Succot simply called the eighth day. It is referred to as Shemini Atzeret, and is often confused with Succot. Many erroneously believe that since it is called "the eighth day" then it must part of Succot. Essentially they treat it as the eighth day of Succot. The problem is that Succot is clearly a seven day Feast. There is no eighth day to the Feast of Succot. The confusion exists primarily because of the very vague references that we find in the Scriptures.

Here is what we read in Vayiqra: "*on the eighth day shall be a set apart gathering unto you; and you shall offer an offering made by fire unto YHWH: it is a atzeret; and you shall do no servile work therein.*" Vayiqra 23:36. We read that the eighth day is a Shabbaton. "*Also in the fifteenth day of the seventh month, when ye have gathered in the fruit of the land, you shall keep a Feast unto YHWH seven days: on the first day shall be a Shabbaton, and on the eighth day shall be a Shabbaton.*" Vayiqra 23:39.

There are specific sacrifices on this day, separate and apart from Succot. "*[35] On the eighth day you shall have a atzeret: you shall do no servile work therein: [36] But you shall offer a burnt offering, a sacrifice made by fire, of a sweet savour unto YHWH: one bullock, one ram, seven lambs of the first year without blemish: [37] Their grain offering and their drink offerings for the bullock, for the ram, and for the lambs, shall be according to their number, after the manner: [38] And one goat for a sin offering; beside the continual burnt offering, and his grain offering, and his drink offering.*"

Bemidbar 29:35-38.

So what is the mystery concerning the eighth day? To begin, while many English translations call it a "solemn assembly" the Scriptures clearly describe it as a "atzeret." Remember that the seventh day of Unleavened Bread is an atzeret. Now the eighth day - the day after Succot is a atzeret. These are the only two atzerets that occur in the Appointed Times of YHWH.

To gain some further insight it might be helpful to look at some references to "the eighth day" in the Scriptures. First of all we must immediately think of something that occurs on the eighth day of every male child's life - circumcision.

This day has great significance with the Covenant. It is a day when the mark of the Covenant is received. (Vayiqra 12:3). So after the new birth of a male child into the Covenant, a seven day count begins, followed by the eighth day when blood is shed, a mark is given and a name is sealed. This is a vital day in the life of one born into the Covenant.

It is also the day that the firstborn are given to YHWH. "*29 Thou shalt not delay to offer the first of thy ripe fruits, and of thy liquors: the firstborn of thy sons shalt thou give unto Me. 30 Likewise shalt thou do with thine oxen, and with thy sheep: seven days it shall be with his dam; on the eighth day thou shalt give it me.*" Shemot 22:29-30. (see also Vayiqra 22:27).

Here we see a powerful connection, once again, with the firstborn. So on this day, the eighth day, a firstborn male child would not only be circumcised, he would be symbolically given to YHWH through the Levites and would be redeemed. "*And every firstling of an ass thou shalt redeem with a lamb; and if thou wilt not redeem it, then thou shalt break his neck: and all the firstborn of man among thy children shalt thou redeem.*" Shemot 13:13.

The eighth day was a day of redemption for the firstborn males of the Covenant. This, of course, makes us think of Passover, when the firstborn males were saved from death, and Yisrael was redeemed by YHWH. "*Wherefore say* unto the children of Yisrael, I am YHWH, and I will bring you out from under the burdens of the Egyptians, and I will rid you out of their bondage, and I will redeem you with a stretched out arm, and with great judgments." Shemot 6:6.

Another great secret that is revealed by the Creation Calendar is that the Passover, when the firstborn of Yisrael were redeemed, occurred on "the eighth day" – the day after the weekly Sabbath. The Passover occurred on Yom Rishon, on the first day of the week in 1437 BCE.

Shemini Atzeret is a mysterious day, although the patterns of the past help us to see its importance in the future. The past redemption of Yisrael was accomplished *"with an outstretched Arm and with great judgments."* The Arm of YHWH is clearly a Messianic reference that can be seen throughout the Scriptures.[154] So we should expect to see this day of redemption in the future involving the Messiah and great judgment, not just in the Land of Egypt, but upon the entire planet.[155]

Amazingly, it was on "the eighth day" that the Tabernacle was "open for business" after seven days of preparation at the door. (Vayiqra 9:1). The Tabernacle was an essential part of the Covenant. Dwelling with YHWH was the goal, although He would be living in separate quarters since the golden calf incident.

While the Tabernacle was set up on Day 1 of Month 1, "the eighth day" was not Day 8 of Month 1. This is part of the mystery associated with "the eighth day." The eighth day was the conclusion of a perfect weekly cycle. It was the beginning of a new cycle that started after the Sabbath. It was the first day, Yom Rishon on Day 10 of Month 1 in 1436 BCE.

So on this "eighth day" the House was ready and opened up so that the firstborn of Yisrael (represented by the Levites) could enter in. This has prophetic implications for the day when Yisrael will enter the House on the first day of the Millennial Kingdom. (Yeshayahu 30:26, Revelation 19:1-

10). It is also the pattern for when New Jerusalem descends from heaven at the end of seven millennial days. (Revelation 3:12, 21:2).

If you examine the Scriptures and tradition you will see numerous things that began for Yisrael when the Tabernacle service began on the eighth day. This was the first day that Aharon stood as High Priest and blessed the children of Yisrael. It was also the day that the Levitical priesthood began their service. This was the first day of the daily offering - the morning and evening lambs. This was the day that fire came from YHWH and lit the Altar before the Tabernacle. It was the first day of eating of the sacrifices that were presented before at the Tabernacle, and it was the day when a new commandment concerning altars was prescribed.

All of these events occurred "on the eighth day" on the first day of the week on Yom Rishon. It was also the day YHWH told Yisrael that He would accept them when the Second temple was dedicated on Day 8 of Month 1 in 456 BCE. (Ezekiel 43:27).[156]

So this eighth day was a day of new beginnings for the Covenant people in their relationship with YHWH. This fact is profoundly demonstrated by other Scriptures concerning the eighth day. It is the day that male children are given the sign of the Covenant in their flesh. The eighth day is the day that the diseased person, the leper, is cleansed. This symbolized a cleansing from sin. (see Vayiqra 14). The cleansing occurs at the door of the Tabernacle, the House of YHWH, on the eighth day. (Vayiqra 14). It is the day when men and women are declared clean from an unclean state. (Vayiqra 15). In all of these cases we can see washing with water, followed by blood and the cleansing is accomplished at the door to the Tabernacle.

The message was clear. The Children of Yisrael had to be clean to enter into the Courts of the House of YHWH - the Tabernacle. They needed to be washed clean, and blood needed to be shed to accomplish the cleansing. Once they were cleansed, they could visit His House and commune with Him. Of course, this was why the man and woman were expelled from the Garden. The man and woman became defiled, and therefore could no longer commune directly with a set apart Elohim. That is why YHWH used messengers to communicate with His Creation. This was the problem that needed to be resolved. Through the Torah, YHWH was teaching Yisrael this very important lesson, and revealing the patterns that would be fulfilled to get them back into the House.

So it should be clear that this eighth day has profound significance as we learn to approach and fellowship with YHWH. In fact, eight is the Gematria value of the Hebrew word "ahab" (ロ५४), which means "love." The aleph (४) is equivalent to the number 1, the hey (५) is equivalent to the number 5, and the bet (ロ) is equivalent to the number 2. So the "breath or spirit" of the "first or head" leads to "the house." This is the essence of love - the love of YHWH. So we can see that the number eight is all about relationship.

Incredibly, the first time that we read the word "ahab" (ロ५४) in the Scriptures is when Yaacob was planning to deceive his father. Ribkah sends Yaacob for two kid goats to make a meal that the father Yitshaq "loves." While Yaakob often takes the fall for this deception, the plan was formulated by the wife and mothe Ribkah.

This was a meal for one person. There was no need for two kid goats, and therefore the text seems to be drawing our attention to a mystery that is not immediately evident. It should remind us of the two goats of Yom Kippur and the Atonement that He provides us through His Son - the ultimate act of love. This is even more powerful when we recognize the context of the text. It was when Yaacob received the blessing of the firstborn - the Covenant promises.

The Hebrew letter "chet" (ㅐ) has the numerical equivalent of 8. You might notice that in the Ancient Script

it looks like a fence, and indeed that is the meaning of the symbol. This is because the eighth day is a day of separation. It marks the end of the seventh day, and the beginning of a new week. In fact, we see how time has been segmented into seven day cycles, so this day is actually beyond our time. It is essentially "time beyond time."

It is a new time, a new beginning, when the fence, or gate, is opened for those in the Covenant. The fence is a barrier, a separation between those in the House and those outside. There were always walls and fences around the House of YHWH, and there is a description of another wall around the Renewed Jerusalem being 144 cubits thick and made of jasper. (Revelation 21).

The twelve gates around the City have the names of the Twelve Tribes of Yisrael. (Revelation 21:12). In other words, you must be in the Covenant to enter in, and *"there will be no way to enter into it anything profane, or one who causes an abomination or a lie, but only those who are written in the Lamb's scroll of life."* (Revelation 21:27).

As has already been mentioned, the number 8 is closely associated with new beginnings since it essentially starts a "new" or "renewed" cycle after the completion of seven. So we can see that this eighth day is intimately associated with the Covenant, and it is a time of renewal for those in the Covenant cycle. It has profound implications for the future.

How interesting that it immediately follows the seven days of Succot, and is an eighth day Shabbaton. Even though we are not specifically commanded to be at the House of YHWH, since it is not a Pilgrimage Feast, we will be there if we are obeying the commandment concerning Succot. That is why it is known as an "atzeret."

Since we are commanded to be at the House for seven days we will definitely be in His presence at the beginning of the eighth day, so we should stay another day and find rest with Him. As Mosheh and Aharon were commanded to stay

in front of the door of the Tabernacle for seven days prior to the service on the eighth day, we can see that we are supposed to dwell in succas, which are temporary dwellings. The succa is to remind us that Yisrael dwelled in temporary structures prior to moving into the Covenant Land.

So this very special Covenant day also involves dwelling with YHWH. It is when the House is opened to those in the Covenant. It is when we leave our temporary dwellings, transcend time and abide with Him. As we shall see, these Appointed Times of the seventh month – the Sabbath month - are intimately associated with a future work of the Messiah, as are all the Moadim.

14

Messiah and the Moadim

Hopefully by now, the reader can see how important the Appointed Times are to YHWH and His plan to restore Creation. This creates a dilemma for the Christian religion which has essentially rejected His Times, and implemented different "holy days," many of which are completely separate from the Appointed Times of YHWH.[157]

One would think that a group of people professing to believe and obey the Creator of the Universe - the One Who Created Time and marked special times - would observe those times. This is particularly significant when we examine the life of Yahushua, the One they claim as their Messiah. His life was intimately tied with the Appointed Times, which would appear to be a resounding affirmation of the continuing significance of the Appointed Times.

Of course, as mentioned previously, the Appointed Times are intimately connected with the Covenant and the restoration process. Therefore we should expect the Messiah to operate around these special times. In fact, a careful reading of the Messianic Writings will reveal that Yahushua observed the Appointed Times, and it could be argued that almost every instance of His being in Jerusalem was at an Appointed Time.[158]

So let us briefly examine His life, and look at some of the examples where Yahushua the Messiah is associated with the Appointed Times. Our examination begins on the First Day of the Seventh Month - Yom Teruah. It was the day when Kings of Yahudah would mark the beginning of their

reign.[159] This was a good day for a King to begin his reign.

Remember that this was a day of blasting so it was a very powerful day. It was a day when sound was reverberating across the Land as a remembrance of the voice of YHWH that blasted from Sinai - the same voice that uttered the words at Creation. So we also have a connection with Creation on this day

Indeed, this was likely the day of Creation when YHWH created Day One and made it echad. It was also the echad of month seven. Here is what the Scriptures declare: "*Speak unto the children of Yisrael, saying, In the seventh new moon, in the first (echad) of the new moon, shall you have a shabbaton, a memorial of blowing, a set apart gathering.*" Vayiqra 23:24.

Notice the "echad," and there is no reference to a "day" in the Hebrew text. This moment of time appears to be the seam in the cycle of a year. Just as YHWH stitched together night and day and made them into a "yom echad," so it appears that He did the same with a year. This day unifies the year, and it occurs at the first visible sighting of the seventh new moon.

This special day was also the moment that Yahushua was born. On September 11, 3 BCE at around 5:53 pm [+/- 10 minutes], Yom Teruah began at the moment of the setting of the sun. Shortly after this, the renewed moon would have been visible, assuming there was no cloud cover. At around 6:12 pm [+/- 10 minutes], Spica, the brightest star in the constellation Bethulah, also known as Virgo, would have touched the horizon. The Hebrew name of this star is "Tsemach" which means "The Branch" – a title for the Messiah. (Yeshayahu 4:2, 11:1; Yirmeyahu 23:5, 33:15; Zechariah 3:8, 6:12). The Latin name "Spica" means "kernel of wheat." It was around the time that Tsemach/ Spica touched the earth that the Messiah was born, having left the waters of the womb at the time when blasts of the shofar would have been resounding throughout the Land.

We know this because it was also the moment when a great sign occurred in the heavens announcing the Birth of The Messiah. 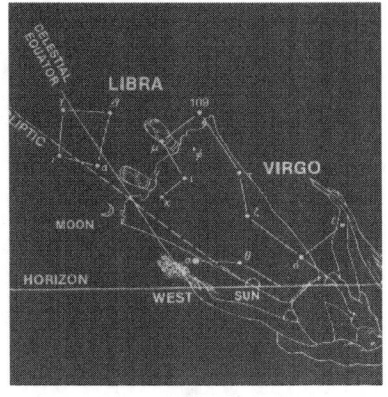 *"' And there appeared a great sign in heaven; a woman clothed with the sun, and the moon under her feet, and upon her head a crown of twelve stars:* [2] *And she being with child cried, travailing in birth, and pained to be delivered."* Revelation 12:1-2. Anyone with a computer and the appropriate astronomical software can see this event as it occurred over 2,000 years ago.[160]

The Prophet Yeshayahu alluded to this sign involving a virgin giving birth. (Yeshayahu 7:14). The birth of the Messiah occurred in Bethlehem, the City of David. It did not occur in Jerusalem as the Messiah had to be born in Bethlehem to fulfill the prophecy of Micah 5:2. The Messiah was not born at Succot, as at the time of His birth, every man of Yisrael returned to the city of his birth for a census. (Luke 2:3). As Succot was an important Pilgrimage Feast for the people of Yisrael, they would not be required to travel away from Jerusalem on Succot. This would have caused a rebellion. As such, it is quite certain that the Messiah was not born at Succot.

Yahushua was circumcised on the eighth day according to the Torah, on Day 8 of Month 7 in 3 BCE. How incredible that we see the Messiah shedding the blood of the Covenant of Circumcision, receiving the mark, on the eighth day of the Sabbath month. It was also at this blood shedding event that His Name was sealed – Yahushua "YHWH saves His people." Yahushua being circumcised on the eighth day of the Sabbath month is highly significant.

The parents of Yahushua surely went to Jerusalem for the Feast of Succot when "the Word (ᛉᛒ) became flesh and tabernacled with men." (see Yahanan 1). Bethlehem, after all, is very close to Jerusalem. Interestingly though, we first read about Yahushua being in the City of Jerusalem when Miryam went to the House of YHWH, after her purification was complete according to the Torah. This would have occurred after 40 days, so it was then that they redeemed Yahushua as the Firstborn Son. Yahushua's dedication was on Day 11 of Month 8 in Year 3984 on Yom Shli-shi which is the third day of the week on Tuesday, October 22, 3 B.C.E.*

The Scriptures then describe a time when "wise men" visited the "Child," not the "infant." They most likely found Yahushua home in the Galilee and anointed Him on a subsequent birthday - Yom Teruah.[161] The Scriptures tell how Yahushua was taken to Egypt, and then they remain silent until we read about an Appointed Time involving Yahushua when He was 12 years old. (Luke 2:42).

The text indicates that Joseph and Miryam went up to Jerusalem every year at Passover. (Luke 2:41). Interestingly, the number 12 represents the people of YHWH, and a perfect year, so how appropriate that that was the age when Yahushua went to Jerusalem at Passover. At the conclusion of the Feast His parents left without Him, and after 3 days He was found in the House of YHWH where people marveled at Him.

The texts then record Him beginning His ministry by being immersed in the Jordan River - at the same spot where the waters were divided, and Joshua (Yahushua) led Yisrael into the Land. This event occurred on Day 28 of Month 13 on the Creation Calendar, three days before the wedding at Cana. (Yahanan 1:29-2:1).[162]

We read that after being immersed and being declared to be the "Lamb of Elohim" by Yahanan the Immerser, who was a Priest, Yahushua began His work as the Lamb. Yahushua began by going into the desert for 40 days and 40 nights, symbolic of Yisrael's journey in the wilderness with Mosheh and Joshua (Yahushua).

Where Yisrael, and even Mosheh, failed in the

wilderness, Yahushua was victorious. He came out of the wilderness as Joshua (Yahushua) and led the Children of Yisrael out of the wilderness. Yahushua was fulfilling the patterns previously provided by Yisrael and the Patriarchs. Those historical activities were actual prophetic pictures of the Messiah. Yahushua was walking out those events and revealing the meaning in them. Many of those patterns involved the Appointed Times.

This is what Yahushua meant when He proclaimed: "*Think not that I am come to destroy the Torah, or the Prophets: I am not come to destroy, but to fulfill.*" Mattityahu 5:17. Many believe that Yahushua came to put an end to the Torah, which they call "The Law." This thinking reveals their ignorance of the purpose of the Torah, which is the Instruction of YHWH. The Torah points the way to YHWH and to Life. Therefore, by fulfilling the Torah, Yahushua in no way intended to destroy or change the Torah, that is an absurd notion. His life was the very embodiment of the Torah. He revealed the meaning and the patterns of the Torah through His walk.

Part of the fulfillment was to reveal some of the patterns in the Appointed Times. The Torah is full of patterns and instructions all intended to get us in a position and on a path where we can be restored with YHWH. It leads us back to the House, and the Appointed Times essentially provide an outline for that process.

This book is not intended to show all instances of Yahushua's fulfillment of the Torah. That is simply not possible to accomplish in a chapter. For further discussion of that issue the reader is referred to the Walk in the Light series book entitled "The Messiah."

Here it is important to understand that the Messiah came to "fulfill" the patterns of the Torah. We cannot appreciate His teaching, His life, death or resurrection unless we view them within that context. Upon close examination we can see that He mainly went to Jerusalem for the

Appointed Times.[163] He spent much of His time in the North, the land known as the Galilee of the Nations. This was the Land of the House of Yisrael. They had been removed from the Land and replaced, but this was where Yahushua was harvesting.

In fact, throughout His life He often spoke in parables, and made numerous agricultural references in His teachings. You see, the Covenant people and the Covenant land were supposed to operate in synchronicity, within the framework established by YHWH, His Calendar and His Appointed Times. Yahushua used those references because in large part, He was speaking to a people who were still identified with the Covenant. He did make reference to other sheep - sheep not of the fold of the House of Yahudah. In fact, He proclaimed that He came for the Lost Sheep of the House of Yisrael. (Mattityahu 15:24).

Remember that the House of Yisrael had been divorced, exiled and scattered to the ends of the earth by YHWH. (Yirmeyahu 3:8). Through that process they lost their identity, which was based upon their relationship with YHWH. The Prophets declared that the House of Yisrael would one day return, and be reunited with the House of Yahudah.

The House of Yahudah had been exiled and while some returned, others willingly stayed out of the Covenant Land. They did not lose their identity, as did the House of Yisrael. The Yahudim knew who they were, even as they remained scattered. The Passover was a pattern for redeeming and delivering the Lost Sheep of Yisrael and the House of Yahudah. It was about regathering and reuniting the divided people of am Yisrael – the family of Elohim.

"They shall come with weeping,
and with supplications I will lead them.
I will cause them to walk by the rivers of waters,
In a straight way in which they shall not stumble;

*For I am a Father to Yisrael,
and Ephraim is My firstborn."*
Yirmeyahu 31:9.

Prior to and including the Passover in Egypt, the firstborn offered sacrifices to YHWH. With the construction of the Tabernacle, or Succa, of YHWH, the Levites represented the firstborn in the House. The Passover is the event which redeems the Covenant people. The House of Yisrael, as the unfaithful bride of YHWH needed to be redeemed and restored.

Just as all of Yisrael was redeemed from Egypt and the firstborn covered by the blood of the Lamb, so the House of Yisrael and the House of Yahudah needed the Lamb of Elohim to redeem them from their exile. The work of the Lamb of Elohim was what was needed to save the firstborn.

With that understanding, perhaps we can better comprehend the reason for His death, and the Appointed Time when it occurred - Passover. In fact, Yahushua fulfilled every portion of this Feast through His life, death and resurrection.

Yahushua made two Triumphal Entries in which He rode into Jerusalem on a donkey. He made the first entry on Day 8 of Month 1. (Mattityahu 21:1-17, Mark 11:1-11, Luke 19:29-46, Yahanan 12:1-11). He made a second entry the next day on Day 9 of Month 1. (Mattityahu 21:18-19, Mark 11:12-19, Luke 19:47-48, Yahanan 12:12-19). This fulfilled the prophecy in Zechariah 9:9 that the Messiah would come humbly riding on a donkey.

The text described people as waving palm branches and singing Hosanna, which means "save now." (Yahanan 12:13). This was from Psalm 118, a Psalm traditionally sung during Hoshana Rabbah on the seventh day of Succot. Those palms, which would have been used to build succas were laid before the path of Yahushua as He entered the City. Most people probably thought that this was a Hoshana Rabbah event, but they failed to discern His true purpose. He had to atone to make way for the return of the House of Yisrael and the House of Yahudah as the Passover Lamb.

The people believed that Yahushua was the Messiah, and they wanted this to be a seventh day of Succot. Succot was always known as the special time that commemorates Elohim dwelling with His people. How fitting for the Kingdom of Elohim, when it fully comes to the redeemed earth, to be considered the ultimate fulfillment of this special Feast. Elohim Himself will finally dwell with His people in all His fullness

To many people's surprise, this did not occur. Instead, Yahushua allowed Himself to be inspected for the 4 days leading up to the Passover. Throughout this period the religious leaders could find no fault in Him. (Mattityahu 21-26). Yahushua showed Himself to be the true Lamb without spot or blemish. He was an acceptable sacrifice to YHWH.

Remember that the lambs were selected on the 10th day of the 1st month. It is traditionally believed that the lambs were kept in Bethlehem, which means House (Beit) of Bread (Lechem). So the flesh of those lambs could be associated and linked with bread. Yahushua as the Lamb of Elohim was born in the House of Bread. This provides a direct connection between the Messiah and the manna - the Bread of Life that came from heaven. On Day 10 of Month 1 Yahushua, the Lamb of Elohim, entered Jerusalem and was inspected by the Saducees and the Pharisees.

The inspection of Yahushua occurred on Day 10 of Month 1, while the one day of the year where the High Priest enters the Most Set Apart Place was on day 10 of Month 7 at exactly the opposite end of the Calendar.

Passover was on Day 14 of Month 1, and it was shortly after sunset beginning Day 14 of Month 1 that Yahushua participated in what is commonly called The Last Supper. This was a Passover meal where the Lamb of Elohim was personally present. At this Covenant meal, originally conducted under the protection of the blood of the lamb, He renewed the Covenant with His 12 talmidim – representing am Yisrael. Through that renewal process, He revealed that the unleavened bread and the wine represented His flesh and His blood - His Life, which would soon be offered up.

It is helpful to look at the renewed Covenant in context as provided by the Prophet Yirmeyahu. Here is the preface for the promised Renewed Covenant. It is a bit lengthy, but important to set the stage for the following passage.

"*¹ The word that came to Yirmeyahu from YHWH, saying, ² Thus speaketh YHWH Elohim of Yisrael, saying, Write thee all the words that I have spoken unto thee in a scroll. ³ For, lo, the days come, saith YHWH, that I will bring again the captivity of My people Yisrael and Yahudah, saith YHWH: and I will cause them to return to the land that I gave to their fathers, and they shall possess it. ⁴ And these are the words that YHWH spoke concerning Yisrael and concerning Yahudah. ⁵ For thus saith YHWH; We have heard a voice of trembling, of fear, and not of peace. ⁶ Ask ye now, and see whether a man doth travail with child? wherefore do I see every man with his hands on his loins, as a woman in travail, and all faces are turned into paleness? ⁷ Alas! for that day is great, so that none is like it: it is even the time of Yaakob's trouble; but he shall be saved out of it. ⁸ For it shall come to pass in that day, saith YHWH of hosts, that I will break his yoke from off thy neck, and will burst thy bonds, and strangers shall no more serve themselves of him: ⁹ But they shall serve YHWH their Elohim, and David their king, whom I will raise up unto them. ¹⁰ Therefore fear thou not, O my servant Yaakob, saith YHWH; neither be dismayed, O Yisrael: for, lo, I will save thee from afar, and thy seed from the land of their captivity; and Yaakob shall return, and shall be in rest, and be quiet, and none shall make him afraid. ¹¹ For I am with thee, saith YHWH, to save thee: though I make a full end of all nations whither I have scattered thee, yet will I not make a full end of thee: but I will correct thee in measure, and will not leave thee altogether unpunished. ¹² For thus saith YHWH, Thy bruise is incurable, and thy wound is grievous. ¹³*

There is none to plead thy cause, that thou mayest be bound up: thou hast no healing medicines. ¹⁴ *All thy lovers have forgotten thee; they seek thee not; for I have wounded thee with the wound of an enemy, with the chastisement of a cruel one, for the multitude of thine iniquity; because thy sins were increased.* ¹⁵ *Why criest thou for thine affliction? thy sorrow is incurable for the multitude of thine iniquity: because thy sins were increased, I have done these things unto thee.* ¹⁶ *Therefore all they that devour thee shall be devoured; and all thine adversaries, every one of them, shall go into captivity; and they that spoil thee shall be a spoil, and all that prey upon thee will I give for a prey.* ¹⁷ *For I will restore health unto thee, and I will heal thee of thy wounds, saith YHWH; because they called thee an Outcast, saying, This is Zion, whom no man seeketh after.* ¹⁸ *Thus saith YHWH; Behold, I will bring again the captivity of Yaakob's tents, and have mercy on his dwelling places; and the city shall be builded upon her own heap, and the palace shall remain after the manner thereof.* ¹⁹ *And out of them shall proceed thanksgiving and the voice of them that make merry: and I will multiply them, and they shall not be few; I will also glorify them, and they shall not be small.* ²⁰ *Their children also shall be as aforetime, and their congregation shall be established before me, and I will punish all that oppress them.* ²¹ *And their nobles shall be of themselves, and their governor shall proceed from the midst of them; and I will cause him to draw near, and he shall approach unto me: for who is this that engaged his heart to approach unto me? saith YHWH.* ²² *And you shall be My people, and I will be your Elohim.* ²³ *Behold, the whirlwind of YHWH goeth forth with fury, a continuing whirlwind: it shall fall with pain upon the head of the wicked.* ²⁴ *The fierce anger of YHWH shall not return, until he have done it, and until he have performed the intents of his heart: in the latter days ye shall consider it."* Yirmeyahu 30:1-24.

So YHWH was identifying the problem. Yisrael had been divided into the House of Yisrael and the House of Yahudah. Two different kingdoms with different exiles resulting from their iniquity. It seemed that their wound was incurable, but YHWH promised a cure. Through a great time, known as Yaakob's Trouble, a solution would come.

The nations that had held the captives would be judged. Yaakob too would be judged, but there would be healing and restoration for Yisrael and Yahudah. They would be restored as a Covenant people and restored to the Covenant Land. This process of restoration would occur through a Renewed Covenant further described by Yirmeyahu.

¹ At the same time, saith YHWH, will I be the Elohim of all the families of Yisrael, and they shall be My people. ² Thus saith YHWH, The people which were left of the sword found grace in the wilderness; even Yisrael, when I went to cause him to rest. ³ YHWH hath appeared of old unto me, saying, Yea, I have loved thee with an everlasting love: therefore with lovingkindness have I drawn thee. ⁴ Again I will build thee, and thou shalt be built, O virgin of Yisrael: thou shalt again be adorned with thy tabrets, and shalt go forth in the dances of them that make merry. ⁵ Thou shalt yet plant vines upon the mountains of Samaria: the planters shall plant, and shall eat them as common things. ⁶ For there shall be a day, that the watchmen upon the mount Ephraim shall cry, Arise ye, and let us go up to Zion unto YHWH our Elohim. ⁷ For thus saith YHWH; Sing with gladness for Yaakob, and shout among the chief of the nations: publish ye, praise ye, and say, O YHWH, save your people, the remnant of Yisrael. ⁸ Behold, I will bring them from the north country, and gather them from the coasts of the earth, and with them the blind and the lame, the woman with child and her that travaileth with child together: a great company shall return thither. ⁹ They shall come with weeping, and with supplications will I lead them: I will cause them to walk by the rivers of waters in a straight way, wherein they shall not stumble: for I am a Father to Yisrael, and Ephraim is My firstborn. ¹⁰ Hear the word of YHWH, O ye nations, and declare it in the isles afar off, and say, He that scattered Yisrael will gather him, and keep him, as a shepherd doth his flock. ¹¹ For YHWH hath redeemed Yaakob, and ransomed him from the hand of him that was stronger than he. ¹² Therefore they shall come and sing in the height of Zion, and shall flow together to the goodness of YHWH, for wheat, and for wine, and for oil, and for the young of the flock and of the herd: and their soul shall be as a watered garden; and they shall not sorrow any more at all. ¹³ Then

shall the virgin rejoice in the dance, both young men and old together: for I will turn their mourning into joy, and will comfort them, and make them rejoice from their sorrow. ¹⁴ And I will satiate the soul of the priests with fatness, and My people shall be satisfied with My goodness, saith YHWH. ¹⁵ Thus saith YHWH; A voice was heard in Ramah, lamentation, and bitter weeping; Rachel weeping for her children refused to be comforted for her children, because they were not. ¹⁶ Thus saith YHWH; Refrain thy voice from weeping, and thine eyes from tears: for thy work shall be rewarded, saith YHWH; and they shall come again from the land of the enemy. ¹⁷ And there is hope in thine end, saith YHWH, that thy children shall come again to their own border. ¹⁸ I have surely heard Ephraim bemoaning himself thus; Thou hast chastised me, and I was chastised, as a bullock unaccustomed to the yoke: turn thou me, and I shall be turned; for thou art YHWH my Elohim. ¹⁹ Surely after that I was turned, I repented; and after that I was instructed, I smote upon my thigh: I was ashamed, yea, even confounded, because I did bear the reproach of my youth. ²⁰ Is Ephraim My dear son? Is he a pleasant child? For since I spake against him, I do earnestly remember him still: therefore My bowels are troubled for him; I will surely have mercy upon him, saith YHWH. ²¹ Set thee up waymarks, make thee high heaps: set thine heart toward the highway, even the way which thou wentest: turn again, O virgin of Yisrael, turn again to these thy cities. ²² How long wilt thou go about, O thou backsliding daughter? For YHWH hath created a new thing in the earth, A woman shall compass a man. ²³ Thus saith YHWH of hosts, the Elohim of Yisrael; As yet they shall use this speech in the land of Yahudah and in the cities thereof, when I shall bring again their captivity; YHWH bless thee, O habitation of justice, and set apart mountain. ²⁴ And there shall dwell in Yahudah itself, and in all the cities thereof together, husbandmen, and they that go forth with flocks. ²⁵ For I have satiated the weary soul, and I have replenished every sorrowful soul. ²⁶ Upon this I awaked, and beheld; and My sleep was sweet unto Me. ²⁷ Behold, the days come, saith YHWH, that I will sow the House of Yisrael and the House of Yahudah with the seed of man, and with the seed of beast. ²⁸ And it shall come to pass, that like as I have watched over them, to pluck up, and to break down, and to throw down, and to destroy, and to afflict; so will I watch over them, to build, and to plant, saith YHWH. ²⁹ In those days they shall say no more, The fathers have eaten a sour grape, and the children's teeth are set on edge. ³⁰ But every one shall die for his own iniquity: every man that eateth the sour grape, his teeth shall be set on edge. ³¹ Behold, the days come, saith YHWH, that I will make a renewed Covenant with the House of Yisrael, and with the House of Yahudah: ³² Not according to the covenant that I made with their fathers in the day that I took them by the hand to bring them out of the land of Egypt; which My covenant they brake, although I was an husband unto them, saith YHWH: ³³ But this shall be the covenant that I will make with the House of Yisrael; After those days, saith YHWH, I will put My Torah in their inward parts, and write it in their hearts; and will be their Elohim, and they shall be My people. ³⁴ And they shall teach no more every man his neighbour, and every man his brother, saying, Know YHWH: for they shall all know Me, from the least of them unto the greatest of them, saith YHWH: for I will forgive their iniquity, and I will remember their sin no more. ³⁵ Thus saith YHWH, which giveth the sun for a light by day, and the ordinances of the moon and of the stars for a light by night, which divideth the sea when the waves thereof roar; YHWH of hosts is His Name: ³⁶ If those ordinances depart from before Me, saith YHWH, then the seed of Yisrael also shall cease from being a nation before me throughout the ages (olam). ³⁷ Thus saith YHWH; If heaven above can be measured, and the foundations of the earth searched out beneath, I will also cast off all the seed of Yisrael for all that they have done, saith YHWH. ³⁸ Behold, the days come, saith YHWH, that the city shall be built to YHWH from the tower of Hananeel unto the gate of the corner. ³⁹ And the measuring line shall yet go forth over against it upon the hill Gareb, and shall compass about to Goath. ⁴⁰ And the whole valley of the dead bodies, and of the ashes, and all the fields unto the brook of Kidron, unto the corner of the horse gate toward the east, shall be set apart unto YHWH; it shall not be plucked up, nor thrown down any more throughout the ages." Yirmeyahu 31:1-40.

So there you have it. This was the work of the Messiah, and it is not yet complete. The Last Supper was a continuation of the process that began from the beginning. A Covenant process to plant and harvest a people for YHWH. The Messiah came to renew the Covenant which the House of Yisrael and the House of Yahudah had broken.

After the Passover meal, Yahushua was later crucified on a stake for 6 hours between the 3rd hour and the 9th hour, which is between 9:00 am to 3:00 pm, after which He gave up His Spirit. Interestingly, this was at the same time that the Temple priests were sacrificing an additional Passover offering called the "Chagigah."

We know that His body was placed in a tomb before sunset, and by His own testimony He would be in Sheol for 3 days and 3 nights. During this time, the High Priest was offering the first (resheet) barley offering to YHWH on Day 16, which was a Friday. Yahushua was still in Sheol, although He was later resurrected after three days and three nights on the weekly Shabbat on Day 17.

Now some try to make the resheet barley offering into a Feast, which it is not. They erroneously call it the Feast of Firstfruits, but the Feast of Firstfruits (bikkurim) is Shabuot. In fact, the time for the people to bring their firstfruits (bikkurim) was between Shabuot and Succot.[164]

Some also try to show that Yahushua was resurrected on the day of the resheet barley offering, which He was not. No matter how you calculate this offering, it did not occur on the weekly Shabbat in the year Yahushua died in 34 CE. However, this fact does not detract from the point that Yahushua is clearly the "first" (resheet) of YHWH. The barley was cut and presented before YHWH on Day 16 of Month 1, and Yahushua rose on Day 17 of Month 1 on the third day of Unleavened Bread in 34 CE.

Yahushua, as the Lamb of YHWH, was cut off in the midst of the week - Wednesday. His blood was shed and His life was removed from His body. He was in the Tomb, "cut

off," while the resheet offering was made, and He was later resurrected on the weekly Shabbat.

We read something very interesting in the New Testament text at the death of Yahushua. "*50 Yahushua when He had cried again with a loud voice, yielded up the Spirit. 51 And, behold, the veil of the Temple was rent in twain from the top to the bottom; and the earth did quake, and the rocks rent; 52 And the graves were opened; and many bodies of the set apart ones which slept arose, 53 And came out of the graves after His resurrection, and went into the Set Apart City, and appeared unto many.*" Mattityahu 27:50-53.

So Yahushua was the resheet, and others were resurrected after Him on the weekly Sabbath on Day 17 of Month 1. Yahushua did this as a sign to all those who believe in Him, that He will raise them up to live with Him in the Sabbath of millennia in the Age of Life. By doing so, He decisively answered the debate of the time concerning the resurrection.

The timing of all of these events was no coincidence. It occurred exactly as planned by a perfect Elohim. It all makes perfect sense if you understand the Feast of Passover along with the special Sabbaths and weekly Sabbaths included within the Festival.

After His resurrection, Yahushua continued to walk on the Earth in His renewed body for 40 days. He ended His ministry as He began. This 40 day period occurred within the omer count. It was the midst of the grain harvest, and it was a perfect bookend to His ministry. He started at the Jordan when the Spirit descended upon Him and He ended at the Mount of Olives, where He ascended into the heavens. As we read from Zechariah, this is also where He will return. (Zechariah 14:4).

Before Yahushua departed, He instructed His followers to stay in Jerusalem (Acts 1:4-5). He gave this instruction because the Feast of Shabuot was soon approaching. On that day, all obedient Yisraelites would gather at the House of YHWH in Jerusalem. This was a memorial of Sinai when the Torah was given to the people. In that particular year, the Spirit fell upon those who belonged to Yahushua - those in His harvest. This was part of the Covenant renewal when YHWH promised to write His Torah on the hearts and minds of His people. (Ezekiel 36:26).

Many years later, Yahushua appeared to Yahanan in a vision. Yahanan found himself transported into the future to Year 6,000 and the Day of YHWH. Yahushua spoke like a "trumpet" and appeared as a menorah. In English translations we read Him saying: "*I am the Alpha and the Omega, the First and the Last.*" (Revelation 1:11). This seems a bit cryptic until we recognize that He was a Hebrew Messiah speaking to a Hebrew disciple, more properly called a "talmid."

Therefore, Yahushua was not saying He was the Greek letter alpha (**A**) and the Greek letter omega (Ω). The letter alpha is the first letter in the Greek alphabet, which equates to the Hebrew aleph (ℵ). The letter omega is the last letter in the Greek alphabet, which equates to the Hebrew taw (✗). Therefore, Yahushua was revealing that He is the Aleph Taw (✗ℵ). He is the beginning and the end of the Hebrew language which was how everything was Created, and He is everything in between. He is the very embodiment of the Torah.

Yahushua also spoke of "living waters" in His ministry which is a veiled reference to immortality. The Hebrew letter representing water is mem (ᵐ). When the mem (ᵐ) is placed between the aleph (ℵ) and the taw (✗), it spells a new word "emet" (✗ᵐℵ) – which means: "truth." Yahushua said that He was the Way, the Truth and the Life. (Yahanan 14:6).

By making this profound statement Yahushua was explaining many mysteries concerning the Aleph Taw (✗ℵ). He is revealing Himself throughout the Torah and demonstrating His presence in the Covenant journey. He is providing for the restoration of Creation through the Torah on the schedule set forth through the Appointed Times.

This was aptly summarized in the following text. "*²⁰ But now Messiah is risen from the dead, and has become the First Fruits of those who have fallen asleep.²¹ For since by man came death, by Man also came the resurrection of the dead. ²² For as in Adam all die, even so in Messiah all shall be made alive. ²³ But each one in his own order: Messiah the First Fruits, afterward those who are Messiah's at His coming. ²⁴ Then comes the end, when He delivers the kingdom to Elohim the Father, when He puts an end to all rule and all authority and power.*" 1 Corinthians 15:20-24.

The word for "first fruits" is "aparche" (ἀπαρχὴ) in the Greek. According to Thayer's Greek Lexicon Strongs number 536 (aparche) is equivalent to the Hebrew resheet - "a beginning of sacrifice." Yahushua as the "first" is gathering together the firstfruits of Yisrael. He is all about the Harvest of "the Planting of El" - am Yisrael. The patterns are all there to see in the Covenant Land and the Covenant People.

Just as Adam was taken out of the ground, he was connected to the planet. His sin affected the very balance of Creation and opened the door for corruption, chaos and destruction. The restoration of Creation also includes the restoration of the earth, and therefore the Covenant people remain connected with the Covenant Land.

Yahushua "fulfilled" the Torah, and He did this through certain Appointed Times, but much remains to be fulfilled. This was made clear through Paul (Shaul) when he declared that the Appointed Times, the New Moons and the Sabbaths are a shadow of things to come. (Colossians 2:16-17) In fact, the early believers were all Hebrews, and were very familiar with the Scriptural calendar, the times and the seasons.

This is why Shaul wrote: "*But concerning the times and the seasons, brethren, you have no need that I should write to you.*" 1 Thessalonians 5:1-2. Whenever the word "seasons" is used, it is typically referring to the Moadim. So Shaul was clearly stating that the Thessalonians did not need any instruction concerning the Appointed Times. They knew them, and were

expecting further fulfillment. Things simply did not happen as quickly as they anticipated. (see I and II Thessalonians).

No matter what your opinion is regarding Shaul, it is clear that he dealt with many controversies within the early Assembly. The fact that he did not deal with calendar issues essentially demonstrates that there was no major discord within the early Assembly on Calendar issues. Also, He continued to keep the Appointed Times and continued to make vows according to the Torah. (see Acts 18:18-21).

Shaul said under oath that he kept the instructions of the Torah. (Acts 24:14-16). In fact, he made it his life's ambition to teach Gentiles to do the same. By all accounts he kept the Appointed Times, and even dated his letters by them. Shaul told people to imitate him as he imitated the Messiah. (1 Corinthians 11:1).[165]

The life of Yahushua revolved around the Appointed Times, and as He lived He revealed the fulfillment of some of those times. Because of that fact, we would expect Him to provide correction if the traditions of the people concerning the Calendar and the Appointed Times were wrong. Yahushua did not rebuke or give specific instruction regarding calendar issues although His actions did speak volumes.

He did not provide instruction or correction regarding the New Moon, which is currently an issue in great dispute. The New Moon was the first crescent - period. Yahushua followed the Torah by observing Passover on Day 14 of Month 1. He also counted the omer from the day after the High Sabbath, from Day 16 of Month 1, just like Mosheh did. (Yahanan 5:46).

Of one thing we can be certain, He will return again, and that return will also revolve around the Appointed Times and their continued fulfillment. Sadly, the Appointed Times have, in large part, been forgotten by much of the world. This happened in the past and it is happening now. *"YHWH has caused the Appointed Times and Sabbaths to be forgotten in Zion."*

Lamentations 2:6.

As a result, those who proclaim to believe in the Messiah fail to understand many of the teachings and actions of the Messiah. His Life and Words must be viewed within the context of the Appointed Times and the Covenant as a whole.

Thankfully, many eyes are being opened to the Appointed Times, and their significance is again being understood. Just as Nehemiah and Ezra read the Torah and discovered that they had not been keeping the Appointed Times, so have many of the elect forgotten their appointments with YHWH, but this is changing as we continue toward the end of days.

15

In the End

At this point, the reader should now understand that time is the arena within which the spiritual and the physical come together. It is the framework within which all of creation exists and functions. Time was created in the beginning as a current to gather the Harvest of YHWH – His Covenant people who will fill His House. Within this framework of time there are weekly Appointed Times and annual Appointed Times.

The weekly seven day cycle began at creation, and has continued ever since. This seven day cycle is completed when the earth has made seven revolutions on its axis. After the passage of six complete days, the weekly Sabbath occurs on the seventh day - from sunset to sunset. Therefore, the moment of sunset determines when each day begins and ends.

There are other Appointed Times that operate on an altogether different cycle. They occur annually and they are reliant upon both the sun and the moon. These annual Appointed Times start with a meal - the Passover. It is followed by The Feast of Unleavened Bread, the Feast of Shabuot, The Day of Blasting, The Day of Atonements and The Feast of Succot. The cycle ends with "the Eighth Day."

There are seven annual Appointed Times and three Pilgrimage Feasts, known as hags, that occur within those seven Appointed Times. Neither the first Appointed Time, on Day 14 of Month 1 nor the last Appointed Time on Day 22 of Month 7 is classified as a Pilgrimage Feast, yet in both

instances, a person would certainly be in the location where YHWH placed His Name. That, of course is where the Pilgrimage Feasts were to occur, at the dwelling place of YHWH. (Debarim 12).

These seven annual Appointed Times occur within a seven month period. They start with a meal followed by a seven day Feast. They are then followed by another Feast which is determined from a count of seven sevens. The seventh month cycle ends with a seven day Feast followed by the eighth day - a new beginning. The pattern of sevens cannot be ignored.

So what do we do with these Appointed Times? The answer to that question depends upon your relationship with YHWH. We have seen that there are some very technical issues with the calendar, and for those who are willing to dig there is great treasure awaiting them. If you were born into Judaism, then you know to follow the Torah of Mosheh, which includes the Appointed Times.

In fact Rabbi Samson Hirsch is known for explaining "The catechism of the Jew consists of his calendar. On the pinions of time which bear us through life, [Elohim] has inscribed the eternal words of His soul – inspiring doctrine, making days and weeks, months and years the heralds to proclaim His truths. Nothing would seem more fleeting than these heralds of time, but to them [Elohim] has entrusted the care of His [set apart] things, thereby rendering them more imperishable and more accessible than any mouth of priest, any monument, temple or altar could have done."[166]

Sadly, Rabbinic tradition and interpretation has often clouded and confused the simplicity of the Torah of Mosheh, and the Messiah which it reveals. Today, adherents of Rabbinic Judaism do not properly understand what it means to be in Covenant with YHWH. They mistakenly believe that their religious system is the exclusive entry point, and conduit, for the Covenant with Yisrael. They have been taught to follow the rabbis and profess belief in Elokim,

Hashem and Adonai. They do not profess belief in Yahushua the Messiah who is YHWH – the image of the invisible Elohim.

They also follow a clearly unscriptural tradition for determining their dates to observe the Appointed Times. Most in Judaism are taught that the Appointed Times are Jewish Holidays, strictly for those of Jewish descent or for those who converted to the religion of Judaism. We have already demonstrated the error of that position.

If you are a Christian then your relationship with YHWH rests upon the shed blood of the Messiah – the Lamb of Elohim. Most Christians understand that the blood provides a covering, and that it was accomplished through the Passover. Typically though, Christians ignore or neglect the fact that Passover is a Covenant meal. You must be in Covenant with YHWH in order to participate in the all important Covenant meal Passover, which most neglect. Indeed, they are supposed to be observing the Passover in remembrance of Yahushua, as He instructed. (Luke 22:19; 1 Corinthians 24-25). So admittedly, they are not identifying with the Elohim of Yisrael – the One Who makes Covenant with His people. In fact, some attempt to replace the Passover with a ritual known as the Eucharist or Communion.

Most Christians are actually taught, and believe, that they are in a new and different Covenant than the one made with Yisrael. This has led many astray because there is no different Covenant, only one renewed through the Messiah. As a result, the majority of Christians, either knowingly or unwittingly, end up rejecting the Torah of YHWH, which includes the Appointed Times that direct the way of the Covenant path.

Christianity has willingly relinquished the Appointed Times to the religion of Judaism, because they think they no longer have any use for them. Christianity has developed its own way of worshipping YHWH, and its own times. By

changing the Appointed Times of YHWH, Christianity has a different sabbath and different feasts, many of which derive from pagan sun worship.[167] This is specifically prohibited in the Scriptures. (Debarim 12:1-4 and 12:32). The bottom line is this: The Appointments that you keep determine whom you serve. If you claim to believe in YHWH, and love Him, then you keep His Commandments. (Proverbs 7:2, Yahanan 14:15; 15:10).

Some put little to no effort into discerning the times, while others diligently seek out the truth. This is the distinction between those who will be considered wise, and those who will be considered foolish. This entire process reveals the heart and level of commitment of those who claim to serve YHWH.

Yahushua gave a very interesting parable about 10 servants - 5 wise and 5 foolish. "¹ Then shall the kingdom of heaven be likened unto ten virgins, which took their lamps, and went forth to meet the Bridegroom. ² And five of them were wise, and five were foolish. ³ They that were foolish took their lamps, and took no oil with them: ⁴ But the wise took oil in their vessels with their lamps. ⁵ While the Bridegroom tarried, they all slumbered and slept. ⁶ And at midnight there was a cry made, Behold, the Bridegroom cometh; go ye out to meet Him. ⁷ Then all those virgins arose, and trimmed their lamps. ⁸ And the foolish said unto the wise, Give us of your oil; for our lamps are gone out. ⁹ But the wise answered, saying, Not so; lest there be not enough for us and you: but go ye rather to them that sell, and buy for yourselves. ¹⁰ And while they went to buy, the Bridegroom came; and they that were ready went in with Him to the marriage: and the door was shut. ¹¹ Afterward came also the other virgins, saying, Master, Master, open to us. ¹² But He answered and said, Verily I say unto you, I know you not. ¹³ Watch therefore, for ye know neither the day nor the hour wherein the Son of Man cometh." Mattityahu 25:1-13.

The virgins represent those waiting for their Groom. They represent those anticipating the return of the Messiah Who is coming for His Bride - Yisrael. There is a wedding on the horizon, and they need to be ready. They are all slumbering and sleeping, and when the cry is given at midnight they will all arise and trim their lamps. All the virgins are expecting Him, but the foolish virgins will not be prepared. When the Groom comes, the foolish virgins were "off shopping." Their preparations were too late. They missed their opportunity to join the wedding Feast, and they were shut out.

They were not permitted into the Feast because the Bridegroom does not know, and will not recognize, anyone working lawlessness (ἀνομίαν) or unrighteousness (ἀδικίας). (see Mattityahu 7:23; Luke 13:27). These are people who are not observing the Torah, and violating the Instructions.

We have already discussed the marriage aspect of the Covenant, and the entire process is to lead us to the House of YHWH, so that we can enter into relationship and dwell with Him. You must be known by the Master, which means your name must be written in His Scroll. Those in His Scroll are those in the Covenant - those who have been covered by the blood and obey the Commandments. They will be remembered by YHWH.

You need to have enough oil so that you have light - so that you can see in the darkness. The Scriptures clearly indicate that the Torah is a Lamp. *"Thy Word is a lamp unto my feet, and a light unto my path."* Tehillim 119:105. *"For the commandment is a lamp; and the Torah is light; and reproofs of instruction are the way of life."* Proverbs 6:23. *"The light of the righteous rejoiceth: but the lamp of the wicked shall be put out."* Proverbs 13:9. The Scriptures clearly define the righteous as those who obey the commandments, and the wicked as those who do not obey the commandments.

The five wise virgins are the firstfruits of the harvest. *"These are they which were not defiled with women; for they are virgins. These are they which follow the Lamb whithersoever He goeth. These were redeemed from among men, being the firstfruits unto Elohim and to the Lamb."* Revelation 14:4. If you want to be

ready for the Master's return then you had better not delay. You need to prepare and make sure that your lamps are lit and full of oil. That involves knowing the Word of YHWH, and keeping the instructions found in the Torah.

Those in Covenant receive the blessings of the shed blood of Messiah, and are cleansed from the past adultery of Yisrael. They are "virgins" ready for the Wedding Feast. (Yirmeyahu 31). Those who have oil are those who are walking in righteousness and obeying the Torah, which includes the Appointed Times. The Appointed Times will be a guide through darkness and judgment, just as they were for Yisrael when they were enslaved in Egypt. Those who keep the Appointed Times will be ready for the Master's arrival.

The Appointed Times clearly reveal the Covenant path, and as we saw with Yisrael in Egypt, the Passover is the beginning of that path. Those who desire to journey on that Covenant path must first be in the Covenant. They must bear the sign of the Covenant – circumcision.

Once in that Covenant they must enter the house through the door, which is covered by the blood of the Lamb. As they partake of the Covenant meal, and eat of the lamb whose blood was shed, they are acknowledging that the firstborn require the protection of the lamb. This of course is symbolic of the Lamb of Elohim, the Messiah. The First (Resheet) of YHWH died so that the firstborn of Yisrael might live on the Passover.

That Appointment revealed that the son of YHWH, the Lamb of Elohim, was the fulfillment of the pattern of the Passover Lamb. While the religion of Christianity essentially understands this fulfillment by the Messiah, they fail to understand the relevance and significance of all of the Appointed Times. They have been taught that they are in a "New Covenant," something different from the Covenant described within the Tanak – the Torah, the Prophets and the Writings. This is simply not true. Both Judaism and Christianity have developed traditions about the Torah, and the Appointed Times which distract many from the true meaning.

Once we partake of the Covenant meal, we are delivered and are given a Sabbath rest. Following that Sabbath, the Priest would cut a sheaf of barley, and specific provision was made for presenting unripened barley. The reason being that this was an early resheet (first or beginning) offering made by the Priest. This offering was quantified by a single omer. This did not involve everyone bringing the firstfruits from their individual crops, that would come later at the actual Feast of Firstfruits – the Feast of Weeks - Shabuot.

This resheet offering was the first cutting of the harvest waved by the Priest on behalf of the people on Day 16 of Month 1. It then began a count of seven sevens, or rather seven weeks, which is why the Scriptures call it the Feast of Weeks. During this period of time the people were harvesting their grain: first the barley and then the wheat. Toward the end of the wheat harvest, on the 50th day, the people gathered at the House and presented their bikkurim - the firstfruits of their crops. Through this act, they were really presenting themselves as firstfruits.

This 50th day, called Shabuot (weeks), is connected to the Feast of Unleavened Bread through the counting of weeks and days. Due to this connection, it is often considered the "atzeret" of Passover, although the Scriptures never describe it as such. The combined barley and wheat harvest involved grain crops that needed to be separated from weeds (tares), which grew among them. After the separation, the grains are threshed and winnowed and placed in a barn. Once the grain is secured, the tares are then destroyed by fire. How appropriate that the people would come with their harvest offerings to the House of YHWH built on a threshing floor. (see 2 Shemuel 24:24-25). The symbolism cannot be ignored.

Of course, Yahushua often taught in parables which would expound upon the meaning of the times. "[24] *Another* parable put He forth unto them, saying, The Kingdom of Heaven is likened unto a man which sowed good seed in his field: [25] But while men slept, his enemy came and sowed tares among the wheat, and went his way. [26] But when the blade was sprung up, and brought forth fruit, then appeared the tares also. [27] So the servants of the householder came and said unto him, Sir, didst not thou sow good seed in thy field? From whence then hath it tares? [28] He said unto them, An enemy hath done this. The servants said unto him, Wilt thou then that we go and gather them up? [29] But he said, Nay; lest while ye gather up the tares, ye root up also the wheat with them. [30] Let both grow together until the harvest: and in the time of harvest I will say to the reapers, Gather ye together first the tares, and bind them in bundles to burn them: but gather the wheat into my barn." Mattityahu 13:24-30.

This is one of many parables that Yahushua used relative to the agriculture and harvest season, which was at the heart of the Appointed Times. Remember that not all of the Appointed Times are designated as Feasts. There are instances when we observe a time in our homes, and there are instances when we go up to the mountain of the House of YHWH and celebrate a Hag - a Feast. The Feasts involve a space and time event at the House of YHWH, and they are specifically coordinated around the harvest of crops in the Covenant Land. These Hags are when the Harvest of the Master is gathered to Him.

The patterns of the Covenant Land are meant to symbolize the spiritual teaching, and plan of YHWH for His Covenant people. All of the patterns are applicable to our spiritual walk. Indeed, Yisrael is referred to as "trees of righteousness, the planting of YHWH." Yeshayahu 61:3. Therefore, those in the Covenant, the people of Yisrael, should be bearing good fruit which they can present to YHWH at His House.

We can see this in the progression of the crops as they begin as seeds. Some seeds are good while others are bad. The seeds planted fall upon various types of ground. Yahushua showed this in a parable. Some seed falls on good ground and produce a great yield, while others fall on bad soil and produce less. There are also weeds, known as tares, which grow up with the good seed. In the end they will all be separated. (See Mattityahu 13).

So the first omer offering made during Unleavened Bread began the grain harvest, and it was presented without yeast. It was pure and represented the Messiah as the First (Resheet) offering of the Harvest of YHWH. Messiah, of course, was the First, and as the Lamb of Elohim, His blood covers the house, saves the firstborn from death and makes way for the adoption of the firstborn of Yisrael, represented by the Levites. The firstborn are then able to enter into the House, partake of the meal and join into the wedding celebration.

The seven weeks are then counted when the people are harvesting their crops. The harvest season culminates with the 50th day when the people gather together at the House of YHWH to celebrate the Feast of Weeks. This is the harvest of YHWH. This process is revealing one aspect of the Covenant plan, when YHWH would gather His people to thresh and sift them.

Of course, the fact that it occurs on the 50th day then connects us to the 50th year - the Jubilee. For the Appointed Times in seven months give us a reduced picture of much larger cycles of righteousness operating in Elohim's universe. The weekly Sabbath is a miniature rehearsal of the Sabbath Year and the seventh millennium. The 50 day omer count, counting 7 weeks and one day, are a miniature rehearsal of the 50 year Jubilee Cycle. The 50 year Jubilee Cycle consists of seven Shemitah cycles, each containing seven years, followed by one Jubilee Year.

The cycles of seven are highly prominent in Elohim's economy, from the seventh hour (Yahanan 4:52), to the seventh day, seventh week, seventh month, seventh year, seventh Shemitah cycle and the seventh millennium. The New Moons are also special to Elohim.

The New Moon of Month 7 is unique in that it is a New Moon and a High Sabbath – no matter what day of the week it falls on. It is marked by blasting and calls us to repentance. We then count 10 days until Yom Kippurim, the Day of Atonements. Those who are covered by the blood are atoned, and those who are not covered receive no atonement.

Those who receive atonement proceed to the Feast of Ingathering. Instead of grain, now the harvest is fruit. This occurs at the end of the harvest - the end of days. This is aptly described in the Book of Revelation.

"14 *I looked, and there before me was a white cloud, and seated on the cloud was One 'like a Son of Man' with a crown of gold on His head and a sharp sickle in His hand.* 15 *Then another messenger came out of the Hekal and called in a loud voice to him who was sitting on the cloud, 'Take your sickle and reap, because the time to reap has come, for the harvest of the earth is ripe.'* 16 *So he who was seated on the cloud swung his sickle over the earth, and the earth was harvested.* 17 *Another messenger came out of the Hekal in heaven, and he too had a sharp sickle.* 18 *Still another messenger, who had charge of the fire, came from the Altar and called in a loud voice to him who had the sharp sickle, 'Take your sharp sickle and gather the clusters of grapes from the earth's vine, because its grapes are ripe.'* 19 *The messenger swung his sickle on the earth, gathered its grapes and threw them into the great winepress of Elohim's wrath.* 20 *They were trampled in the winepress outside the city, and blood flowed out of the press, rising as high as the horses' bridles for a distance of 1,600 stadia.*" Revelation 14:14-20.

According to this passage it becomes quite apparent that the earth will be harvested around Sukkot – The Feast of Ingathering. So during the final Sabbath month during the 120th Jubilee, the Final Blast will sound and the earth will be harvested. The firstfruits of the Covenant will be gathered to dwell with YHWH.[168] The grapes will be thrown into the winepress of Elohim's wrath.

So this process of harvesting over the course of seven months, within the framework of seven Appointed Times, involving seven Sabbaths and culminating with the eighth day is the context for the entire Covenant process involving the people of YHWH. If you are in a Covenant relationship with YHWH, then you should keep the Commandments. Those commandments include the Appointed Times. We keep (shamar) them by watching over, protecting and guarding these times because they are our guide back to Eden.

We know how to calculate those times according to the Creator's Calendar and as we determine the times, we proclaim them. As we keep and proclaim the Times we are participating in rehearsals that will affect our future. The prophets foretold an exciting future for the Covenant people known as "am Yisrael."

This divided people will soon be reunited and there will be a deliverance involving the Appointed Times. The patterns of the past are there for future generations to learn from. (1 Corinthians 10:1-11). As we observe these Appointments we are actually rehearsing our futures.

With that in mind, the importance of discerning the times cannot be emphasized enough. Yahushua repeatedly warned His followers to watch.[169] When He approached Jerusalem before His crucifixion, He wept because the people failed to discern the times. (Luke 19:41-44). They failed to recognize Him, and they were blinded concerning their impending doom. Many were killed when Jerusalem and the Hekal were destroyed in 70 CE.

Today I hear people proclaim that, "we cannot keep the Appointed Times because there is no Temple." What they fail to recognize is that the Appointed Times are not simply about sacrifices. They are about meeting with the Creator at a specific time and place – both of which can be determined and "kept" (shamar) without a Temple. And for those not living in the land of Israel, those who are scattered throughout the world, it is still possible to meet with YHWH at the right time wherever you live. This will insure that when the rehearsal becomes a reality, you will be found watching, prepared and ready – like a wise virgin.

YHWH has stated many times that He does not desire the blood of sacrifices. "*For I desire mercy and not sacrifice, and the knowledge of Elohim more than burnt offerings.*" Hoshea 6:6. The offerings and sacrifices presented during the Appointed Times were meant to instruct us, but the Appointed Times are not dependent upon the shedding of blood or the presentation of offerings. As we saw at Sinai, there were no sacrifices specified for the 3 Pilgrimage Feasts when they were first described.

YHWH wants His Covenant people to be living offerings. "*¹ O Yisrael, return to YHWH your Elohim, for you have stumbled by your crookedness. ² Take words with you, and return to YHWH. Say to Him, Take away all crookedness and accept the bulls of our lips.*" Hoshea 14:1-2. "*¹⁰ Thus says YHWH: Again there shall be heard in this place—of which you say, It is desolate, without man and without beast in the cities of Yahudah, in the streets of Jerusalem that are desolate, without man and without inhabitant and without beast, ¹¹ the voice of joy and the voice of gladness, the voice of the bridegroom and the voice of the bride, the voice of those who will say: 'Praise YHWH of hosts, for YHWH is good, for His mercy endures forever' and of those who will bring the sacrifice of praise into the House of YHWH. For I will cause the captives of the land to return as at the first, says YHWH.*" Yirmeyahu 33:10-11. (see also Hebrews 13:15).

As we approach the end of days, the m'qetz yomim, it is vitally important to discern the times. Through the Appointed Times, YHWH has provided the outline for His plan. Those Times were established from the beginning, and are there to guide the Covenant people in the end and to the end.

"*³ Hearken unto Me, O House of Yaakob, and all the remnant of the House of Yisrael, which are borne by Me from the belly, which are carried from the womb . . . ⁹ Remember the former things of old: for I am Elohim, and there is none else; I am Elohim, and there is none like Me, ¹⁰ Declaring the end from the beginning, and from ancient times the things that are not yet done, saying, My counsel shall stand, and I will do all My pleasure.*" Yeshayahu

46:3, 9-10.

Hopefully the reader is now ready to view history and the future in a new light, recognizing that YHWH operates His Plan according to His Calendar. He is precise, never late, and always on time – His time. History is not simply a progression of random occurrences, but rather a pattern of events that fall perfectly and exactly when planned.

As such, the Appointed Times are not simply historical events from days gone by. They are special rehearsals in the plan of YHWH, which lead up to a crescendo at the end of the age. In fact, it can be safely stated that the Appointed Times are more important today than ever before as we approach the end of days.

Remember that the mathematical value of the word "moad" is 120. We saw that the time of mortal man is 120 Jubilee cycles. In fact, Mosheh was 120 years old when he died at the threshold of the Covenant Land – at the door so to speak. So the moad are essentially the framework for mortal man's time upon this earth. After 120 Jubilee cycles, the Redeemed of YHWH will be granted immortality. The moad are the references in time that make up the framework of how YHWH operates during those 120 cycles and beyond. The moad lead us to the door of the House, where we rely upon the Messiah to gain entrance.

"For the vision is yet for an Appointed Time, but at the end it shall speak, and not lie: though it tarry, wait for it; because it will surely come, it will not tarry." Habakkuk 2:3. With this understanding it is imperative for all who claim to be in Covenant with YHWH, to walk within the Covenant Appointments. This is how we synchronize our lives with the plan of YHWH. When we observe the Appointed Times, we can know with certainty that we are doing the will of YHWH, and we will be "in the right place at the right time."

It could mean the difference between life and death in the future. Just as the Yisraelites in Egypt needed to precisely follow the commandments concerning the Passover in order to be spared from death - those same commandments will prove critical in the end, but we need to watch. If the Children of Yisrael had not diligently obeyed the commandments concerning the Passover in Egypt, their firstborn would have perished. The same will be true in the end. Those who are not watching, those who are not wise, those who do not have sufficient oil in their lamps will find themselves in darkness, shut out of the House and the Feast occurring therein.

Yahushua Himself warned: *"Remember therefore how thou hast received and didst hear; and keep it, and repent. If therefore thou shalt not watch, I will come as a thief, and thou shalt not know what hour I will come upon thee."* Revelation 3:3. In other words, if we do not watch we will be surprised, but if we watch we will not be surprised.

Within the Appointed Times we have a pattern for all time. We see that the Creator established the pattern for His universe by creating it in six days and resting on the seventh. This cycle which, He started in the beginning continues to this very day. Within and along side of this continuous seven day cycle we have Feasts that occur at three times each year. Within the first and the seventh month we see seven day feasts. In the months between these seven day feasts we see a seven week count leading to Shabuot, a one day Feast.

This seven week count that occurs every year points to the seven Shemitah Year, or Sabbath Year, count that leads to the Jubilee. Ultimately, we see this pattern stretched out to 7 millennium, patterned from the seven day week created in the beginning.

The existence of a Hekal does not control the calendar. Time continues without a physical Hekal on the planet Earth. As long as the sun and the moon continue in their courses we can still calculate the passage of time. The sun and the moon control the calendar. The Moadim still occur at their Appointed Times. Indeed, the very pattern of the original Tabernacle revealed that the people of Yisrael will be the Hekal – the House. Also, remember that the word for "keep" is shamar (ᐤᗰᗯ) in Hebrew which means: "watch, guard and protect." As we observe the Calendar and rehearse the times we are, in fact, "keeping" them as living Tabernacles.

Jerusalem is still at the heart of the Covenant Land. There were periods in the past when there was no standing Tabernacle or Hekal, but things were rebuilt and restored. We are currently in a period of restoration which makes the Appointed Times especially important. Also, it is vital to recognize that while there is no Hekal, no Priesthood and no Altar, individuals have obligations separate and apart from the Temple service. While I may not be a Levite priest, I can still go to the place YHWH established at the right time and meet with Him.[170] In fact, as living Tabernacles, when we join together at the Appointed Times we see the House being rebuilt. This is one of the pictures provided through Succot.

The Appointed Times were always rehearsals meant to teach us the Covenant path. While there may not be a standing Hekal in Jerusalem, we can still rehearse the times, and seek out the meanings contained within them.

In fact, we live them out so that we can understand the Covenant plan, and so that we can be in a place where He wants us to be. These Appointed Times synchronize our lives with the Creator. The cycle is like a calibrating tool or tuning instrument. We meet with YHWH on Shabbat and at the Appointed Times, and He places His tuning fork on us to check whether we are operating on His frequencies.[171] The Appointed Times are meant to align and unify us - they also identify us. There is only one Covenant people - Yisrael, and there is only one Calendar for the Covenant people.

In the end, your life is in your hands, and it is your responsibility to work out your salvation with fear and trembling (Philippians 2:12). You cannot delegate this responsibility to your parents, or your spouse or to some other person that you hold in high esteem. It is your choice whether to enter into covenant with YHWH through the blood of the Lamb of Elohim. The only one who will be holding your hand on judgment day is an angel sent by the Son of Man (Matthew 24:31, Mark 13:27) – if you are keeping the commandments of Elohim and believe in Yahushua the Messiah. (Revelation 14:12). The Messiah was very straight forward on this issue. *"He who believes and is immersed will be saved; but he who does not believe will be damned."* Mark 16:16

It should be noted here that in Hebraic thought, belief is always linked with obedience. Although the Christian religion teaches that your salvation is assured if you believe the Messiah, but disobey Him, this is simply not the case according to the Messiah. *"You are My friends if you do whatever I command you."* Yahanan 15:14. *"He who believes in the Son has eternal life; and he who does not obey the Son shall not see life, but the wrath of Elohim abides on him."* Yahanan 3:36. So it all comes down to what you believe about the Messiah – do you believe His words? Do you believe He is the image of the invisible Elohim (Colossians 1:15) who does not change (Malachi 3:6) and does not lie (Hebrews 6:18)?

Do you believe that Elohim would send a prophet like Mosheh (Debarim 18:15-19), and that He will *destroy* anyone who will not hear Yahushua (Acts 3:22-23)? Yahushua said, *"I am the way, the Truth and the Life, no man comes to the Father but by Me."* Yahanan 16:6. Do you believe Yahushua when He said, *"If you have seen Me you have seen the Father."* (Yahanan 14:9)?

If you believe in YHWH, you will come into Covenant with Him, and if you do not believe in YHWH, you will not come into Covenant with Him. Many people think that keeping the Appointed Times on the correct calendar is a relatively minor issue. However, Yahushua said that the way to life is narrow, hard pressed and difficult, and few people find it. (Mattityahu 7:14).

Some do not think that the proper observance of the Appointed Times is a matter that could affect a person's salvation, and that whether one observes New Moons and Sabbaths is of little consequence. However, the spiritual journey into the Covenant that will result in admission into the House most definitely involves the proper observance of Appointed Times, New Moons and Sabbaths (Revelation 22:14-15). For it is the Appointed Times that mark the path on a person's spiritual journey. That is why New Moons and Sabbaths are integral to the worship of YHWH according to YHWH. (Yeshayahu 66:23).

Yahushua said before He left that many would come in His Name, saying He was the Messiah, but would deceive many. (Mattityahu 24:5, 24:11, Mark 13:6). The Christian religion fulfills this prophecy perfectly, for it admits that the Yahushua spoken of in Mattityahu, Mark, Luke and Yahanan is the Messiah. However, Christianity deceives many into thinking that *obedience* to the covenant is *unnecessary*, even *detrimental*, to obtaining eternal life – when nothing could be further from the truth.

Yahushua prophesied that at this time in history, there would be those who would deceive the very elect (Mattityahu 24:24). The elect are the Covenant people of Yisrael – how could they be deceived? In fact, there are some sincere people today, who desire to be in Covenant with YHWH, but who are not observing the Appointed Times.

Some fail to observe the Appointed Times because they think they are irrelevant. Others, who think they are relevant, question whether the sun and moon were made for Appointed Times. (Beresheet 1:14), or whether the moon really is a faithful witness in heaven. (Psalm 89:37).

They are ignorant of how the Covenant people of Yisrael observed the Appointed Times of YHWH in the past, and are therefore led about by every wind of doctrine and false teaching of men in the present. (Ephesians 4:11-14). And so many sincere people are today being deceived on the issue of when to observe the Appointed Times – but this must be, for Yahushua said it would happen. (Mattityahu

24:25).

Peter prophesied that the heavens will release Yahushua the Messiah at the restoration of all things – in a Jubilee Year. (Acts 3:21). YHWH revealed through Noah that this would be in Jubilee Year 120 (Beresheet 6:3), so the Covenant people of Yisrael should be expecting the Messiah's return soon. And as His return is intimately connected with the Appointed Times, the Appointed Times of YHWH become of paramount importance.

YHWH is in the process of building a spiritual nation – a nation that will be led by the Spirit of Elohim – the Spirit of YHWH – the Spirit of Yahushua the Messiah. Revelation 19:10 proclaims: *"Worship Elohim! For the testimony of Yahushua is the Spirit of prophecy."* It is time for the Covenant people of Yisrael to properly observe the Appointed Times of YHWH, and to come to grips with the way YHWH reckons time. For only in doing so, will Yisrael understand her past, and in turn fulfill her destiny.

The river of time that was referred to at the beginning is soon approaching the end of its journey – the end of an age. The river that sprang from the Garden flows back to the garden, the New Jerusalem. The New Jerusalem, better known as the Renewed Jerusalem contains a river. The Scriptures begin with a river, and end with a river - the River of Life.

The Appointed Times chart our course back to the Garden where only one river flows. To properly navigate our passage on this river, YHWH provided us with the Torah which acts as a lighthouse, channel markers and warning beacons. It keeps us on course, on the way to life.

Contained within the Torah are the instructions concerning Appointed Times which act as currents in the cycles of time. These cycles of righteousness continue from the beginning to the end, and are there for our benefit. (Psalm 23:3). They are ports of harbor along our journey where we are able to rest, refresh, resupply and fellowship with YHWH. They help to correct our course and keep us from the shallows, the rocks, the winds and the waves that would send us into harms way.

If you were suffering from a terminal disease and had an appointment with a physician who had the cure for your ailment, I do not suspect that you would miss that appointment or take it lightly. You would not try to change the appointment or send someone else in your place. You would want to meet personally with the physician, and spend a lot of time with him. You would be serious about this appointment with anxious anticipation, and probably be there early.

Even more importantly, we have appointments with our Creator, the One Who breathed life into us, the One Who gives us life and redeems us from death - the One Who can truly heal us body, soul and spirit. With that in mind, we should keep His Appointed Times which are regular appointments that YHWH has made with His people. They are meant to bless and heal us, to teach us and help prepare us for everlasting life.

What a privilege to participate in this process. Sadly, while YHWH always faithfully keeps His Appointments, all too often His people are no shows. We are expected to know these times, and observe these appointments so that we are walking in the light of His perfect will and plan. Once we become aware of the need to walk in the Appointed Times, the question is whether we will keep (shamar) them. Many find excuses not to observe the Appointed Times, raising issues such as the need for a Priesthood, or the presence of a Temple.

These arguments miss the point altogether. While there were clearly rituals and sacrifices that Yisrael was to follow once in the Covenant Land, Yisrael has not been restored from their punishment and exile. We are essentially coming out of a period of bondage likened to the time of the Passover in Egypt. Just as it was critical to meticulously

observe the Passover at the right time then, the same holds true now. Thankfully, if you are reading this book you have fair warning. It is time to get in synchronicity with the Calendar before it is too late.

This book is by no means an exhaustive analysis of the Appointed Times. That was not the purpose. The goal is to highlight the importance of the Appointed Times for those in Covenant with YHWH. The Moadim had significance in the past, and they have continuing relevance to the present and future. They are not just interesting historical events, they are a treasure map that guides us back to paradise.

Hopefully, the reader will understand the need to step into synchronicity with the plan of YHWH as it plays out through His Appointed Times. It may seem foreign at first, especially when you start discerning tradition from Scriptural commandments. This is to be expected, and it is part of the process where we learn to meet with YHWH and learn His ways. Just as a newborn learns to crawl before it can walk, the same holds true as we are "born again" into the Covenant, and begin to traverse the Covenant journey back to the Garden.

The point at first is simply obedience. We may not always know why we are required to do things, but that is exactly why we must obey. Through our continuous obedience, we begin to learn and understand the purpose of these rehearsals. There will be a time when they will no longer be rehearsals. Just as Yisrael once journeyed from slavery to freedom, protected from the judgments of YHWH, there will be a time in the future when Yisrael, the Covenant people, will be gathered and delivered through their diligent obedience to these rehearsals.

The Appointed Times must be examined within the context of the Covenant. They are Times established by YHWH to perfect and establish His Covenant. If you are a part of His Covenant then you must understand the Moadim – The Appointed Times.

Endnotes

¹ Time is often described as a physical dimension. Just as height, length and width constitute the dimensions of our three dimensional physical world, so time is another dimension in the world as we know it.

² While we often think of time as a straight line from point A to point B, or from the beginning to the end, time is much more than just the passage of seconds, minutes or hours. It permeates all aspects of the physical realm and cannot be simply measured on a clock. This typifies the western mentality of viewing matters in a linear sense. To truly understand time from the perspective of the Creator, one must learn to view time from a cyclical perspective, because that is how creation flows. Our physical existence is contained within the dimension of time, while the Creator exists both within and without the Created dimension of time.

³ *Philosophiae Naturalis Principia Mathematica*

⁴ en.wikipedia.org/wiki/Time

⁵ See Bureau International des Poids Mesureswikide, www.bipm.org.

⁶ Evolution has been debunked many times over but it continues to be promoted as truth by those who desperately desire to live a life free from the One Who created them. This is not a treatise on evolution, but the reader is encouraged to seek out the abundant evidence disproving the notion of evolution.

⁷ There are ample studies which reveal on numerous levels the statistical impossibility of evolution, as well as the Big Bang Theory, neither of which can even explain the existence of the matter or energy which are required for their theories of chaos to result in the order that we observe in the universe. See *Evolution: Possible or Impossible?* by James F. Coppedge, Zondervan 1976.

⁸ "Occam's razor" *Merriam-Webster's Collegiate Dictionary* (11th ed.). New York: Merriam-Webster. 2003. ISBN 0-87779-809-5.

⁹ The NESS » The Razor in the Toolbox see Wikipedia.

¹⁰ The term "god" is a generic term which can be attached to any number of powerful beings described in mythology and worshipped in pagan religions. Some use a capital "G" to refer to "the God of the Bible" but I find it a disservice to apply this label to the Creator of the Universe when the Hebrew Scriptures clearly refer to Him as Elohim. The pagan origins of the word "god" are discussed in the Walk in the Light series book entitled

"Names." Elohim ($ᄊᄼᄊᄼ$) is technically plural, but that does not designate more than one Creator. The singular form is El ($ᄼ$) and could refer to any "mighty one," but because the plural is used to describe the Creator, it means that Elohim is qualitatively stronger or more powerful than any singular El ($ᄼ$). In Hebrew, the plural form can mean that something or someone is qualitatively greater not just quantitatively greater. We see in the first sentence of the Scriptures that "In the Beginning Elohim created." The Hebrew for "created" is "bara" ($ᄼᄊᄼ$) which literally is "He created." It is masculine singular showing that while Elohim is plural He is masculine singular. For an excellent discussion of the Hebrew Etymology of the Name of Elohim I recommend *His Name is One* written by Jeff A. Benner, Virtualbookworm.com Publishing 2002. The Hebrew language currently in use, often called modern Hebrew, is not the language used when the Scriptures were first spoken and written. The original Hebrew language is often called "ancient" or "paleo" Hebrew.

[11] There are many different Ancient Hebrew scripts discovered through archaeology. Since they were all written by different individuals there are stylistic variances between them. The modern Hebrew used today is not the same language as the Ancient or Paleo Hebrew used by Ancient Yisrael. Therefore, throughout this text we will attempt to provide examples of words and phrases in their Ancient Script in order to glean the depth of their meaning.

[12] The Paleo Hebrew font primarily used in this book is an adaptation and interpretation of the various examples of Paleo Hebrew found throughout archaeology. Since there are a variety of scripts found in academia, this one script font developed by the author is being used for consistency and clarity in an attempt to represent the Creator's meaning in the "original" language.

[13] It is important to recognize that there is no such thing as a Hebrew numeral set, separate and apart from the Hebrew letters. As a result, each Hebrew character has a corresponding numeric value. This adds an interesting dimension to the study of Scriptures. Commonly called gematria, the study of the numeric values of characters and words can be quite revealing.

[14] The Hebrew Scriptures contain numerous instances of what are commonly called jots and tittles. These typically include enlarged, diminished or reversed characters intended to draw the readers attention to something. No one knows exactly how they came into existence, although the popular opinion is that Mosheh included them in the original Torah. One thing is certain, they

are not considered to be scribal errors and they have been maintained in all copies of the Hebrew texts, although you will not see them in a translation.

As discussed in Footnote 12, there are a variety of examples of the Ancient Hebrew Script. The author has developed a Font intended to represent the ancient language as might have been written by an individual person thousands of years ago.

The word et (×ᵝ), otherwise known as the Aleph Taw, consists of two Hebrew characters - the aleph (ᵝ) which is the first character in the Hebrew alphabet, and the taw (×) which is the last letter in the Hebrew alphabet. "This word ×ᵝ is used over 11,000 times (and never translated into English as there is no equivalent) to point to the direct object of the verb." (from Benner, Jeff A., *Learn to Read Biblical Hebrew*, Virtualbookworm.com 2004 Page 41.). It is embedded throughout the Hebrew Scriptures and while it has a known grammatical function, the Sages have long understood that it has a much deeper and mysterious function – many believe that it is a direct reference to the Messiah. As such, it plays an important part in understanding the Scriptural Covenants so we will, at times, examine its existence and relevance throughout this text.

To view exactly where we are in time visit www.torahcalendar.com

It is well established that every person needs sleep, and that a person needs darkness to allow the body to create melatonin and human Growth Hormone. The body requires sound sleep to heal, and the failure to get enough sleep under the proper conditions can be very damaging to health - both mental and physical.

The Kabbalists say that the world was created by the letters of the alphabet (Aleph Bet), meaning through the use of sound and vibration. The **Hebrew Scriptures** embody the very sound of creation, the vibrations that actually were used to create and manifest. Therefore words are "creative," and if they are creative they can also be destructive. This is why the spoken word is so important, particularly the Scriptures spoken in the pure language in which they were originally written.

YHWH (ᴴᴵᵂᵞ) is the four letter Name of the Elohim described in the Scriptures. This four letter Name has commonly been called the "Tetragrammaton" and traditionally has been considered to be ineffable or unpronounceable. As a result, despite the fact that it is found nearly 7,000 times in the Hebrew Scriptures, it has been replaced with such titles as "The Lord," "Adonai" and "HaShem." I believe that this practice is in direct violation of the First and Third Commandments. Some commonly accepted pronunciations are: Yahweh, Yahuwah and Yahowah. Since there is debate over which pronunciation is correct, I simply use the Name as it is found in the Scriptures, although I spell it in English from left to right, rather than in Hebrew from right to left. For the person who truly desires to know the nature of the Elohim described in the Scriptures, a good place to start is the Name by which He revealed Himself to all mankind.

21 The word "Bible" has traditionally been the word used to describe the collection of documents considered by Christianity to be inspired by Elohim - I prefer the use of the word Scriptures. The word Bible derives from Byblos which has more pagan connotations than I prefer, especially when referring to the written Word of Elohim. This subject is discussed in greater detail in the Walk in the Light Series book entitled *Scriptures*.

22 It is important to recognize that some things get "lost in translation." This is particularly true when translating from an eastern language to a western language. This does not mean that the Word of Elohim is not perfect. We are talking about imperfect men translating words from one language to another while attempting to maintain their complete power and meaning. For a detailed discussion of this matter read the Walk in the Light series book entitled *Scriptures*.

23 Anyone who is familiar with the Modern Hebrew language might notice that there are no sofits in the Paleo Hebrew used. In Modern Hebrew certain characters have a different "final form" than their regular usage. For instance the word for darkness "choshech" appears as ᚻwᚻ in the Ancient Hebrew, and חשך in Modern Hebrew. In the Modern Hebrew the chet (ח) at the beginning looks different from the chet sofit (ך). This is not the case in the Ancient language where the chet (ᚻ) looks the same no matter where it is located.

24 Picture of Black Hole from wikimedia.org

25 Interestingly, this was also done after Noah and the Flood. It was a new beginning - a new day for mankind and creation. (Beresheet 8:5, 8:13). In the Shema, YHWH is described as Echad (See Appendix D).

26 There are many ways that people reckon days, but the Scriptures provide that a day begins in the evening. Therefore, for the purposes of The Appointed Times, they are always reckoned beginning at evening.

27 One cannot ignore the parallels with the book of Revelation where there are 144 thousand and 24 elders before the throne to YHWH Echad. It appears that time was fashioned to reveal the

Kingdom of YHWH. This will be discussed further in the Walk in the Light series book entitled *The Final Shofar*.

28 See en.wikipedia.org/wiki/Planck_time.

29 "Pardes refers to (types of) approaches to biblical exegesis in rabbinic Judaism (or - simpler - interpretation of text in Torah study). The term, sometimes also spelled PaRDeS, is an acronym formed from the name initials of the following four approaches: Peshat (פְּשָׁט) — "plain" ("simple") or the direct meaning[1]. Remez (רֶמֶז) — "hints" or the deep (allegoric: hidden or symbolic) meaning beyond just the literal sense. Derash (דְּרַשׁ) — from Hebrew *darash*: "inquire" ("seek") — the comparative (midrashic) meaning, as given through similar occurrences. Sod (סוֹד) (pronounced with a long O as in 'bone') — "secret" ("mystery") or the mystical meaning, as given through inspiration or revelation." en.wikipedia.org/wiki/Pardes_(Jewish_exegesis).

30 This likely is revealing the Covenant between the day and night mentioned in Jeremiah. It also seems to show the Arm of YHWH working from within the house and then progressing through the door and leaving the house to shepherd His flock. Again, this happened on the fourth day, the fourth millennium when Yahushua the Messiah appeared. See the Walk in the Light Series book entitled *The Messiah*.

31 December 25 used to be the summer solstice and thus the day when sun worshippers would celebrate the "rebirth" of the sun. It is a day traditionally associated with the birth of sun gods throughout the planet. For a further discussion of this matter see the Walk in the Light series books entitled *Restoration* and *Pagan Holidays*.

32 Sadly, Christianity, which claims to follow the teachings of the Messiah of Yisrael has adopted the pagan celebration of the christ mass "Christmas" as the date of the birth of their messiah. The Messiah of Yisrael was not born on December 25. For a further discussion of this matter see the Walk in the Light series books entitled *Restoration, The Messiah* and *Pagan Holidays*.

33 The term "Jewish" can have a variety of interpretations. A person can be considered "Jewish" if they subscribe to the religion of Judaism. A person can also consider themselves to be Jewish if they can trace their lineage to a Jewish mother. A person can be of Jewish ancestry without subscribing to any form of Judaism.

34 According to Chuck Missler of Khouse, there is something profoundly special about this single occurrence that can only be seen using Equidistant Letter Sequencing, also known as EDLS.

It has been said that using EDLS you would statistically expect to find the word moadim couched within Beresheet 5 times. Instead, only once at an interval of 70, and it is focused on Beresheet 1:14. The subject of equidistant Letter Sequencing is discussed further in the Walk in the Light Series book entitled The Scriptures.

³⁵ The date of the birth of Isaac (Yitshaq) is quite significant as his life has many Messianic patterns built in. This will be discussed later in the text and was discussed in the Walk in the Light series books entitled Covenants and The Messiah.

³⁶ Yisrael (ﬡﬢﬤﬥﬦ) is often translated to mean "he will rule as El." This is because the name actually contains the root of the name of Sarah – sar (ﬧﬨ). Sar means: "ruler or prince." Interestingly, we can break the name Yisrael (ﬡﬢﬤﬥﬦ) down further in the Ancient Script, which provides even more detail. We could define the word as "the possession (ﬤﬥ) of El (ﬡﬢ) with El in the center, as the head (ﬧ)." The root yisr (ﬧﬤﬥ) means "straight" so Yisrael could mean "those who belong to El, who follow El and walk straight in His path."

³⁷ The first time that we read about Yisrael is when the son of Yitshaq, named Yaakob, was returning to the Promised Land with his family. He wrestled with a mysterious man and would not let go. The man then told him: "Your name will no longer be Yaakob, but am (ﬦﬨ) Yisrael, because you have struggled with Elohim and with men and have overcome." Beresheet 32:28. He then blessed Yaakob, but He would not tell him His Name. There is another very interesting item in the passage describing the name change. If you were simply reading a translation you would miss it completely. In the Hebrew text the word am (ﬦﬨ) appears right next to the name Yisrael. This was the am (ﬦﬨ) that we discussed earlier, and it was signifying that the Covenant points to Yisrael. The people of Yisrael are the Covenant people promised from the beginning. They are the noble family that would be in the Kingdom.

³⁸ The Red Sea crossing occurred during the Barley Harvest. We know this because the Scriptures record that the Barley was Aviv when the plague of hail reigned down upon Egypt. (Shemot 9:31). Aviv means: "green ears" or "unripe." The Scriptures also record that the banks of the Jordan were overflowing when the Children of Yisrael crossed over because it was the harvest time (Joshua 3:15). Shortly thereafter they were circumcised and partook of the Passover and ate the crops of the land.

³⁹ Gematria is the study of the numerical values of Hebrew words and letters. For more information see Appendix B or visit the

website at www.shemayisrael.net.

40 It is well established that YHWH has a 7,000 year plan for creation patterned upon the first seven words of the Hebrew Scriptures and the seven day weekly cycle. There are six days for man, or flesh, and the seventh is the Sabbath of YHWH. This time is divided into 50 year Jubilee cycles so the time allotted to man is 120 Jubilee Cycles, which is 6,000 years. (see Beresheet 6:3).

41 Qayin (ᐟᐣᐟᵠ) means: "acquired" and is an accurate transliteration of the name commonly referred to as Cain.

42 Hebel (ᐟᐧᐟ) means: "breath" and is an accurate transliteration of the name commonly referred to as Abel. This name also can mean "vanity," and the Book of Yasher actually states that this was the intended meaning of the name as Hawah declared: "In vanity we came into the earth, and in vanity we shall be taken from it." Book of Yasher 1:13.

43 See Yeshayahu 41:26, 46:10, 48.

44 Yisrael should not be confused with the Modern State of Israel or the Jewish people. Yisrael always represents those in Covenant with YHWH. The Modern State of Israel is not a Torah observant Covenant people. While many of the citizens may be ethnically Jewish and descend from different tribes of Yisrael, that does not automatically mean that they are in Covenant with YHWH. You must join the Covenant and obey the commandments to be in Covenant with YHWH and belong to His Set Apart Assembly called Yisrael.

45 For a more detailed discussion on this subject see the Walk in the Light series book entitled *Covenants*.

46 Yirmeyahu (ᐟᐧᐟᐧᐟᐧᐟ) is the proper transliteration for the Hebrew name of the prophet commonly called Jeremiah.

47 The Covenant with the day and with the night is spoken, but not explained in Yirmeyahu 33:20, 33:25. So what is the Covenant with the day and with the night? If we look back at the first day of creation we recall that YHWH combined the day and the night into a Yom Echad - a unified day. That was the Covenant that the day would always follow the night, and that after the dark there would be light. This Covenant is at the heart of our existence and creation because it means that the order which YHWH established at the beginning continues. Obviously, that Covenant is at the very heart of the Appointed Times which rely upon the sun and the moon, as do the day and the night.

48 For a more detailed discussion on the Scriptural dietary instructions see the Walk in the Light series book entitled *Kosher*.

49 It is a well established Hebraic concept that 1,000 years are like a

day to YHWH. This idea was first taught by Mosheh in Psalm 90:4. Peter said in II Peter 3:8 that the brethren should not be ignorant of this one thing. The 1,000 years for a day concept is also to be found in the Talmud in Sanhedrin 97A-97B, the Epistle of Barnabas 15:1-9 and the Secrets of Enoch 33:1. It was also spoken of by Irenaeus in *Against Heresies* Book 5/28/3, by Cyprian in chapter 11 of *The Treatises of Cyprian*; by Lactanius in *The Divine Institutes* Book 7 Chapters 25-26; by Methodius in *The Banquet of the Ten Virgins* Discourse 9, Chapter 1; by Latimer and by Hippolytus of Rome. Sir Isaac Newton who was very interested in the subject apparently said, "About the times of the end, a body of men will be raised up who will turn their attention to the prophecies and insist upon their literal interpretation in the midst of much clamor and opposition."

[50] Michael Wise, Martin Abegg Jr., and Edward Cook, *The Dead Sea Scrolls - A New Translation*, Harper Collins, 2005, p. 94.

[51] For further discussions concerning this issue, reference is made to the Walk in the Light series books entitled *The Messiah* and *The Final Shofar*.

[52] The instructions of YHWH are known as the Torah. In a very general sense, the word Torah is used to refer to the first five books of the Scriptures which some call the Pentateuch, or the five books of Moses. Torah may sound like a strange word to anyone who reads an English translation of the Scriptures, but it is found throughout the Hebrew text. The reason is because it is a Hebrew word which translators have chosen to replace with "the Law." Whenever the word "Torah" is found in the Hebrew, it has been translated as "the Law" in English Bibles. Therefore, if you grew up reading an English Bible then you would never have come across this word. On the other hand, if you read the Hebrew Scriptures the word Torah is found throughout the text. The word Torah (𐤄𐤓𐤅𐤕) in Hebrew means: *"utterance, teaching, instruction or revelation from Elohim."* It comes from horah (𐤄𐤓𐤅𐤄) which means *to direct*, *to teach* and derives from the stem yara (𐤄𐤓𐤉) which means to **shoot** or **throw**. Therefore there are two aspects to the word Torah: 1) aiming or pointing in the right direction, and 2) movement in that direction. The Torah (𐤄𐤓𐤅𐤕) is the first five books of the Hebrew and Christian Scriptures. The Torah is more accurately defined as the "instruction" of YHWH for His set apart people. The Torah contains instruction for those who desire to live righteous, set apart lives in accordance with the will of YHWH. Contrary to popular belief, people can obey the Torah. (Devarim 30:11-14). It is the myriads of regulations, customs and traditions

that men attach to the Torah that make it impossible and burdensome for people to obey. The Torah has been in existence as long as Creation and arguably forever, because the instructions of YHWH are the ways of YHWH. The names of the five different "books" are transliterated from their proper Hebrew names as follows: Genesis – Beresheet, Exodus – Shemot, Leviticus – Vayiqra, Numbers – Bemidbar, Deuteronomy – Debarim. While it is generally considered that the Torah is contained exclusively within the 5 Books of Moses, in a broader sense one might argue that they are included in the entire Tanak – The Torah, The Nebiim (The Prophets) and the Ketubim (The Writings).

53   Yeshayahu (𐤉𐤔𐤏𐤅𐤔𐤉) is the proper transliteration for the Prophet commonly called Isaiah. His name in Hebrew means "YHWH saves."

54   The description of the rainbow in the Throne Room in Heaven is actually found in the Book of Revelation at 4:3.

55   *Nechama Leibowitz*, New Studies in Bereshit, p. 86.

56   As we continue to examine the Covenant process between YHWH and man, including the Appointed Times, it becomes increasingly clear that the Messiah, represented by the Aleph Taw, is at the center of it all. The Aleph Taw and the Messiah are discussed in greater detail in the Walk in the Light series book entitled *The Messiah*.

57   Throughout this text you may find that the words "Jewish," "Jews" and "Jew" are in italics because they are ambiguous and sometimes derogatory terms. At times these expressions are used to describe all of the genetic descendants of the man named Yaakob (Jacob), later named Yisrael (Israel). At other times the words are used to describe those who adhere to the religion of Judaism. The terms are commonly applied to ancient Israelites as well as modern day descendants of those tribes, whether they are atheists or Believers in YHWH. The word "Jew" originally referred to a member of the tribe of Judah (Yahudah) or a person that lived in the region of Judea. After the different exiles of the House of Yisrael and the House of Yahudah, it was the Yahudim that returned to the Land while the Northern Tribes, known as the House of Yisrael, were scattered to the ends of the earth (Yirmeyahu 9:16). The Yahudim retained their identity to their culture and the Land and thus came to represent all of Yisrael, despite the fact that the majority of Yisrael, the 10 tribes of the Northern Kingdom, remained "lost". As a result, the word "Jew" is erroneously used to describe a Yisraelite. While this label became common and customary, it is not accurate and is the

cause of tremendous confusion. This subject is described in greater detail in The Walk in the Light Series book entitled *The Redeemed*.

58 See Vayiqra 19:15, Debarim 1:17 and 16:9, 2 Samuel 14:14, 2 Chronicles 19:7, Proverbs 24:23 and 28:21, Ezekiel 18:20-32, Matthew 22:16, Acts 10:34, Romans 2:11, Ephesians 6:9, Colossians 3:25, James 2:1 and 2:9, 1 Peter 1:16-17.

59 Some believe a great planetary event may have occurred resulting in the breakup of the continents. This would have created diversity among the population on the planet. See *Worlds in Collision*, Immanuel Velikovsky, Paradigma Ltd. 2009. Seder Olam I says that Abram was 48 at the time of the dispersion. Midrash Yalkut Divrie HaYamim I says that construction on the Tower of Babel ended when Abram was 48.

60 The Third Day, known as Yom Shli-shi (ישלישי יום) has great significance in the Scriptures and should be the subject of much study for the serious student.

61 The Book of Yasher is not a "canonized" text, but it is referenced in "canonized" Scriptures which would appear to validate its existence and validity. See Joshua 10:13 and II Samuel 1:18. The issue of canonization is discussed in the Walk in the Light series book entitled *Scriptures*.

62 The Hebrew Scriptures are the original texts and the Hebrew language was uniquely chosen by the Creator to transmit His message. There is critical information below the surface of the text that often gets lost, particularly when you start translating this ancient eastern language into a modern western language. As a result, I encourage students of the text to learn and study in the original Hebrew whenever possible.

63 Shaul of Tarsus, commonly referred to as the Apostle Paul in Christianity, recognized that the Seed of Abraham was the Messiah. In his Torah teaching to the Galatians he writes: *"Now to Abraham and his Seed were the promises made. He does not say, 'And to seeds,' as of many, but as of one, 'And to your Seed,' who is Messiah."* Galatians 3:16. Shaul was a well educated man, allegedly taught by the renowned Sage Gamaliel. Through his various writings he was apparently attempting to instruct Gentiles in the Hebrew Scriptures. Sadly, many of his writings have been twisted and misconstrued, and some actually believe that he was the founder or a co-founder of the Christian religion.

64 The ashes of the Red Heifer mixed with water were necessary to cleanse a person who was defiled from a dead body, in order that the person might enter the Tabernacle or the temple – the House. Every person is tarnished from sin, which is the transgression of

the Torah perpetuated from the Garden. All must be made clean before they can be reconciled to YHWH. This process of becoming clean, so that you can enter into the House of YHWH is provided through the picture of the Red Heifer, which is slaughtered "outside the camp," not on the Altar which is within the courts of the House of YHWH. The Red Heifer sacrifice provides cleansing so that one can approach YHWH to do business with Him. Only when you have entered the House do you receive atonement, and offer up sacrifices on the Altar before the House. The description of the Red Heifer slaughtering can be found in Numbers (Bemidbar) 19.

65 *Jewish and Early Christian Methods of Bible Interpretation*, Judah Gross, Hashtaumd, Quoting [ix] Levenson 181 [x] Manns 60.

66 The number 70 has great significance in the Scriptures. One thing that it represents is all of the nations or people on the Earth. This derives from the fact that there were seventy nations who repopulated the earth after the flood. (Beresheet 10). 70 was also the number of beings, or souls, who went into Egypt with Yisrael. (Beresheet 46).

67 The Scriptures detail many matters that relate to time and the number seventy. For instance there are 70 years for the life of a man (Psalm 90:10). The House of Yahudah was exiled for 70 years for the seventy Sabbath years that they failed to let the Land and Jerusalem rest. (Yirmeyahu 35:11). The Book of Daniel also speaks of 70 weeks. (see Daniel 9). Therefore, the number 70 is quite significant when examining time. We can see this with the multiples of seven involving the week and the seven week count in Shabuot as well as the 7,000 year plan of YHWH for creation.

68 Mosheh (YwM) is the proper transliteration for the name of the Patriarch commonly called Moses. Most agree that the name Mosheh is actually an Egyptian name which refers to his miraculous appearance from the waters of the Nile.

69 The mixing and deliverance from Egypt was a precursor for another greater fulfillment of this Covenant that will occur through another cycle in the end. The Covenant people are currently mixed within the nations, and will some day be delivered from the Nations as Yisrael was once delivered from Egypt. This issue is discussed further in the Walk in the Light series books entitled *Covenants*, *The Redeemed* and *The Final Shofar*.

70 *Pharaoh's and Kings – A Biblical Quest*, David Rohl, Crown Publishers, New York p. 252-256.

71 The Book of Yasher 68:17, 71:1 and 72:25. The Book of Yasher is

not a canonized text, but it is referred to twice in the Tanak and recent research has been performed verifying the historicity of the dates within it, making it a valuable resource for "filling in the gaps" that are present throughout the Torah. Research performed by Eliyahu David ben Yissachar, Jerusalem, Israel.

72 The man Aaron, whose Hebrew name is better transliterated as Aharon, was the brother of Mosheh. They both were born into the Tribe of Levi, although Mosheh had been adopted into the household of Pharaoh. Aharon often functioned as the mouthpiece for Mosheh. He was a High Priest although he received the instructions of YHWH through Mosheh.

73 The first born is a very important subject, especially in ancient days. The first born was typically entitled to a "double portion" of the father's estate, and was expected to carry on in the father's stead after death. In the Exodus we see YHWH killing the firstborn of all in Egypt that were not under the "covering" of the blood of the slaughtered lambs and kids of the first year. Because of this incident, the Tribe of Levi was later set apart to YHWH. "[11] *YHWH also said to Mosheh,* [12] *'I have taken the Levites from among the Israelites in place of the first male offspring of every Yisraelite woman. The Levites are mine,* [13] *for all the firstborn are mine. When I struck down all the firstborn in Egypt, I set apart for myself every firstborn in Yisrael, whether man or animal. They are to be mine. I am YHWH.*" Bemidbar 3:11-13.

74 Beresheet 33:17.

75 The mikvah is where the Christian doctrine of baptism derives, although it did not begin with Christianity and was commanded by YHWH long before Messiah came. It was a natural thing for Yisraelites to do. In fact, there were numerous mikvaote (plural form of mikvah) at the Temple and it was required that a person be immersed in a mikvah prior to presenting their sacrifice. The Hebrew word for baptize is tevila (ͻ⌣□⊕), which is a full body immersion that takes place in a mikvah (ᛘᑭᑭᴍ). This comes from the passage in Beresheet 1:10 when YHWH "gathered together" the waters. The mikvah is the gathering together of flowing waters. The "tevila" immersion is symbolic for a person going from a state of uncleanliness to cleanliness. The priests in the temple needed to tevila regularly to insure that they were in a state of cleanliness when they served in the Temple. Anyone going to the Temple to worship or offer sacrifices would tevila at the numerous pools outside the Temple. There are a variety of instances found in the Torah when a person was required to tevila. It is very important because it reminds us of the filth of sin, and the need to be

washed clean from our sin in order to stand in the presence of a set apart Elohim. Therefore, it makes perfect sense that we be immersed in a mikvah prior to presenting the sacrifice of the perfect lamb as atonement for our sins. It also cleanses our temple which the Spirit of Elohim will enter in to tabernacle with us. The tevila is symbolic of becoming born again and is an act of going from one life to another. Being born again is not something that became popular in the seventies within the Christian religion. It is a remarkably Yisraelite concept that was understood to occur when one arose from the mikvah. In fact, people witnessing an immersion would often cry out "Born Again!" when a person came up from an immersion. It was also an integral part of the Rabbinic conversion process, which, in many ways is not Scriptural, but in this sense is correct. For a Gentile to complete their conversion, they were required to be immersed, or baptized, which meant that they were born again - born into a new life. Many people believe that immersion is a newly instituted Christian concept because of the exchange between Messiah and Nicodemus. Let us take a look at that conversation in the Gospel according to Yahanan: *"¹ Now there was a man of the Pharisees named Nicodemus, a ruler of the Yahudim. ² He came to Yahushua at night and said, 'Rabbi, we know you are a teacher who has come from Elohim. For no one could perform the miraculous signs You are doing if Elohim were not with him.' ³ In reply Yahushua declared, 'I tell you the truth, no one can see the kingdom of Elohim unless he is born again.' ⁴ 'How can a man be born when he is old?' Nicodemus asked. 'Surely he cannot enter a second time into his mother's womb to be born!' ⁵ Yahushua answered, 'I tell you the truth, no one can enter the kingdom of Elohim unless he is born of water and the Spirit. ⁶ Flesh gives birth to flesh, but the Spirit gives birth to spirit. ⁷ You should not be surprised at My saying, You must be born again. ⁸ The wind blows wherever it pleases. You hear its sound, but you cannot tell where it comes from or where it is going. So it is with everyone born of the Spirit.' ⁹ 'How can this be?' Nicodemus asked. ¹⁰ 'You are Yisrael's teacher,' said Yahushua, 'and do you not understand these things? ¹¹ I tell you the truth, we speak of what we know, and we testify to what we have seen, but still you people do not accept our testimony. ¹² I have spoken to you of earthly things and you do not believe; how then will you believe if I speak of heavenly things? ¹³ No one has ever gone into heaven except the One who came from heaven - the Son of Man. ¹⁴ Just as Mosheh lifted up the snake in the desert, so the Son of Man must be lifted up, ¹⁵ that everyone who believes in him may have eternal life.'"* Yahanan 3:1-15. From this exchange it seems that Nicodemus is unfamiliar with immersion, but he was not surprised by the fact that a person needed to be "born again." His first question: *"How can a man be born when he is old?"* demonstrated he did not see how it applied to him, because he was already a Yahudim. His second question *"How can this be,"* only affirmed that fact. And this is why Yahushua asked: *"You are Yisrael's teacher and do you not understand these things?"* In other words, "you're supposed to be the one teaching Yisrael about these spiritual matters and you're not. You think only the Gentiles need to be immersed and born again, but you all need it because you are all sinners and this needs to be taught to everyone, not just the Gentiles." So you see, being born again through immersion was not new to Yisrael. This is why many readily were immersed by Yahanan the Immerser - they understood their need. It was often the leaders who failed to see their need for cleansing because they were blinded by the notion that their Torah observance justified them. It is important to note that the tevila must occur in "living waters" - in other words, water which is moving and ideally which contains life. These living waters refer to the Messiah. In a Scriptural marriage, a bride would enter the waters of purification prior to her wedding. These are the same waters that we are to enter when we make a confession of faith and become part of the Body of Messiah - His Bride.

[76] Undoubtedly, the most significant prayer in the Torah is known as The Shema found at Debarim 6:4. In fact, it was declared to be the first (resheet) of all the commandments by Yahushua. (see Mark 12:29). The Shema proclaims: *"[4] Hear, O Yisrael: YHWH our Elohim, YHWH is one. (echad) [5] Love YHWH your Elohim with all your heart and with all your soul and with all your strength. [6] These commandments that I give you today are to be upon your hearts. [7] Impress them on your children. Talk about them when you sit at home and when you walk along the road, when you lie down and when you get up. [8] Tie them as symbols on your hands and bind them on your foreheads. [9] Write them on the doorframes of your houses and on your gates."* Debarim 6:4-9. The command to write the commands on our doorposts and our gates means that YHWH is in control of that space. His Commandments are the rule of that property, which represents His Kingdom on the Earth. So we are instructed to essentially establish the Kingdom of YHWH in every area of our lives. The text of the Shema in Hebrew is quite profound and contains an enlarged ayin at the end of the word "shema" and an enlarged dalet at the end of the word "echad". The ayin dalet is essentially announcing that we should "see" the "door." The Shema text is provided in Appendix D.

[77] Elim was a very special place and one cannot ignore the

numerical significance of twelve (12) and seventy (70). Some interpret Elim to mean: "Palm trees" or better yet "strong trees." Twelve is a number typically associated with the 12 Tribes of Yisrael, the Community of YHWH or governmental perfection. Seventy (70) is a number typically associated with "the Nations." Here at this place we see a picture of the Nations being nourished by Yisrael. This was an oasis in the desert and a picture of a future event when the Nations leave their bondage in the Egypt system that now envelopes the world and they come together to the waters that flow through Yisrael. This is not only a place, but a time which is rehearsed yearly called Succot, when Palm Branches are waved. This subject is discussed further in the Walk in the Light series book entitled *The Final Shofar*.

78 A Ketubah (ⵯⵍⵏⵅ⵴) is simply a marriage contract. It was quite common in ancient cultures and continues to be common primarily in eastern cultures. It established the rights and responsibilities of the parties and often included the damages for a parties' breach of the contract. In western culture similar contracts are used and called pre-nuptial agreements.

79 We have already mentioned the concept of Gematria and the study of numbers in the Scriptures. Along that line the numbers 4, 40, 400 are repeatedly linked with Messiah. This subject is discussed further in the Walk in the Light book entitled *The Messiah*. Indeed, when Yisrael was delivered from Egypt after the 400 years had expired, it was the blood of the lamb that protected the firstborn from death.

80 There are new theories concerning the new moon which attempt to persuade people to believe that the new moon occurs at the conjunction, rather at the sighting of the first sliver. This notion is not warranted by any historical information, and borrows on the astronomical determination of a conjunction which actually only lasts for a matter of minutes. The moon is in darkness before and after the actual conjunction and can be in darkness for days at a time. Therefore, the determination of the moment of conjunction requires great mathematical precision. The conjunction would have been very difficult to determine in ancient days, and because it is so brief, the determination of when to recognize the new moon day would have involved great debate and discussion, none of which is found in the historical records. The first sliver is a visible sign, or "owt" that can be seen by all, verses a dark moon which remains unseen for days. There is ample historical proof that the new moon was considered to be the crescent moon when the first sliver was observed. See Philo, *Treatise on the Special Laws*, Book II, XI (41) which states: "[It] is

that which comes after the conjunction, which... [is] the day of the new moon in each month . . . at the time of the new moon, the sun begins to illuminate the moon with a light which is visible to the outward senses, and then she displays her own beauty to the beholders." Etymologically, it has been asserted that the word chodesh (ש ח ה) derives from chadash (ש ח ה) which can mean "to polish with a sword." So the chodesh would appear as a chadash, a scimitar or curved sword common in the Middle East. See Gesenius' Hebrew-Chaldee Lexicon.

[81] It has been well documented that most probable exodus route went through Wadi Watir on the Sinai Penninsula and the Red Sea crossing occurred at Nuweiba, Egypt, where an underwater land bridge has been located containing remnants of Egyptian chariot wheels. The Scriptures specifically provide that YHWH made the Egyptian's chariot wheels fall off. (Shemot 14:25). The location of Mt Sinai is found in Saudi Arabia according to Galatians 4:25 where altars and other relics have been found confirming the presence of the Yisraelites along with the mixed multitude that departed Egypt. For a detailed discussion of this issue see the book entitled *The Exodus Case New Discoveries Confirm the Historical Exodus* by Dr. Lennart Möller, Scandinavia Publishing House 2002.

[82] It is interesting to read that YHWH has a Scroll with names written in it. While this verse does not have any added detail, the point is clear - YHWH has a register of those who are included in His Covenant. If you join in and obey the terms, your name gets written in the Scroll. If you refuse to obey, your name can be blotted out. This flies directly in the face of a popular Christian doctrine "once saved always saved." Sadly, many in Christianity believe that their destiny relies upon whether they said a simple prayer at some point in their lives. The plain fact is that actions speak louder than words and while we all need the atonement freely provided by the Messiah, once we join the family of YHWH we are expected to obey His rules.

[83] This entire renewal process turns out to be a Messianic allusion. The Messiah is the one who meets with YHWH and transmits His Words, He came with the esteem of YHWH hidden behind a veil of flesh. They fasted 40 days and 40 nights, which would turn out to be a Messianic trademark.

[84] "According to Rashi, Moses ascended Mount Sinai no less than three times for forty days and forty nights. The first ascent began on the 6th of Sivan [month 3], 50 days after the Exodus, when Moses first received the Ten Commandments . . . When he descended and saw the people worshipping the Golden Calf,

however, he smashed the tablets (Exod. 32:19). According to tradition, this occurred on the 17th of Tamuz [month 4] . . . On the following day Moses burned the Golden Calf and judged the transgressors. He then reascended on the 19th of Tamuz [month 4] and interceded on behalf of Israel for 40 more days (until the 29th of Av [month 5]) . . . [Elohim] then called Moses the following day, on Elul [month 6] 1, to ascend a third time to receive a new set of tablets. Forty more days and nights were spent receiving the revelation of Torah at Sinai. Moses finally descended on Tishri [month 7] 10 - Yom Kippur - with the second set of tablets in hand and the reassurance of [Elohim's] forgiveness." Quoted from www.hebrew4christians.com (correct month numbers inserted). With recent technological advances we can now discern with precision when these events took place. According to the work of Eliyahu David ben Yissachar the First ascent occurred on Day 8 of Month 3 and the descent occurred on Day 18 of Month 4. The Second ascent occurred on Day 19 of Month 4 and the descent occurred on Day 29 of Month 5. The Third ascent occurred on Day 30 of Month 5 and the descent occurred on Day 10 of Month 7.   The Golden Calf was worshipped on Day 17 of Month 4 and the Tablets were broken on Day 18 of Month 4. Interestingly, there can only be 143 days between Day 8 of Month 3 and Day 10 of Month 7 in a year where Month 3, 4, 5 and 6 each contain 30 days, which is indeed the case in the year of the Exodus. According to 1 Kings 6:1, the year of the Exodus occurred 480 years before year 4 of King Solomon's (Shlomo's) reign.

85 Wikipedia, Roman Calendar.
86 Wikipedia, Gregorian Calendar.
87 There are also weeks of years, Jubilee cycles and millennia, but these will be discussed later. There is actually one reference to hours in John (Yahanan) 11:9.
88 While the House of Yisrael went into exile, that did not mean that YHWH gave up on His Firstborn. In fact, Mosheh and the Prophets were very clear that they would be regathered and restored with the House of Yahudah. First, the Messiah had to make atonement for the sins that caused the exile and the time of the punishment needed to expire. That time was revealed through the very unusual prophecy "acted out" by Ezekiel (Yehezqel) (see Yehezqel 4). This matter is discussed in greater detail in the Walk in the Light series book entitled The Redeemed.
89 The current modern Hebrew character set is sometimes referred to as Chaldean flame letters. This language came with the Yahudim after their Babylonian exile. There is a great deal of

mystery associated with this language, which is really not so modern at all. One thing is certain, it is not the original language of Yisrael. In fact, it is really a language that exclusively belongs to the Yahudim. Those from the House of Yisrael who desire to truly learn about their Hebrew Roots should be looking at the original Hebrew Language often referred to as Ancient Hebrew or Paleo Hebrew. This would have been the language used by Abraham, Yitshaq, Yaakob, Mosheh and the Assembly of Yisrael.

90 Both the religions of Judaism and Christianity are guilty of mixing pagan traditions and practices. This issue is discussed in greater detail in the Walk in the Light series books entitled *Restoration* and *Pagan Holidays*.

91 This was specifically prophesied by Hoshea - that the House of Yisrael would be called "Not My People." In fact, the House of Yisrael was given a certificate of divorce. (Yirmeyahu 3:8). They were unfaithful to the Covenant relationship with YHWH, and were therefore evicted from the Covenant Land. While away, Yahudah stepped in and assumed a role not necessarily theirs. The House of Yisrael consists of the Tribe of Joseph, Ephraim and Manasseh, who essentially lays claim to first born status. YHWH has a long memory, and as the punishment ends we can look forward to the reemergence of the House of Yisrael, exactly as prophesied by Hoshea (see Hoshea 1).

92 The Calendar Court, also referred to as The Calendar Council originally consisted of priests who examined the evidence of witnesses who reported seeing the new moon. This clearly reveals that the first sliver sighting was the means of determining the new moon. While the Calendar Court developed into a tradition, the sighting of the moon was the historically recognized means of determining the new month. For further discussion on the Calendar Court see See *Rabbinical Mathematics and Astronomy*, W.M. Feldman, M.L. Cailingold, London 1931. See also Alfred Edersheim, *The Temple Its Ministry and Services*, Updated Edition, Hendrickson Publishers, 1994.

93 The notion that there is an oral Torah as well as a written Torah has opened the door for much confusion. There was an Oral Torah which was spoken by YHWH and then it was written by Mosheh. Thus, the Oral and the written were the same. Rabbinic tradition has not only proposed the idea that there is an oral torah, but they have also placed the Torah into the realm of men and made it flexible and subject to the majority opinion. The Rabbis profess that the Torah was given to man, for man, thus

placing it within man's dominion. This is a grievous mistake in that while the Torah was given to man, it was a gift to provide instruction and direction. It is not something to be altered or tampered with in any way.

94 www.jewfaq.org/calendar.htm

95 As YHWH is not an Elohim of confusion, all of the dates contained in the Scriptures can be mathematically calculated on His Calendar. This means that every date, past, present and future in the Scriptures, from Beresheet to Revelation, originates from the Creator's Calendar. Although there have been counterfeit calendars throughout Yisrael's history, including the Enoch calendar, the Qumran calendar, the Karaite calendar and the Rabbinic calendar, YHWH keeps time on His Calendar. For further discussion on the development of the calendar up until the Rabbinic calendar in 359 CE, see the book entitled *Calendar and the Community* A History of the Jewish Calendar Second Century BCE - Tenth Century CE by Sacha Stern, Oxford University Press 2001.

96 www.torahcalendar.com see article entitled *Determining the Hebrew Year*.

97 *Calendar and the Community* A History of the Jewish Calendar Second Century BCE - Tenth Century CE by Sacha Stern, Oxford University Press 2001, Section 4.2.2 Calendrical rules. The Creation Calendar found at www.torahcalendar.com follows the rule as described in the first rescension. The rule of the equinox is attested in a single passage of the Babylonian Talmud (B. RH 21A), which exists in two different rescensions.

98 As one might expect, the Land bears witness to the accuracy of the true Scriptural Calendar. The Rule of the Equinox, which relies on no opinion from any man or religious ruling body has repeatedly and faithfully been confirmed by the harvests in the land of Israel. I have travelled to Israel on many occasions to confirm this fact and document the evidence, especially in years, that have been controversial such as 2008 and 2011. The Creation Calendar has been perfectly in synch with the harvests of the Land, while other manmade calendars have been in error, which would have been devastating to those in the Land if they were relying upon an accurate rendering of the harvest cycles. Proofs can be found at www.shemayisrael.net and www.torahcalendar.com.

99 By using the powerful algorithms underlying the Creator's Calendar found on www.torahcalendar.com we are able to go backward in time. We are able to confirm certain days, months and years that have been provided in the Scriptures, which

confirms that the Rule of the Equinox was used by Ancient Yisrael and more importantly, YHWH Himself. Supporting research and evidence remains unpublished at the time of this printing, but is hoped to be available in the near future. For updates please visit www.torahcalendar.com.

Those who follow the conjunctionist position essentially equate a Scriptural new moon (rosh chodesh) with an astronomical New moon or dead moon. The astronomical new moon is not observed because it is a dark moon. The astronomical definition is not the method historically used by Yisrael. While modern science may define a dark moon as a new moon, it is not a good idea to let science interpret the Scriptures. We have seen the problems in this regard with Creation and evolution. Science is often at odds with the Scriptures. The Sun and Moon were specifically called the greater light and the lesser light. The operative word being "light." They were meant to be a visible witness of the calendar. The first sliver of the renewed moon is a visible sign of renewal when we actually see the light. We know that the moon was made for Signs and Appointed Times. (Beresheet 1:14; Tehillim 104:19). A sign is something that is meant to be seen and observed. The moon is in a dark phase for more than a day and so there is no precision and nothing to observe. Therefore the conjunctionists rely upon darkness for their sign, which is inconsistent with the Scriptures. Their primary argument is premised upon the interpretation of one word in Psalm 81:3, which states: "*Blow the chodesh shofar fullness (kesah) in the day of our solemn feast.*" Some translations provide for blowing the shofar at "the full (kesah) moon." The conjunctions position then points out that the word kesah (Ч𐤟Ш) means: "clothed or covered." They then indicate that this must mean it is covered in darkness, but that is an incorrect assumption. When something is in darkness it is not covered with anything. While the word can certainly mean covered or clothed, the intention is that it is clothed in light, not in darkness. Indeed, this is aptly demonstrated in a Psalm that speaks of the majesty of creation. "*¹ Bless YHWH, O my soul. O YHWH my Elohim, You are very great; You are clothed with honor and majesty. ² Who coverest Thyself with light as with a garment: who stretchest out the heavens like a curtain.*" Tehillim 104:1-2. So the covering is light and light is the sign we should be looking for. As we shall see later in the discussion, there are two Feasts that occur in the middle of the month. So there are Appointed Times that occur around the Full Moon, in the middle of the month. The full moon of Passover/Unleavened Bread and Succot are wonderful signs.

There is a false doctrine that has infiltrated the Christian Religion causing tremendous harm and confusion as people attempt to identify with YHWH and His Covenant. The doctrine is referred to as Replacement Theology and it essentially teaches that the Christian Church has replaced Yisrael - the Covenant people of YHWH. It teaches that the Church is now "Spiritual Yisrael" and makes a separation between that which is considered to be "Old" and that which is considered to be "New." As a result, the "New Testament" is often considered to be newer, better and more relevant than the "Old Testament." As a result, many are not taught the Covenant Path found within the Torah, and they end up rejecting the path established by YHWH, believing that it is old, outdated and irrelevant to the new Yisrael - the Church. This, of course, is not consistent with the Torah or the Prophets, but it is the framework within which many in the Christian religion find themselves, and it ends up controlling their reading and interpretation of the Scriptures which leads them away from the Covenant into a life of confusion and lawlessness. The Messiah does not have good things in store for those who reject the Torah and live lawless lives contrary to His commandments. (See Mattityahu 7:23; Luke 13:27).

102
Strong's Hebrew Concordance Number 8104

103
For a discussion of the Messiah and events involving the Appointed Times see the Walk in the Light series book entitled *The Messiah*.

104
The Lunar Sabbath is a fairly new idea that seems to be circulating in the Messianic/Hebrew Roots movement and has caused a tremendous amount of confusion. It has no basis in history and essentially promotes the notion that the weekly Sabbath cycle is controlled by the lunar cycle, which is exactly the opposite of what is demonstrated by Vayiqra 23, which clearly separates and sets apart the weekly Sabbath from the other Appointed Times. The weekly Sabbath is a memorial of Creation week and exists on a completely independent seven day count separate from the lunar-solar reckoning of the annual Appointed Times. The matter is discussed in an Appendix in the Walk in the Light series book entitled *The Sabbath*.

105
For an in depth discussion regarding the Sabbath day the reader is referred to the Walk in the Light series book entitled *The Sabbath*.

106
It is important to understand the distinction between "am Yisrael" and Judaism. The Assembly of Yisrael consists of all

who enter into Covenant with YHWH. This includes anyone from the nations regardless of genetics, lineage or culture. Judaism is a religion that originated from ancient Yisrael, namely the Pharisaic sect. It has adapted and evolved since the destruction of Jerusalem in 70 CE. While it may contain many physical descendants of the House of Yahudah, called Yahudim or Jews, it is by no means the exclusive conduit of the Covenant. In fact, in many ways, Judaism has added to and taken away from the Torah which is specifically prohibited according to Debarim 5:32.

107 For a detailed discussion of the Scriptural Covenants see the Walk in the Light series book entitled *Covenants*.

108 For further discussion and analysis of the significance of the number 4 as it relates to the Messiah can be found in the Walk in the Light series book entitled *The Messiah*.

109 Shemot 12:47-48.

110 *Encyclopaedia Judaica* Vol. 13, p. 169. The full text records the following: "The Feast of Passover consists of two parts: the Passover ceremony, and the Feast of Unleavened Bread. Originally, both parts existed separately; but at the beginning of the [Babylonian] exile they were combined." There is no direct evidence to support this claim as to when the change occurred. The Babylonian exile involved 7 different captivities beginning in the year 618 BCE through the year 595 BCE, with the fall of Jerusalem in 599 BCE, not in 586 BCE as is traditionally held. It involved the punishment of the House of Yahudah, also known as the Southern Kingdom. The period of the exile from the last captivity in 595 BCE until the Decree of Cyrus, was prophesied in Yirmeyahu 29:10-14 to be 70 years. It occurred well after the exile of the House of Yisrael by the Assyrian Empire which consisted of 5 different exiles between 723 BCE and 714 BCE.*

111 See en.wikipedia.org/wiki/Council_of_Jamnia

112 There is much confusion surrounding the term "Jew" which has resulted because of the division and exiles of the various tribes of Yisrael. This issue is discussed in detail in the Walk in the Light series entitled *The Redeemed*. It is important to note that the people known as the Jews derive primarily from the House of Yahudah. A remnant from all 12 tribes, including Ephraim and Manasseh were essentially mixed into the House of Yahudah after the division of the Kingdom under Jeroboam and Rehoboam. We can see an example of this in Luke 2:36 where Hanna the prophetess is mentioned as being the daughter of Phanuel of the tribe of Asher. She was living in the region of Judea, and thus would be considered a Judean, despite the fact

that she was not from the tribe of Yahudah.

[113] Shemot 12:9.

[114] At the original Pesach each family slaughtered their lamb or goat so this process could be done simultaneously at the homes of the individuals. After the establishment of the Levitical Priesthood and the ordinances of the House of YHWH, this process took more time. While the males of the house would continue to slaughter their own lambs, it was done in a single location which resulted in the service being done in intervals to accommodate all the people. The Mishnah was redacted in 220 CE by Rabbi Yehudah haNasi long after the destruction of the Second Temple. The Mishnah provides an elaborate description of when the Passover sacrifice was slaughtered. There is good reason to believe that the description of "between the evenings," being between noon and sunset, was fabricated, in an attempt to erase the memory of Yahushua the Messiah from Judean history.

[115] Matzah is the Hebrew word for unleavened bread. It is typically flat, but can be baked in loaves as was done with   the   bread placed upon the Table of Showbread in the Tabernacle and the Temple. See Edersheim, *The Temple Its Ministry and Services*, id.

[116] Many of the photos that are currently circulating in public depicting the real Mount Sinai in Saudi Arabia are the result of the adventures of Jim and Penny Caldwell. For more information concerning their work visit splitrockresearch.org.

[117] There are potentially great health benefits to removing leaven from your diet. There are many people affected with digestive yeast infections and a yearly fast from leaven may help avoid those problems.

[118] See Alfred Edersheim, *The Temple Its Ministry and Services*, Updated Edition, Hendrickson Publishers, 1994.

[119] See Vayiqra 23:17. The tenth part is what belongs to YHWH. So whenever you see the tenth, such as the resheet offering we recognize that it is about returning to YHWH what belongs to Him. This becomes significant with both the Messiah and the firstfruits.

[120] See en.wikipedia.org/wiki/Septuagint.

[121] See en.wikipedia.org/wiki/Masoretic_Text.

[122] See Article entitled *An Overview on How To Count the Omer* at www.torahcalendar.com. See also Flavius Josephus *Antiquities* 3/250-254, Rosh Hashanah 6B, Mishnah Menachot 10.

[123] Joshua is the name in the Scriptures more properly transliterated Yahushua. This was, very appropriately, the same name as the Messiah. Many argue about the spelling and pronunciation. They claim that it is spelled with five Hebrew characters ⳥ש וּ הⳣ and

should therefore be pronounced Yahushua. Interestingly, contained within the Dead Sea Scrolls, is an example of the Name spelled with 6 letters ⊙𝕗w𝕗Ɐᴗ thus validating the pronunciation as Yahushua. The simple fact is that the Scriptures contain the Name of Yahushua using 4 letters, 5 letters and 6 letters. There are variations on the same name and they all have the same essential meaning: "YHWH saves."

[124] For more information on this subject see the Walk in the Light series book entitled *The Redeemed*. It is important to understand that modern Rabbinic Judaism can trace its roots to the Pharisaic sect of Yisrael, but the religion of Judaism is a separate and distinct religion from the faith of Yisrael described by Mosheh in the Torah. Judaism has added to, and taken away from the Torah. It has developed traditions as well as a system of leadership and decision making different from Yisrael.

[125] Tim Hegg, *Counting the Omer An Inquiry into the Divergent Methods of the 1ˢᵗ Century Judaisms*, torahresource.com   2002. Simeon b. Beothus was appointed in 23 BCE according to Eliyahu David ben Yissachar, Jerusalem, Israel.

[126] History is full of examples where the Priests were pressured, coerced and even killed if they deviated from what was considered to be proper Torah observance. (See Edersheim, *The Temple* at p. 279, Sukkah 9). The Pharisees were clearly zealous for the Torah, their main problem was that they developed traditions which were given equal or greater weight than the Torah. This was one of the main areas that Yahushua corrected the Pharisees – their traditions. Relative to the operation of the Temple, they scrutinized the Temple service, since they were active observers and constantly present in the Temple. They were held in high esteem by the people, and therefore they were a force to be reckoned with. So even though the position of High Priest became politicized and corrupted, there were likely many righteous Levites serving in the House of YHWH, and the Pharisees helped to keep things in check to an extent by adding pressure from the inside.

[127] While Hanukah is traditionally called a Feast, it should not be confused with a hag, designated as an Appointed Time in the Scriptures.

[128] For a further and more detailed discussion of the Sabbath see the Walk in the Light series book entitled *The Sabbath*.

[129] The Roman Catholic Church was essentially founded by the sun worshipping Roman Emperor Constantine. Through various edicts, adherents were directed away from the Torah and the Appointed Times toward festivals and days associated with

pagan sun worship. This issue is discussed in greater detail in the Walk in the Light books entitled *Restoration* and *Pagan Holidays*. The Roman Catholic Church essentially was the antithesis of the Council at Jamnia. Each group worked hard to divide and separate from the other. As a result, each subsequent religion (Judaism and Christianity) has moved away from the Torah in their own unique ways. Sadly, the Torah, the Prophets and the Writings (The Tanak) are supposed to be held in high esteem by both religions, yet the traditions of man have caused division and strife between the two.

130   For a further discussion see the Walk in the Light series book entitled *The Messiah*.

131   Sheol is the proper rendering of the place where souls go when they exit the body. Christianity has adopted many misunderstandings relative to heaven and hell.

132   Jonah was in the belly of the fish for three days and three nights (Jonah 1:17). Yahushua said that this would be the only sign given to an evil generation. (Luke 11:29-30).

133   After being crucified on a Wednesday, Yahushua was raised "on the third day" according to Matthew 16:21, 17:23, 20:19, 27:64, Mark 9:31, 10:34, Luke 9:21-22, 13:32, 18:33, 24:7, 24:46, Acts 10:40 and 1 Corinthians 15:4. Yahushua was raised on the weekly Sabbath on Day 17 of Month 1, which was the third day of Unleavened Bread. This was the day after the First (Resheet) Barley offering that was offered on Day 16 of Month 1. Yahushua was also raised "after three days" according to Mark 8:31. So He was crucified and buried on Passover on Day 14 of Month 1, and raised after three days on Day 17 of Month 1 in 34 CE. This constitutes further proof that the Passover was being held at the correct time on Day 14 of Month 1 at this time in Yisrael's history. For a further discussion on the timing and dating of the death and resurrection see the Walk in the Light series book entitled *The Messiah*.

134   For a further discussion see the Walk in the Light series book entitled *The Messiah*. See also www.torahcalendar.com.

135   Matthew 12:8; Mark 2:28; Luke 6:5.

136   The method of counting is confirmed by Mosheh through a careful analysis of the Scriptures and tradition. Yisrael left Egypt in 1437 BCE,* 480 years before the fourth year of King Solomon in 957 BCE as stated in 1 Kings 6:9. The Yisraelites crossed the Red Sea and left Egypt on Day 21 of Month 1 according to Exodus 12:16B-17. The crossing occurred on Yom Rishon – the first day of the week. (see www.torahcalendar.com and view Day 21 of Month 1 in 1437 BCE). The Yisraelites arrived at the Wilderness

of Sinai on the selfsame day they came out of Egypt according to Shemot 19:1. They therefore arrived at the wilderness of Sinai on Yom Rishon, the first day of the week, on Day 5 of Month 3. (see see www.torahcalendar.com and view Day 5 of Month 3 in 1437 BCE). Mosheh received revelation from YHWH three days later according to Shemot 19:11 on Day 7 of Month 3. Hebrew tradition holds that this day was Shabuot. It is a fact that Shabuot falls on Day 7 of Month 3 in 1437 BCE. Therefore, we know that Mosheh started the count on Day 16 of Month 1, which is consistent with the method used during the time of Yahushua. If something this important were awry, He surely would have corrected them. We now have the Creation Calendar available through www.torahcalendar.com. As a result, we have the ability to essentially travel back in time to that month and year and confirm these dates and methods. The New Testament also confirms that they were counting weeks and Sabbaths and that on Day 17 of Month 1, after the crucifixion of Yahushua they had already begun the count. We read in all the Gospels the phrase "mia ton shabbaton" when referencing Day 17, which was a Sabbath. (see Mattityahu 28:1; Mark 16:2; Luke 24:1; John 20:1). In the Greek "mia ton Shabbaton" means: "first of the Sabbaths." There will always be seven weekly Sabbaths in the seven week count, and this means that they were counting the Sabbaths, and the weeks by Day 17. The Priest had made the resheet omer offering on Day 16, which was a Friday in 34 CE.

137   See Endnote 136 for various examples of Scriptural support. The Targum Jonathan uses "weeks" instead of "sabbaths" as does the Chumash. Also, Yom Kippur is called a Sabbath. It is clearly not a weekly Sabbath, but rather a High Sabbath. (see Vayiqra 23:26-32). Also, if you begin the counting of the omer on the day after the weekly Sabbath there will be years when Day 21 of Month 1 lands on a weekly Sabbath, when the first (resheet) offering will be outside the Feast of Unleavened Bread, after the Feast is over. This is clearly not supposed to happen. The last day of the Feast of Unleavened Bread is not only a Sabbath, it is deemed a solemn assembly, an atzeret. (Debarim 16:8). The Feast is concluded on that day. The resheet barley offering must be accomplished within the confines of Unleavened Bread in order for the people to leave and start their own harvesting.

138   Flavius Josephus, *Antiquities*, III, 253 [x, 6].

139   The story of Ruth is truly a story for our day - you should stop and read it now. It is not a difficult story to read and understand, so I will simply point out some things to think about when you read it. Notice that the family of Naomi were from Bethlehem in

the Land of Yahudah. They were from the Tribe of Yahudah, although they were in the land of Moab because Yisrael was under a famine. Yisrael had no king – they were in the period of the judges yet the name of Naomi's husband Elimelech means: "my Elohim is King" which gives us a hint that this story is about YHWH as King. The only reason Yisrael would be in famine is if they were being cursed, which means that they were not obeying the terms of the Covenant made at Sinai and renewed at Moab. So where do Naomi and her family go? They went "back to the Torah" – back to Moab where the Torah and the Covenant were renewed prior to Yisrael entering the Promised Land. There Naomi's two sons marry Moabite women - who would then become part of their family. Again, it was in Moab that the strangers were included within the renewed Covenant. (Debarim 29:11). Not only did Naomi's husband die while they were in Moab, but so did   her sons.   Typically when one son would die he would take on the responsibilities of his brother's family, but in this case, all of the men had died and the women, and their hope of producing seed had effectively been "cut off." The women were free to leave their connection with Yisrael and remain in Moab, but Ruth "clung" to Naomi and took Naomi's Elohim as her own. They then return to Yisrael together and the story of Ruth coming to the Land of Yisrael starts "in the beginning" (beresheet) of the barley harvest. This is highly significant because we know that the first month coincides with abib barley and the harvest. The barley is harvested, followed by the wheat harvest as the people gather their firstfruits (bikkurim) and prepare for Shabuot, the Festival of Firstfruits (Bikkurim). The story of Ruth takes place between these two harvests. In fact, the book of Ruth is traditionally read during the Feast of Shabuot. The Torah provides something specific concerning these times. *"When you reap the harvest of your land, you shall not wholly reap the corners of your field when you reap, nor shall you gather any gleaning from your harvest. You shall leave them for the poor and for the stranger: I am   YHWH your Elohim."* Vayiqra 23:22. YHWH is specifically showing that He will make provision for the Gentiles through His Appointed Times, and this sets the stage for the process of being redeemed and grafted in like Ruth, who was previously joined to Yisrael and cut off. Ruth was gleaning the fields of Boaz and she went about the business of redemption with Boaz at the threshing floor. (Ruth 3). The year when Ruth gleaned in the fields was 1066 BCE. The famine in the story of Ruth took place when Eli was High Priest according to Josephus in Antiquities 5/318-319 in 1076 BCE. The

10 years spoken of in Ruth 1:4 occurred between 1076 – 1066 BCE. Eliyahu David ben Yissacher, Jerusalem, Israel.

140 Interestingly, the only time that the term "Rosh Hashanah" is found in the Scriptures refers to a Day 10 of Month 1 in a Jubilee year. See Yehezqel 40:1.

141 Shemot 16:23; 31:15; 35:2 and Vayiqra 23:3.

142 The Scriptures declare that the Yisraelites "saw the sound." (Shemot 20:15). This may have been the same effect that we see when a jet breaks the sound barrier, or it may have been some other phenomenon. Regardless, it must have been quite an event. There are several texts that speak of the awesomeness of the voice of YHWH.

143 The Melchizedek priesthood is one of the most mysterious aspects of the Torah. Very little information is provided except when Abraham actually paid tithes to Melchizedek – The Righteous King of Jerusalem. Abraham, a man who met and Covenanted with YHWH paid an honor to this King/Priest that should give us pause for reflection. This Priest was not a Levite, because there were no Levites at that time. The Levitical Priesthood would later come from Abraham's descendants. As a result it is vital that we understand that YHWH has another priesthood that operated before Abraham, and one that is in operation even now, which is separate and apart from the line of Aharon and the Levitical Priesthood established in the Torah. The Levitical Priesthood requires an earthly sacrificial system, but the Melchizedek line transcends both time and space. This has great Messianic significance and it should help us understand the dual nature of the Messiah as both King and High Priest. To understand the Melchizedek priest, it is important to understand the role of the firstborn prior to Sinai. It was the firstborn who would offer sacrifices as the head of the house. Recall the word "beresheet" which combines the house, the firstborn son and the resheet all in the first word of the Scriptures. So Melchizedek was from the beginning, the Priest and King of all Creation which is the House of the Messiah.

144 Shemot 31:7, 35:12, 37:6, 39:35.

145 Mikayahu is the proper translation for the prophet commonly referred to as Micah. Mikayahu means: "Who is like YHWH?"

146 It is tradition that Mosheh descended with a second set of tablets on Yom Kippur, Day 10 of month 7. This fits perfectly with the notion that Yisrael is given a second chance. It was through the work and mediation of Mosheh that this was accomplished. Therefore we see the pattern of a Mediator involved in providing

the requisite atonement for the Covenant people of YHWH. Therefore, in order to receive that provision of atonement, you must be in the Covenant. The atonement is essentially the provision of YHWH through the Covenant to allow His people access into the House.

147   *Jerusalem The Eye of the Universe*, Aryeh Kaplan p21.

148   Reference is made to Joshua 6 which describes the Battle of Jericho. Much of the symbolism is meant to teach us how the Messiah will lead Yisrael into the Covenant Land in the end times. When read prophetically, in light of the information contained in the Book of Revelation, it is really quite profound. Some of the symbolism was discussed in the Walk in the Light series book entitled *The Messiah*. More in depth analysis is provided in the Walk in the Light series book entitled *The Final Shofar*.

149   The adoption of the sons of Joseph is detailed in Beresheet 48. It occurred just prior to the death of the man Yisrael. The incident is full of mystery. For instance, when Joseph initially relates to his father or vice versa, Yisrael is called Yaakob. He then tells Joseph that his two sons Ephraim and Manasseh, who were born in Egypt would become his, like Reuben and Simeon. Recall that Reuben and Simeon were the first and second sons of Yaakob. Thus Ephraim and Manasseh would now become the first and second of Yaakob. He then speaks of the promises that were made to him by YHWH, that he would become a multitude (qahal) of people. He recounts the death of his beloved wife Rachel at Bethlehem, but does not mention that it was the result of the birth of his youngest son Benyamin. Then Yisrael looks at Joseph's sons and asks who they are. This is quite profound as he is now specifically called Yisrael. He had already called the boys by name and indicated that he would be adopting them. It seems that he did not recognize them or could not see them. This is very interesting, as Joseph was not recognized by his brothers when they first met him in Egypt. Now Yisrael does not see the two Egyptian born boys that he will be adopting. Yisrael then places his right hand upon the head of Ephraim, the second born son of Joseph, and his left hand upon Manasseh, the first born son of Joseph. By doing so he elevated Ephraim to the firstborn of Yisrael and Manasseh as the second born of Yisrael. This has very powerful implications for the culmination of the Covenant in the end of days, which of course centers around the Appointed Times. See Appendix 45 of The Companion Bible by E.W. Bullinger for the 20 different lists of the 12 Tribes in Scripture in all their various orders and groupings.

150   The Scriptures record that King Solomon (Shlomo), renowned for his wisdom (1 Kings 4:29), fell away from the ways of YHWH. He began by loving YHWH and following the commandments (1 Kings 3:3). As a result, he was permitted to build the House of YHWH. Sadly, he strayed and failed to continue in the ways of his father and ended up committing some of the worst abominations possible. (1 Kings 11). YHWH grew angry with him, and upon his death, tore part of the Kingdom from him. The Kingdom of Yisrael was divided into two houses. The House of Yisrael in the north, led by Joseph, and the House of Yahudah in the South led by Yahudah. Jereboam was chosen to lead the ten tribes that joined the House of Yisrael. He was promised great things, but sadly he quickly erred. He set up two golden calves - one in Bethel and one in Dan. He did this to divert worship away from Jerusalem for fear that his people would rejoin with Rehoboam, the son of Shlomo. (1 Kings 12). This resulted in the House of Yisrael being completely removed from the Land by the Assyrians by 714 BCE. But this was not the end of David's throne or the House of Yisrael. All will be restored at the Appointed Time.

151   This subject is discussed in more detail in the Walk in the Light series book entitled *The Redeemed*. The important thing to recognize is that the purpose of scattering the House of Yisrael throughout the earth was so that they could later be regathered through the nations.

152   We know from the Prophet Yehezqel that the punishment for the House of Yisrael was originally established at 390 years. (See Yehezqel 4). Because they failed to repent, their punishment would be multiplied seven times (Vayiqra 26). As a result, the duration of the punishment for the House of Yisrael was 2,730 years. The House of Yisrael (Joseph) experienced 5 different exiles between 723 BCE and 714 BCE. Thus we would anticipate the punishment of Joseph to be concluded somewhere between 2007 and 2016 CE. As a result, the revelation of Joseph appears to be imminent.

153   See Nehemiah 8.

154   For a further discussion see the Walk in the Light series book entitled *The Messiah*.

155   For a further discussion see the Walk in the Light series book entitled *The Final Shofar*.

156   Many believe that the prophecies of Ezekiel chapters 40-48 are entirely about the Millennial Kingdom and the Third Temple. Although many of the prophecies are as yet unfulfilled, some of Ezekiel's prophecies, particularly those involving the Temple

Service, were fulfilled at the beginning of the Second Temple Period. Information concerning the eight day occurrences provided by Eliyahu David ben Yissachar, Jerusalem, Israel.

[157] For a further discussion see the Walk in the Light series books entitled *Pagan Holidays*, *Restoration* and *The Sabbath*.

[158] Typically, in the Messianic writings the only instances when Yahushua was in Jerusalem was for an Appointed Time. Interestingly, Yahushua arose on a weekly Sabbath on the third day of Unleavened Bread on Day 17 of Month 1 in 34 CE. He was seen 40 days (Acts 1:3) and then ascended into heaven on Day 41 of the Omer count on Day 27 of Month 2 in 34 CE. The only other occasion was when He was present in Jerusalem for the Feast of Dedication commonly referred to as Hanukah. (Yahanan 10:22), however, Hanukah is not an Appointed Time.

[159] Yom Teruah was the day that the ancient kings of Yahudah reckoned their regnal years from. This procedure was followed consistently in the time of Solomon, Yirmeyahu and Ezra. Interestingly, Kings of Yisrael would mark their regnal years from the First Day of the First month. (Ernest L. Martin, *The Star That Astonished the World* ASK Publications 1998 quoting Edwin Thiel, *The Mysterious Numbers of the Hebrew Kings*, see also Talmud - Mas. Rosh HaShana 2a Chapter 1). This has profound significance when considering not only the actual dates from past reigns, but also future prophetic dates concerning the Messiah and His role as King over both the Houses of Yahudah and Yisrael.

[160] For a further discussion see the Walk in the Light series book entitled *The Messiah*. For more detailed information you can also read *The Star that Astonished the World* by Ernest L. Martin, and the article *The Birth of the Messiah* at www.torahcalendar.com.

[161] For a detailed discussion concerning the dating of this event see the Walk in the Light series book entitled *The Messiah* at pages 387-394.

[162] See the Walk in the Light series book entitled *The Messiah* at p. 240 - 241. See also www.torahcalendar.com.

[163] Hanukah is not an Appointed Time prescribed in the Scriptures, although it is a very significant time and worthy of commemoration. It essentially is a tradition which belongs to the House of Yahudah as it commemorated the rededication of the House of YHWH, although history shows that it was not a complete restoration and renewal. Therefore, celebration of this special day is really a sober reminder of our need for Messiah. Interestingly, Yahushua is recorded as being in Jerusalem for Hanukah - The Feast of Dedication which essentially places His

164   stamp of approval on this celebration. (see Yahanan 10:22).
       Mishnah Bikkurim 1 Sections 3 and 6.

165   For a further discussion see the Walk in the Light series book
       entitled *The Law and Grace*.

166   Judaism Eternal, Vol. 1, p. 3. Words in brackets changed by the
       author for accuracy and consistency.

167   For a further discussion see the Walk in the Light series book
       entitled *Pagan Holidays*.

168   For a further discussion see the Walk in the Light series book
       entitled *The Final Shofar*.

169   *See Matthew 24:42; Matthew 24:43 Matthew 25:13 Mark 13:35; Mark
       13:37; Luke 12:38; Luke 21:36.*

170   We see through the Appointed Times the work that the Messiah
       accomplished through His life, death and resurrection. We read
       in the Messianic texts that the veil in the Hekal was torn. The
       way to the Most Set Apart was made available. Some things
       were finished but still more needs to be done for the Covenant
       plan to be completed. Yahushua fulfilled   many of the patterns
       in the Torah, but that does not mean it is all over or done away
       with. We still memorialize and rehearse in anticipation of future
       fulfillment of prophecy.

171   The entire creation is filled with frequencies and operates on
       various levels through frequencies. For an interesting discussion
       on the interrelationship of all of creation based upon the
       mathematics of YHWH see *Number in Scripture* by E.W.
       Bullinger, Kregel Publications. Our senses are tuned to
       frequencies, and the spoken Word of YHWH both creates and
       destroys through the power of frequencies. This is why the
       Appointed Times are so critical. We must essentially get "tuned
       in" to the frequencies of Creation established by the Creator.

A Note on Dates

Historical dating has long been a subject of controversy and debate in the
academic community. While certain dates involving particular aspects of
a civilization may be agreed upon, others remain in dispute. This
sometimes leads to problems creating a complete timeline of history.
Very recently some intensive and compelling work has been completed
by using astronomical data, particularly eclipse data, which can then be
used to lock together histories of various cultures, thereby providing an
accurate view of history in totality. The dates used in this book may not
always be the same as academia purports, but they are believed to be the
most accurate available. Dates provided by Eliyahu David ben Yissachar,
Jerusalem, Israel, through the work displayed on www.torahcalendar.com
have been denoted by placing an asterisk (*) next to them.

Author's Note

I completed this book in Jerusalem during the Feast of Unleavened Bread in the year 2012. This was a very unique year because all of the major Calendars coincided with the Creator's Calendar relative to the High Sabbaths of Unleavened Bread. Even the date for the resheet offering was the same, as Day 16 of Month 1 landed on a Sunday. Despite all of the religious divisions that exist, for this brief period in time there was some semblance of unity during this very important Appointed Time. It is times such as this when we are able to taste just a small portion of the joy and unity that the Feasts are intended to relate to the people of YHWH. It is truly sweet, and creates a real expectation for the fulfillment of the times by and through Yahushua the Messiah.

Jerusalem, Israel
April 11, 2012
Day 20 of Month 1

Appendix A

Tanak Hebrew Names

Torah (Instruction)

English Name	Modern Hebrew	Transliteration
Genesis	בראשית	Beresheet
Exodus	שמות	Shemot
Leviticus	ויקרא	Vayiqra
Numbers	במדבר	Bemidbar
Deuteronomy	דברים	Debarim

Nebi'im (Prophets)

Joshua	יהושע	Yahushua
Judges	שופטים	Shoftim
Samuel	שמואל	Shemu'el
Kings	מלכים	Melakhim
Isaiah	ישעיהו	Yeshayahu
Jeremiah	ירמיהו	Yirmeyahu
Ezekiel	יחזקאל	Yehezqel
Daniel	דניאל	Daniel
Hosea	השוע	Hoshea
Joel	יואל	Yoel
Amos	עמוס	Amos
Obadiah	עבדיה	Obadyah

Jonah	יונה	Yonah
Micah	מיכה	Mikhah
Nahum	נחום	Nachum
Habakkuk	חבקוק	Habaquq
Zephaniah	צפניה	Zephaniyah
Haggai	חגי	Chaggai
Zechariah	זכריה	Zekaryah
Malachi	מלאכי	Malachi

Kethubim (Writings)

Psalms	תהלים	Tehillim
Proverbs	משלי	Mishle
Job	איוב	Iyov
Song of Songs	שיר השירים	Shir ha-Shirim
Ruth	רות	Ruth
Lamentations	איכה	Eikhah
Ecclesiastes	קהלת	Qohelet
Esther	אסתר	Ester
Ezra	עזרא	Ezra
Nehemiah	נחמיה	Nehemyah
Chronicles	דברי הימים	Dibri ha-Yamim

Appendix B

Hebrew Language Study Chart

Gematria	Letter	Paleo	Modern	English	Picture/Meaning
1	Aleph	ठ	א	A	ox head
2	Bet	◻	ב	B, Bh	tent floor plan
3	Gimel	∧	ג	G	foot, camel
4	Dalet	▽	ד	D	door
5	Hey	५	ה	H	man raised arms
6	Waw	↑	ו	W, O, U	tent peg, hook
7	Zayin	⌂	ז	Z	weapon
8	Het	⊞	ח	Hh	fence, wall
9	Tet	⊕	ט	T, Th	basket, container
10	Yud	↘	י	Y	closed hand
20	Kaph	⨌	כ	K, Kh	palm, open hand
30	Lamed	∩	ל	L	shepherd staff
40	Mem	ᴍ	מ	M	water
50	Nun	↖	נ	N	sprout, seed
60	Samech	╤	ס	S	prop, support
70	Ayin	◔	ע	A	eye
80	Pey	⌐	פ	P, Ph	open mouth
90	Tsade	+	צ	Ts	hook
100	Quph	⌀	ק	Q	back of the head
200	Resh	⌂	ר	R	head of a man
300	Shin	w	שׁ	Sh, S	teeth
400	Taw	✕	ת	T	mark, covenant

Note: Gematria in a very simple sense is the study of the various numerical values of the Hebrew letters and words. Since there is no separate numerical system in the Hebrew language, all Hebrew letters have a numerical value so it is a very legitimate and valuable form of study. There are many different forms of Gematria. The Gematria system used in this chart is mispar hechrachi, also known as Normative value. The Paleo font used is an attempt to blend the ancient variants into a uniform and recognizable font set that accurately depicts the original meaning of each character.

Appendix C

The Walk in the Light Series

Book 1   Restoration – A discussion of the pagan influences that have mixed with the true faith through the ages which has resulted in the need for restoration. This book also examines true Scriptural restoration.

Book 2   Names – Discusses the True Name of the Creator and the Messiah as well as the significance of names in the Scriptures.

Book 3   The Scriptures – Discusses the ways that the Creator has communicated with Creation. It also examines the origin of the written Scriptures as well as the various types of translation errors in Bibles that have led to false doctrines in some mainline religions.

Book 4   Covenants – Discusses the progressive covenants between the Creator and His Creation as described in the Scriptures which reveals His plan for mankind.

Book 5   The Messiah – Discusses the prophetic promises and fulfillments of the Messiah and the True identity of the Redeemer of Yisrael.

Book 6   The Redeemed – Discusses the relationship between Christianity and Judaism and reveals how the Scriptures identify True Believers. It reveals how the Christian doctrine of Replacement Theology has caused confusion as to how the Creator views the Children of Yisrael.

Book 7   The Law and Grace – Discusses in depth the false doctrine that Grace has done away with the Law and demonstrates the vital importance of obeying the commandments.

Book 8   The Sabbath – Discusses the importance of the Seventh Day Sabbath as well as the origins of the tradition concerning Sunday worship.

Book 9   Kosher – Discusses the importance of eating food prescribed by the Scriptures as an aspect of righteous living.

Book 10   Appointed Times – Discusses the appointed times established by the Creator, often erroneously considered to be "Jewish" holidays, and critical to the understanding of prophetic fulfillment of the Scriptural promises.

Book 11   Pagan Holidays – Discusses the pagan origins of some popular Christian holidays which have replaced the Appointed Times.

Book 12   The Final Shofar – Examines the ancient history of the earth and prepares the Believer for the deceptions coming in the end of the age. Also discusses the walk required by the Scriptures to be an overcomer and endure to the end.

The series began as a simple Power point presentation which was intended to develop into a book with twelve different chapters but ended up being twelve different books. Each book is intended to stand alone although the series was originally intended to build from one section to another. Due to the urgency of certain topics, the books have not been published in sequential order.

For anticipated release dates, announcements and additional teachings go to:
www.shemayisrael.net

Appendix D

The Shema
Deuteronomy (Debarim) 6:4-5

Traditional English Translation

Hear, O Israel: The LORD our God, the LORD is one!
You shall love the LORD your God with all your heart, with all
your soul, and with all your strength.

Corrected English Translation

Hear, O Yisrael: YHWH our Elohim, YHWH is one (unified)!
You shall love YHWH your Elohim with all your heart, with
all your soul, and with all your strength.

Modern Hebrew Text

שמע ישראל יהוה אלהינו יהוה אחד
ואהבת את יהוה אלהיך בכל־ לבבך ובכל־ נפשך ובכל־ מאדך

Ancient Hebrew Text

Hebrew Text Transliterated

Shema, Yisra'el: YHWH Elohenu, YHWH echad!
V-ahavta et YHWH Elohecha b-chol l'bacha u-b-chol naf'sh'cha
u-b-chol m'odecha.

The Shema has traditionally been one of the most important prayers in
Judaism and has been declared the first (resheet) of all the Commandments.
(Mark 12:29-30).

Appendix E

Shema Yisrael

Shema Yisrael was originally established with two primary goals: 1) The production and distribution of sound, Scripturally based educational materials which would assist individuals to see the light of Truth and "Walk in the Light" of that Truth. This first objective was, and is, accomplished through Shema Yisrael Publications; and 2) The free distribution of those materials to the spiritually hungry throughout the world, along with Scriptures, food, clothing and money to the poor, the needy, the sick, the dying and those in prison. This second objective was accomplished through the Shema Yisrael Foundation and through the Foundation people were able to receive a tax deduction for their contributions.

Sadly, through the passage of the Pension Reform Act of 2006, the US Congress severely restricted the operation of donor advised funds which, in essence, crippled the Shema Yisrael Foundation by requiring that funds either be channeled through another Foundation or to a 501(c)(3) organization approved by the Internal Revenue Service. Since the Shema Yisrael Foundation was relatively small and operated very "hands on" by placing the funds and materials directly into the hands of the needy in Third World Countries, it was unable to effectively continue operating as a Foundation with the tax advantages associated therewith.

As a result, Shema Yisrael Publications has essentially functioned in a dual capacity to insure that both objectives continue to be promoted, although contributions are no longer tax deductible. To review some of the work being accomplished you can visit www.shemayisrael.net and go to the "Missions" section.

We gladly accept donations, although they will not be tax deductible. To donate, please make checks payable to "Shema Yisrael Publications" and mail to:

Shema Yisrael
123 Court Street • Herkimer, New York 13350

You may also visit our website or call (315) 939-7940 to make a donation or receive more information.